# GI INGENUITY

# The Stackpole Military History Series

## THE AMERICAN CIVIL WAR

*Cavalry Raids of the Civil War*
*Ghost, Thunderbolt, and Wizard*
*Pickett's Charge*
*Witness to Gettysburg*

## WORLD WAR II

*Armor Battles of the Waffen-SS, 1943–45*
*Army of the West*
*Australian Commandos*
*The B-24 in China*
*Backwater War*
*The Battle of Sicily*
*Beyond the Beachhead*
*The Brandenburger Commandos*
*The Brigade*
*Bringing the Thunder*
*Coast Watching in World War II*
*Colossal Cracks*
*D-Day to Berlin*
*Dive Bomber!*
*Eagles of the Third Reich*
*Exit Rommel*
*Fist from the Sky*
*Flying American Combat Aircraft of*
    *World War II*
*Forging the Thunderbolt*
*Fortress France*
*The German Defeat in the East, 1944–45*
*German Order of Battle, Vol. 1*
*German Order of Battle, Vol. 2*
*German Order of Battle, Vol. 3*
*Germany's Panzer Arm in World War II*
*GI Ingenuity*
*Grenadiers*
*Infantry Aces*
*Iron Arm*
*Iron Knights*
*Kampfgruppe Peiper at the Battle*
    *of the Bulge*
*Luftwaffe Aces*
*Massacre at Tobruk*
*Messerschmitts over Sicily*

*Michael Wittmann, Vol. 1*
*Michael Wittmann, Vol. 2*
*Mountain Warriors*
*The Nazi Rocketeers*
*On the Canal*
*Packs On!*
*Panzer Aces*
*Panzer Aces II*
*The Panzer Legions*
*Panzers in Winter*
*The Path to Blitzkrieg*
*Retreat to the Reich*
*Rommel's Desert War*
*The Savage Sky*
*A Soldier in the Cockpit*
*Soviet Blitzkrieg*
*Stalin's Keys to Victory*
*Surviving Bataan and Beyond*
*T-34 in Action*
*Tigers in the Mud*
*The 12th SS, Vol. 1*
*The 12th SS, Vol. 2*
*The War against Rommel's Supply Lines*

## THE COLD WAR / VIETNAM

*Flying American Combat Aircraft:*
    *The Cold War*
*Here There Are Tigers*
*Land with No Sun*
*Street without Joy*

## WARS OF THE MIDDLE EAST

*Never-Ending Conflict*

## GENERAL MILITARY HISTORY

*Carriers in Combat*
*Desert Battles*

# GI INGENUITY

## Improvisation, Technology, and Winning World War II

James Jay Carafano

STACKPOLE
BOOKS

Copyright © 2006 by James Jay Carafano

Published in paperback in 2008 by
STACKPOLE BOOKS
5067 Ritter Road
Mechanicsburg, PA 17055
www.stackpolebooks.com

GI INGENUITY: IMPROVISATION, TECHNOLOGY, AND WINNING WORLD
WAR II, by James Jay Carafano, was originally published in hard cover by Praeger,
an imprint of Greenwood Publishing Group, Inc., Westport, CT. Copyright © 2006
by James Jay Carafano. Paperback edition by arrangement with Greenwood Publishing Group, Inc. All rights reserved.

*Cover design by Tracy Patterson*

Printed in the United States of America

10  9  8  7  6  5  4  3  2  1

ISBN 0-8117-3468-4 (Stackpole paperback)
ISBN 978-0-8117-3468-4 (Stackpole paperback)

**The Library of Congress has cataloged the hardcover edition as follows:**

Carafano, James Jay, 1955–
    GI ingenuity : improvisation, technology, and winning World War II / James Jay
    Carafano
        p. cm. – (War, technology, and history, ISSN 1556-4924)
    Includes bibliographical references and index.
    ISBN 0-275-98698-5 (alk. paper)
    1. World War, 1939–1945—Technology. 2. World War, 1939–1945—Influence.
    3. Soldiers—United States—Intellectual life—20th century. 4. United
    States—Social life and customs—History—20th century. I. Title. II. Series.
    D810.S2C37 2006
    940.54'1273—dc22                                        2006015090

Brigadier General Thomas E. Griess—in memoriam.

# Contents

# Prologue

# A Genius for War

Nothing explains "GI Ingenuity" better than battling invaders from space.

The science fiction films of the 1950s did not distinguish themselves by great acting or stunning special effects. They proved most remarkable for how well they mirrored American popular culture: our fears, our hopes, and how we saw ourselves and the world. Distant planets, dark corners of this world, laboratories of bubbling test tubes, monsters from the deep, dinosaurs from the past, rockets to the moon, and invaders from outer space all served as metaphors for the anxieties of postwar America. Science fiction films were the cinema of the "greatest generation," when the men and women who won World War II went back to school, bought homes, bore children, and took over boardrooms, congressional seats, and commanded garrisons around the world in a Cold War standoff with the Soviet Union.

GIs came home from the Second World War in 1945 with a renewed sense of optimism. They had grown up and survived the economic collapse of the 1930s Great Depression and gone on to liberate the world and preserve freedom and, in the process, build the greatest economic engine history had ever seen—the American industrial free-market democracy. The euphoria, however, did not last. After the outbreak of the Korean conflict brought the Cold War home to Main Street, as America again sent its boys off to battle (less than half a decade after victory in Europe and the Pacific), the hope of a long peace was gone forever. Americans were again afraid for the future.

The anxiety of dealing with a new and terrible challenge was played out on Saturday matinee screens, with space invaders standing in for the "other," the mysterious, deadly, daunting menace of Communism. And, perhaps not surprisingly, to battle the foreign danger Americans looked back to the genius that won World War II to see them through once again—against monsters from space and monsters on earth.

No picture captured the fight for the future better than the RKO Radio Pictures/Winchester Pictures 1951 film, *The Thing from Another World.* Released only a year after the outbreak of the Korean War, it was the first of a generation of alien space invader movies that featured intrepid Americans saving the planet from domination and destruction.

In *The Thing from Another World,* an aircrew dispatched to check out an unusual report from a civilian Arctic research station discovers a spaceship crashed, under the ice. They fan out and raise their arms to determine the shape. The group forms a perfect circle—a "flying saucer." But when they try to cut the craft out, it explodes. Not far away, however, they find a body thrown from the crash. They take the frozen alien back to the research station, keeping it in a storage room until a raging front blows over and they can fly their discovery back to the air base at Dutch Harbor. As in most scary movies, things almost immediately start to go horribly wrong.

One of the crewmen guarding the alien Popsicle inadvertently leaves an electric blanket over the body. When it thaws, the invader from space escapes. The thing from another world (played by James Arness, who later became a famous TV sheriff) turns out to be a creature that feeds and breeds on human blood. For the remainder of the movie, soldiers and civilians battle the space monster in the station's narrow, claustrophobic hallways. In the end, they electrocute the unwelcome visitor.

The movie was well reviewed and popular, in large part because it was extremely well done, genuinely scary. But it also touched movie audiences because it fed on American fears—terrors fueled by Cold War headlines warning of Communist subversion. The 1938 novella upon which the movie was based, *Who Goes There?* by science fiction writer and editor John W. Campbell, served as an even more explicit analogy for the creeping threat of foreign invasion. In Campbell's book, the alien absorbs the shape of anything it attacks and becomes indistinguishable from a normal human. Just as the threat of Communist infiltration warned of by the likes of "red-baiting" Senator Joseph McCarthy and the hearings of the House Committee to Investigate Un-American Activities, at the ice station it was impossible to distinguish friend from foe. They looked just like us. The film's screenplay (the original draft finished only two months after the North Koreans crossed the 38th parallel and invaded South Korea) made the danger more explicit and overtly militaristic—flat out conquest by a big, ugly menacing monster. The thing was the kind of menace that could be fought man to man, in a battle more like World War II where the combatants wore different uniforms and soldiers knew who the enemy was.

What is most telling about *The Thing from Another World* is how the invader from space is defeated. It is not done by the scientists. Science and technology had been the hallmark of America's rise to industrial greatness, yet the scientists at the station turned out not to be of much help at all. In fact, their leader, Professor Carrington (Robert Cornthwaite), proves downright obstructionist, whining that the alien has to be preserved for science. Carrington's character is also oddly effeminate. During part of the movie while everyone else is arming to the teeth to fight off the space invader, he sports a jaunty tweed jacket and turtleneck sweater—and philosophizes. The alien (not unlike the Communists) had "no emotion, no heart—our superior in every way," Carrington gushes, "Knowledge is more important than life. We owe it to our species to stand here and die." The screenwriter, Charles Lederer, did not make the scientists sound like the kind of people in whose hands should be placed the future of the free world. They were not to be the heroes of the postwar age.

The military men battling monsters at the top of the world were the champions of freedom—manly, decisive, uniformed. The same kind of boys who flew bomber missions over Germany, piloted submarines in the Pacific, and fought on the beaches of Normandy. It is the military, the saviors of the nation during World War II, that saves the day on the Arctic Circle. They were America's heroes. *The Thing from Another World* is as much an homage to the greatest generation as it is a metaphor for Cold War terror.

And what was especially noteworthy was how the military saved the day. The traditional view of the American military as a large, industrial-age, bureaucratic organization, where orders came from the top and were executed at the bottom, is turned on its head. The Air Force commander, General Fogarty, who sends his men out to investigate appears in only one scene; after that he is heard from only by a series of befuddled messages and useless orders transmitted to the station's radio operator. He is of no help at all in saving the earth. In fact, he pretty much appears as lost in the "fog" as his name implied.

The nominal hero of the film is the handsome, rugged, self-confident Captain Pat Henry (Kenneth Toby), the pilot. He, of course, gets the girl, and the credit. But the real savior of the world is the young crew chief. Every suggestion on how to adapt technology to the unusual circumstances of fighting a space alien comes from him. It is the sergeant who suggests using thermite grenades to cut the spaceship out of the ice—and he shows everyone how to use them. In the end, it is the sergeant who proposes trying to electrocute the alien and instructs the others in how to set up a makeshift ambush with electrical conduits and fencing. Every initiative, every adaptation of technology, comes from the genius of an American soldier. They do not all work. When the crew tries to set the monster on fire with kerosene, they almost burn down the station. But, in the end through trial and error, and shear creativity and intuition, the American soldier figures it out. The film's depiction of the bond between soldiers and technology reflected perfectly how Americans remembered what their boys had done in World War II. It was GI ingenuity. And that is what *GI Ingenuity* is all about—technology and the American genius in war.

## NICKNAMES

Over the course of the twentieth century, the era that spans the rise of industry to the postindustrial age of the computer chip, Americans always had a genius for war—applying advances in technology to the challenge of combat. The nature of the American genius, however, evolved as the republic's romance with science and technology changed. In the decades between World War I and Desert Storm there was a significant shift in the relationship between war, society, science, and technology, and as that change occurred the American soldier added to the kit bag that made up his genius for war. The GI experience during World War II reflected a pivotal turning point in that shift.

What counted for genius during combat in Normandy was different from what made soldiers successful on the battlefields of World War I and the campaigns at the end of the century. That is why they all had different nicknames.

Americans had a name for the soldiers they sent off to fight the Great War in 1918, "doughboys." Like most popular American slang, not everyone agrees on the origin of the term. The most common explanation is that the nickname was derived from the brass buttons on a soldier's uniform. They resembled doughboys, a popular snack—small round pieces of flat bread fried in fat (the precursor to the modern doughnut).

The doughboys who fought in France deserved a special name. They were unique, a different breed of American soldier. They were farm kids, small town kids, city kids, many who had never been closer to a combustion engine than a ride on a train. They were kids who had never seen an airplane. They discovered modern technology in war. This was a generation that grew up on the farm and after it came home from war went to work in the factories. This was America's first mass army in the industrial age, an army that excelled because it learned how to harness industrial power, technology, and organization to meet the challenge of modern war. That was the genius of the doughboy era.

In 1940, as Americans gradually began to mobilize and confront the Fascist menace posed by the Axis powers (Germany, Japan, and Italy) the American soldiers did not have a nickname. Sometimes they were called "doughs," a shortened, slangy, big-band age version of doughboy. But doughs never won any popularity polls and with good reason. It did not fit. The boys who went off to war listening to Benny Goodman and Artie Shaw on the radio were different. The sons of the veterans of World War I were another new kind of army.

The soldiers of the Second World War did, of course, draw some of their character from the Great War's legacy. They inherited the genius of their fathers as a matter of course. By the eve of World War II, the United States was the leading industrial power on the planet. No country could more aggressively apply science and technology to mass producing the instruments of war. No country could better take the organizational business practices and discipline of the industrial workplace and apply them to military activities more effectively, organizing and directing men on a large scale to a common purpose.

Nevertheless, the World War II generation had something more. This was the first age of soldiers who grew up comfortable with modern industrial-age technology. These were kids who built jalopies in their garages, poured over glossy full-color issues of *Popular Mechanics,* and read "Buck Rogers in the 25th Century" comic books, listened to his adventures on the radio, and watched Buck pilot rocket ships in the Saturday morning serials at the Bijou. They were tinkers, problem solvers, risk takers, and daydreamers. They were curious, gum-chewing, outspoken kids. They were the first generation to elect an engineer, Herbert Hoover, as an American president. They were a generation well prepared to improvise, innovate, and adapt technology on the battlefield. And since they were a generation who had unprecedented technology available to them, their ability to innovate with technology proved an immeasurable combat edge. They were the ones who figured out how to make the armor, artillery, and airpower that American factories provided in such great abundance work on the battlefield.

The American soldier of World War II deserved his own nickname. And he got one. The one that stuck was GI. It is commonly believed the term came from the initials G.I., "Government Issue," stamped on equipment. It was kind of a joke, as if suggesting the government issued infantry, just like artillery shells, off a factory assembly line—but it did not. The American fighting man had the discipline of the industrial-age worker, but he was a well-educated, free thinking, self-confident individual. While the government did not issue soldiers like parts off the factory floor, it did exploit the genius of the American GI to win the war.

GI ingenuity became an enduring feature of the citizen-soldier—and not just in 1950s science fiction films. Though the hot and cold wars of the Cold War had different names (Korea, Vietnam, and the standoff with the Soviets in Western Europe) and different outcomes, through them all the Army placed a premium on retaining or recapturing the GIs' ability to learn, innovate, adapt, and improvise. When William DePuy, who fought with the infantry in World War II and commanded a division in Vietnam, spoke to soldiers about fighting, he preached the value of aggressive, adaptive, imaginative leaders for implementing the orders handed out by generals; he called his way of fighting "centralized idea, decentralized execution." It was an idea he learned fighting in France. Figuring out on the ground how to best make technology meet the situation at hand remained a vital attribute of the American way of war.

At the dawn of the twenty-first century, however, it is rare to hear soldiers called GIs. The term seems old-fashioned now. The soldiers of the post-Cold War world refer to themselves as "warriors." The U.S. Army even calls its high-tech system of instrumentation and combat gear for infantrymen the "Land Warrior." Ironically, the most technologically sophisticated military in history prefers a name that reduces soldiering to its most primitive and elemental state.

American soldiers like the title of warrior because it reflects the recognition that there is a timeless dimension to land combat. "You may fly over a land forever; you may bomb it, atomize it, pulverize it and wipe it clean of life—but if you desire to defend it, protect it and keep it for civilization," T.R. Fehrenbach famously wrote about the Korean conflict in *This Kind of War* (1963), "you must do this on the ground, the way the Roman legions did, by putting your young men into the mud." After the Cold War, Army leaders frequently quoted Fehrenbach to remind that even in an age of high-tech weapons war was still a human contest, a battle of action and counteraction between thinking, determined foes. Wars could never be won by technology alone. There would always be a need for what the generals called "boots on the ground." There would always be a need for warriors.

Twenty-first century American soldiers may celebrate their warrior roots, but they still come to war laden with an awful lot of technology, technology that GIs saw only in Flash Gordon movie serials. The genius of warriors, however, was larger than GI ingenuity. As the greatest generation built on doughboy genius to harness the industrial age, the twenty-first century warrior retained the GI's capacity to innovate and adapt technology on the battlefield. The warriors, however, added something new.

Today's warriors are a special generation because they have something that no other soldier in history has ever possessed—the computer chip. The computer chip represents the greatest technological innovation of the postindustrial age, and its effect on the post-Cold War military has been transformational. Hardened and miniaturized electronics give the technologies available to soldiers speed, capacity, and capabilities of unprecedented measure. Warriors take computers to war.

The special American genius of this age is the means to adapt "systems integration" to the battlefield, using computers to link technologies together, to get the right information to the right place on the battlefield at the right time to do the right thing. That is warrior genius. It is GI ingenuity on steroids.

## A WINDOW INTO WAR

*GI Ingenuity* illustrates the great transition of the American genius in battle from an industrial-age army to a postmodern military. And it does it by looking at the place where the transition happened—on the battlefield.

The battleground is Normandy. The time is the long summer of 1944. The task is great, to liberate Europe. The enemy is a tough veteran combat force. The invading army is American, short on combat experience, but heavily fortified with the weapons of modern combat—armored tanks, powerful long-range artillery, and an abundance of airpower (fighters, bombers, and aerial observation planes). The challenge is to turn man and machine into a war-winning team.

Normandy in 1944 was one of the pivotal moments in modern military history, perhaps the best moment and place to examine the role of the soldier, technology, and the transformation of America's battle genius. Tracing the saga of the Normandy campaign tells the story of how GIs drew on the inspiration of their fathers' way of war, added the ingenuity of the greatest generation, and presaged the military of the twenty-first century. It is the story of GI ingenuity, past, present, and future.

That story can be told only by bringing together three disparate brands of history that hardly ever get mentioned in the same breath: (1) military history, the story of battle, blood, and bugles; (2) the history of science and technology, which examines ideas and the means of production and products created as a result of turning the tools of science to the problems of everyday life; and, (3) social, economic, cultural, and intellectual history, the exploration of how changes in beliefs and relationships among individuals and communities shape the way humans respond to the world around them. All three historical narratives are required to tell the tale of GI genius.

*GI Ingenuity* is not New Military History.

*GI Ingenuity* is unapologetic, old-fashioned combat history, with mayhem and mass slaughter at center stage. This is the story about death and destruction on the killing fields at Normandy, as well as the battlegrounds that provide the prologue and postscript to the transformation of war that occurred in France in 1944. The story of *GI Ingenuity,* however, is about battles in context, battles in the context of the incredible social, economic, scientific, and technological changes that accompanied the evolution of combat from doughboy to GI to warrior.

James Jay Carafano
Washington, D.C.

# CHAPTER 1

# Wrong War, Right War

## THE GHOSTS OF NORMANDY

FEISTY AND FEARED ARE the two words most often used to describe General William E. DePuy. DePuy ran the U.S. Army Training and Doctrine Command (TRADOC), a headquarters established on July 1, 1973, the same day Congress passed a law prohibiting further U.S. combat activities in Vietnam. DePuy had been picked to take over TRADOC, in large part because he fit those two words—feisty and feared—so very well.

Before the TRADOC assignment, from March 1966 to March 1967, DePuy led the storied 1st Infantry Division, the spearhead of the invasion of Normandy during World War II. In Vietnam, DePuy was the general with the red one patch stamped on his shoulder. It was often debated who feared the leader of the "Big Red One," responsible for defending the area from the Cambodian border to Saigon, more—the enemy or the division. No officer wanted to be "DePuyed," a visit from the general complete with a withering barrage of questions and criticisms.[1] His reputation for categorical and brutally frank assessments was legion. "He is a third rate officer," DePuy wrote of one of his infantry commanders, "who should not be entrusted with command of soldiers in combat." A staff officer was, "completely inadequate … . Valueless." Of another, the general recalled that from the first day, "I strongly suspected that he was weak." DePuy could not stand weak leaders. He fired or transferred anyone who did not measure up.[2]

General DePuy's aggressive leadership style did not go unnoticed. "Goddamn it, what I'm going to do with DePuy," railed the Army Chief of Staff in the Pentagon, "He just eats them [officers] up like peanuts."[3] In the end what they did was promote him. DePuy proved to be a commander who got results—a fighter, both brave and brilliant, an innovative tactician, and an imaginative thinker. He was just the kind of leader the Army needed to recover from the Vietnam morass.

The signing of the Paris Peace Accords in March 1973 formally ended America's chance to win the war by force of arms. The Army that left Vietnam was not a proud one. It was often called "the Hollow Force,"[4] an apt term. Most of the money spent on the military during the war went to pay for the cost of fighting. There were scant investments in ensuring the Army was trained and ready for the future. It was used up. America's post-Vietnam military lacked for everything—morale, modern equipment, and soldiers.

Back in the Pentagon, DePuy saw an opportunity to fix part of the problem. Not since World War II, when Lesley J. McNair directed the Army Ground Forces (AGF) command from his headquarters in Washington at the confluence of the Potomac and Anacostia rivers, had the Army had a separate command responsible for training, developing doctrine, and new equipment. DePuy pressed for establishing one again—TRADOC. He not only won the argument. He was put in charge.[5]

General McNair's AGF offered a fitting model for DePuy. McNair also had to rebuild an army. His job was to turn an American interwar army of 190,000 men with little modern equipment into a combat force of 8 million professional soldiers equipped with the latest technology. And he had to do it fast—one year was allowed to raise, arm, train, and certify a division for combat. It was no simple task.

Readying a force for battle required more than just giving it shiny new weapons. Exploiting technology, McNair believed, demanded marrying the right men and machines.[6] "Leadership will be improved," McNair declared, "by the removal of weak officers."[7] He insisted on realistic training to test leaders and equipment. And he removed or transferred officers who did not look as if they would measure up in combat. DePuy intended to use TRADOC to inspire a similar renaissance in the post-Vietnam force. Marrying innovative training and technology, finding leaders who proved they had the knack of making men and machine work together, would be the means to recapture the genius of the American way of war.

That DePuy looked back to the AGF for inspiration was predictable. World War II remained the formative experience in his military career. The 24-year-old regimental operations officer with a face as smooth as a baby's bottom learned about combat in Normandy.

What DePuy mostly learned was how not to fight.

In France, DePuy did not serve with the division he led in Vietnam, the veteran 1st Infantry Division famous for its fighting exploits from North Africa to Normandy. DePuy fought under the 90th Infantry Division, a rookie command bloodied for the first time in the hedgerows and orchards of the Norman countryside. "The 90th Division was a killing machine," DePuy recalled, "of our own troops."[8] From those tragic days of summer DePuy saw the wrong war.

For the 90th, Normandy was a slaughterhouse. Two weeks after D-Day, DePuy was tasked to take a new colonel just assigned to the division on a reconnaissance of the front. When they passed a large column of troops, the colonel asked which battalion it was. "Those are our replacements," DePuy replied.[9] There were 800 men. They needed them. By the end of the month, the division had almost 2,500 killed and wounded—and DePuy mostly blamed incompetent leadership for the losses. It was a lesson on war that haunted him for the rest of his life.

## ISLAND OF THE WHITE WITCH

DePuy was not the only one who did not think much of the 90th Division. Omar Bradley shared his assessment. Bradley's opinion mattered. As the head of the First U.S. Army, he commanded all the U.S. forces in Normandy.

In his memoirs, General Bradley labeled the 90th a "problem division." In a 554-page account of World War II in Africa, the Mediterranean, and Western Europe, it was the only unit he saddled with that unique distinction. In the opening days of the Normandy campaign, it got so bad his staff discussed the advisability of disbanding the division.[10] That there had even been such talk was pretty damning. In the course of the war, the AGF fielded 90 divisions. Only one, the 2nd Cavalry Division, was ever disestablished. The poor combat record of the 90th was especially troubling for the First Army commander on July 22, 1944—the day the division was supposed to take the Island of the White Witch, a small track of high ground surrounded by open, marshy farmland along the banks of the Séves River.

Attacking the White Witch did not seem like a good omen for a bad-luck division. Still, while the name (inherited from an ancient, local superstition) was ominous, the ground appeared less so. It was not much to look at, a treeless, undistinguished piece of farmland. Heavy summer rains swelled the banks of the river turning the high ground into a small island about two miles long and half a mile wide. There was not much real estate in the many miles of front that ran from the boundary between the First U.S. and Second British armies to the east coast of the Cotentin Peninsula. There were 13 divisions covering the front lines. The 90th's sector, bordering on the Séves, covered a little over a mile—not much ground at all.

A hump of dry earth along the Séves River swampland, however, was thought important, ground worth fighting for. Taking "the island" would put the division in better position to exploit the breakthrough attack that Bradley planned would follow in a couple of days.[11] And the success of the breakout was very important to the First U.S. Army commander; his reputation and the fate of the Allied invasion of France rested on the outcome.

Best-selling books and box-office hits recounting the exploits of the Allied soldiers on D-Day abound. In fact, the events surrounding June 6, 1944, marking the invasion of France with the amphibious landings on the Normandy beaches, have become among the most well-known moments in military history. Few tourists to the Norman countryside leave without visiting the famous landing sites code-named Sword, Gold, Juno, Omaha, and Utah. Most intent on seeing the battlefields of Normandy rarely leave sight of the ocean. They miss the real battle for France. For in truth, getting to the beaches was the easy part.

The land beyond the beachhead and the tenacity of the German defenses proved far more difficult than the Allied commanders expected, particularly in the American sector. The French call this the bocage country, famous for good Norman cheese and calvados, a strong drink distilled from good Norman apples. It was farm country, farm country that had not seen war since before the time of Shakespeare. Over that long peace, Norman fields were farmed again and again, an unchanging countryside bounded by thick walls of earth called hedgerows and traversed by narrow sunken country lanes. Thick bushes and rows of trees topped the hedgerows and banks of the farm roads. In the summer of 1944, the hedgerows and full summer foliage created a problem for the Americans—a field of fire problem.

In the Army manuals, a "field of fire" referred to the space of ground in front of a soldier that could be observed and covered by individual arms, such as a soldier's rifle or a crew-served weapon, such as a machine gun, that required one person to aim and fire the weapon and others to help load and carry ammunition and equipment. In short, the idea in a direct-fire engagement was if soldiers could see the enemy, if a German infantryman was in the field of fire, he could be killed or at least suppressed—forcing the enemy to keep his head down so he could not see or shoot you. Having good fields of fire was an essential to exploiting the killing power and long range of modern weapons.

The Army taught its soldiers that the bigger the field of fire the better, the more ground that could be controlled by force of arms … and the more ground controlled by fire the more friendly troops could move on the battlefield. The Army called that "fire and maneuver." "Every movement must be covered by fire," a field report lectured, "so placed so that it neutralizes that part of the enemy's infantry which could otherwise fire on the [friendly]

An Infantry Squad Struggles to Attack across a Hedgerow in Normandy. (Courtesy, Army Signal Corps)

individuals or elements that are moving."[12] Army tactics were all about seeing, shooting, and then moving.

The Army called the other way to bring fire on the battlefield "indirect observed fire." In this case soldiers still had to see where the enemy was, but rather than exposing themselves to shoot at him, the troops could request fire support. This normally came from mortars or artillery, although airborne fighters on occasion also provided supporting fires with bombs or machine guns. An observer would "call for fire," identifying the target, its map location, and the direction from the observer to the target. Ideally, the observer would watch where the projectiles burst and call in adjustments. The observer would report how many meters and in what direction the rounds needed to move to be nearer to the target. The artillery unit would then calculate how to shift the direction and elevation of the artillery tubes to change the projectiles' trajectory, ensuring the rounds landed close enough to the enemy's position to destroy it or at least force the defenders to keep their heads down so that they could not see and fire at the advancing friendly troops.

Fire (either "direct fire" from rifles, machine guns, or tanks or "indirect fire" from artillery, mortars, or air support) and movement was how the

Americans expected to advance against the enemy in Normandy. That is what the books said. DePuy thought it was so important, the first memorandum he wrote in battle discussed directions for improving fields of fire and artillery coordination.[13] Soldiers in their foxholes read the blotchy rain- and dirt-smeared mimeographed sheets looking for answers on how to win the war and stay alive.

What was most remarkable about the Army doctrine of fire and maneuver was how little it had changed since the end of World War I.[14] It was also remarkable how absolutely useless Army doctrine seemed to be in hedgerow fighting. The problem with bocage battles was that GIs could not kill what they could not see, and the enemy used the hedgerows to make sure the Americans could not see very much. The hedgerows masked the fields in front of the advancing infantrymen so they did not know what was behind the next tree line.

When a GI helmet did poke through the bushes that masked the field beyond, the motion and sound of rustled leaves often provoked a spurt of machine-gun fire or a flurry of mortar rounds. If an advancing infantryman could look into the next field without being shot, he found little reward for the effort. The enemy soldiers concealed their positions by digging into the back side of the hedgerows leaving nothing more sticking out than the business end of a machine gun. Even if the American troops survived blindly shooting and racing across the small Norman fields to the other end of the hedgerows, it might be all for naught. In some cases, the Germans would simply withdraw to the next field, and the killing dance would have to be repeated all over again. Alternatively, the enemy would call up small groups of reinforcements (troops that were not on the front lines, but farther back out of range of the enemy guns that were held in reserve), which the Americans could not see either. A sharp German counterattack would drive the GIs back, and they would have to pay in blood again to recover the real estate they had paid a dear price for the first time they attacked.

The difficulty was not much different from the dilemma faced by their fathers when they assaulted the German trench lines in the First World War. Then one technological solution that presented itself was harnessing the combustion engine for war, wrapped in a blanket of steel plating and called a tank. The tanks could plow across no-man's-land through the barbed wire and over the enemy trenches. After they cleared the way, the infantry could follow on.

Armor, however, proved ill-suited to breaking the stalemate in Normandy. Part of the problem was that the tanks, as the infantry, could not kill what they could not see. The other part of the problem was that they proved very vulnerable in bocage warfare. In many cases, the hedgerows were so thick that tanks could not push through. In effect, the Germans found to their very good luck that every field in Normandy was ringed with a natural tank barrier. In addition, when armor could climb over a hedgerow, the angle of the embankment would force the tank up with its gun pointing into the air and exposing the soft underside of the vehicle to the enemy. In that terrifying pause before the tank lurched forward into the field ahead, the crew could not see or shoot at anything and it was totally vulnerable. The Germans waited for that perfect moment, when they could easily take out a tank with a short-range handheld antitank rocket. Likewise German tanks or antitank guns could be hidden behind hedgerows or sunken lanes, waiting for the kill.

The medieval hedgerows of Normandy wiped out the technological advances in modern war. As a result, after seven weeks of fighting, American commanders could stand on high ground and look over their shoulders and see waves break on the shore where material and equipment stacked up on the beaches. A million men, a half-a-million tons of supplies, and 150,000 vehicles piled up along the thin crust of free France.

General Bradley knew that hedgerows did not go on forever. Farther south the ground was much more open, with better roads and open fields, plenty of room to unleash the Allied armies armored forces, plenty of good fields of fire. The challenge was how to get there without losing tens-of-thousands more infantrymen in the bocage meat grinder, infantry that would be needed in the long march to Berlin.

Bradley planned one of the most important battles of the war—the Normandy breakout. The general intended to mass six divisions on a narrow front to break through the enemy lines and then turn west driving to the coast and cutting off and annihilating the left flank of the German defenses. Taking the island, breaching the Séves River, would put the 90th in a good position to exploit the breakthrough and perhaps begin to redeem the division's reputation.

## CHANGE OF COMMAND

Leadership meant a lot to Bradley as well. Before Normandy, during the Sicilian campaign he relieved Terry de la Mesa Allen, the popular commander of the 1st Infantry Division, because Bradley found him "troublesome," and it was a first-class fighting outfit and Allen a proven, courageous combat leader.[15] After the 90th's performance there was little hope that its leaders would be spared. The division commander Jay MacKelvie did not last long.

From the first days of the invasion there were problems. MacKelvie "sat in a room of the French farmhouse that was the division CP [command post] and stared into the distance."[16] Even the division's analysis of its first attacks recognized they were a disaster, poorly planned, led, and executed.[17] The corps commander fired MacKelvie less than a week after D-Day. Bradley offered no objection. When the troops heard he had been removed and reduced in rank, on officer wrote, "no one seems to know how low that is but all agree it wouldn't be low enough."[18] A few weeks later MacKelvie's assistant, Brigadier General "Hanging" Sam Williams, and a regimental commander were sacked as well.

The newly appointed division commander, Eugene Landrum, offered the 90th a fresh start. Landrum was gruff, no-nonsense, old army, and a veteran of the 1918–1919 Siberian campaign. He commanded U.S. troops in the rugged terrain on Attu Island off the coast of Alaska in 1942 and had headed up the 87th Infantry Division. Landrum would set things right. "I sincerely hope he makes good," General Dwight David Eisenhower, the commander of Allied forces in Europe, reported to George Marshall, the Army Chief of Staff at the Pentagon, "because we have been counting on him very much."[19] The problem with the 90th, as Eisenhower explained to Marshall, was that "this unit is less well prepared for battle than almost any other. ... our senior leaders are quite sure that the Division was not well brought up."[20] All it needed was a strong dose of old-fashioned leadership.

Landrum proved eager to tackle the Séves River crossing and exploit the Normandy breakout. He assigned the mission of taking the island to the 358th Infantry Regiment.

The regiment also had new leadership, its third commander since the Normandy landings, Lieutenant Colonel Christian Clarke. Taking over the regiment on June 15, 1944, with over a month of combat time, he was one of the most experienced leaders in the 90th. In his command post at the village of Gonfreville, Clarke's staff mapped out its plan to rescue the division's reputation. This time it would be done the right way—the Army way.

The plan for cracking the Séves was classic Army fire and maneuver.[21] Fire would come from a spurt of artillery and fighter-bombers that would precede the assault. This would not be like the barrages of World War I. Then artillery would pummel the enemy lines for days, churning up earth and making the approaches impossible while the enemy soldiers nestled safely in their bunkers. In the end the barrage made the advance more, not less, difficult. Alerted of an impending attack, the enemy would call up reinforcements. When the rain of fire ended, the enemy positions would prove more difficult than when the shooting began. In contrast, the assault on the Séves would begin with a short, sharp preparatory barrage that would not give the enemy time to react. And, it would be directed by airborne artillery observers in small planes who could look down into the German positions and accurately direct the American guns on to the target. And there would be a lot of

General Landrum Lectures the Troops about Hedgerow Fighting. (Courtesy, Army Signal Corps)

support. The 90th's attack was the only one scheduled in the corps area. Every artillery battalion in range would join in support, giving the infantry enough cover to race across the open ground to the edge of the island. Once the ground artillery observers crossed with the infantry to the point where they could see the German positions, they would call for more artillery to cover the advance as the GIs closed in.

The maneuver called for two battalions to advance on the objective side by side. It was a lot of troops in a small space. A fully manned infantry battalion had about 860 troops. Though battalions in combat were rarely at full strength and every soldier in the unit would not be at the front (some would be wounded or sick, others would be carrying out rear-area duties such as supply details), still a full-scale battalion attack threw hundreds of soldiers at the enemy. They would probably overwhelmingly outnumber the German defenders.

Not only did it have a lot more soldiers than the enemy, the division had some extra days to rest its demoralized and exhausted troops before the assault. It had been an unusually wet Norman summer and overcast skies interfered with the Allies' ability to employ air support on the front. The breakout was delayed while they waited for the clearer weather the forecasters predicted later in the week. As a result, there was no need to rush the attack on the White Witch. The regiment could use that time to rest.

Meanwhile, for a change, while the skies were as gray as a German uniform, there was not much rain. The water level was down. When it came time to strike, the attackers would be able wade onto the island without any difficulty. They would ford the river, setting up a bridgehead. Engineers would come up behind them and lay temporary bridging, followed by tanks and antitank guns to reinforce the position. Later, backed by the armor, they would drive the remaining defenders off the island.

It was a simple plan. There was nothing wrong with that. As Carl von Clausewitz, the great nineteenth century Prussian military philosopher, whom American army officers were encouraged to read and study, wrote, "in war even the simple is difficult." That is why at the academy at West Point future officers were taught the time-tested "principles of war." One of them was "simplicity." Schoolbook learning was reinforced with the experience of battle. While serving at the Infantry School, long before he became the Army Chief of Staff, George Marshall, the service's most senior general during World War II, commissioned a study of the lessons learned from the mistakes of fighting during the First World War. One of the key lessons was "simplicity in plans, methods, and orders should always be striven for and that elaborate and complicated maneuvers should not be adopted except for the gravest reasons."[22] The rule in battle was always to do the simplest thing possible to get the job done.

Nothing could be simpler than Clarke's plan—overwhelm the enemy with fire and then maneuver.

## RUN TO DAYLIGHT

The schedule called for the troops to cross the line of departure, the water's edge bordering the island that marked the starting point for the attack, at 6:30 A.M. as soon as there was enough light for the aerial observers to spot their targets. And the fires went off at the time intended. Exactly as scheduled, for 15 minutes before the assault five battalions of artillery poured fires on the island, almost a thousands rounds of high-explosive projectiles, cracking and flashing across the face of the island. The taking of the White Witch and the redemption of the 90th Division were under way.

Dawn, however, was not quite what they had hoped for. A clear and crisp morning did not come. Sunrise on July 22, 1944, came shrouded in low-level clouds and damp fog, grounding the fighter-bombers and observation planes. The attack, however, could not be delayed any longer. Jump-off for the breakout had been set. It would happen in 48 hours. If the division wanted to be in a position to exploit the breakout, it had to go on July 22.

Without the air observers, there was no way to tell if the artillery rounds were landing on the enemy. Still, if the rounds forced the Germans to keep their heads down and gave the battalions time to race across the stream, that would be good enough.

It was not. The infantry troops could not cross the line of departure. Even before the attack started, they came under enemy artillery fire. A battalion that did not even join in the advance lost 42 men. The first companies that reached the stream took 50 percent casualties.

Studying the map and trying to guess where the enemy guns were situated, the Americans responded, firing artillery at the suspected German positions. It did not work. Likewise, the preparatory fires seemed to have no effect other than to alert the Germans that an attack was on the way. Enemy flares etched the gray morning skies flickering over the American lines and shadowing the heavily burdened infantrymen as they moved forward. The false dawn was followed by a withering blanket of machine-gun fire and more enemy artillery.

At the same time, all of the American artillery rounds fell far behind the forward German positions and well in front of where their reserves were hidden. The enemy infantrymen were not bothered by the bursting projectiles at all as the explosions kicked up clouds of dirt over empty ground.

Still the Germans were vastly outnumbered. If the GIs could get onto the island, they would hold a distinct numerical advantage. In Army doctrine a superiority of three to one of attackers over defenders was thought sufficient to support an advance. The Americans had many times the Germans' numbers.

Initially, the Americans lost part of that advantage. Hundreds of GIs did not make it to the start line. Only one infantry battalion, under the command of Lieutenant Colonel Al Seeger, managed to move over the largely open ground, down the muddy lane, and through the artillery and machine-gun fire that led to the White Witch. The first company did not reach the stream until 8:30 A.M., when it called for a repeat of the artillery preparation, before it attempted to ford the stream. The field artillery fired at the same targets all over again, which proved of little help. The first company to cross did not reach the island until 11 A.M.

Frustrated, the regimental commander watched the slow pace of the advance from a forward command post overseeing the start line. Clarke could think of little else to do.

Meanwhile, the artillery kept firing, shooting for four hours nonstop, over 5,000 rounds. It did not accomplish much. According to the division artillery after-action report, 95 percent of the fires provided during the day were unobserved—no one could see where the exploding rounds landed or the effect they were having on the enemy. Artillery observers had reached the island, but only one was uninjured and he had no communications. His radio had been destroyed and he would not be able to talk to the field artillery battalions until wire lines were run to his position and phone communications could be set up. To do that, however, wiremen would have to cross the belt of fire laid down by the German defenders.

## DESCENT INTO DARKNESS

To their credit, the GIs continued to press the attack. Sometimes numbers do make the difference. Hundreds of soldiers inched their way toward the high ground, too many for the Germans to slaughter with the meager defenses they had on the island. The comfort of numbers combined with the cajoling of the battalion's officers and the sight of American artillery fire pounding the White Witch (even though it had little effect) was enough to sustain the attack. By 1:00 P.M., two more companies from Seeger's battalion had crossed over. The second battalion also kept at it and got some of its soldiers down the lane and on the island before dark. Together, parts of two battalions had pushed half way across to the high ground and breached the German lines. They had achieved their part of the plan.

Seeger, the senior commander on the island, ordered the men to secure their lines, digging trenches and foxholes along some of the hedgerow-bound fields and fortifying the buildings at the St. Germain farm, forming a horseshoe-shaped defense for any German counterattacks that might appear during the night.

There was, however, a problem. Seeger's battalion was over a half a mile from the start line. Troops from the other battalion were only a 150 yards from the shore. There was a big hole in the flank of the horseshoe.

There was another problem as well. The infantry was alone. The tanks could not cross onto the island. Every time the engineers came forward to lay the steel planking for a temporary bridge, they were slammed by German artillery and mortar fire and driven back.

Nor was there any observed fire support. Three soldiers from one of the artillery battalions gamely tried to lay wire lines to the island. They were all shot.

There was also no way to reach the farm at St. Germain or evacuate wounded without coming under enemy fire. The regimental supply officer, Major Mike Knouf, personally led forays throughout the night, ferrying supplies to the forward troops, but it was not much.

For the GIs on the island, all that could be done was to dig in deeper, ignoring the smell and sight of the dead from both sides that littered the battlefield, and wait for reinforcements and the inevitable German counterattack—and hope that the reinforcements got there first.

There was little joy in gaining a foothold on the White Witch. The combination of overwhelming exhaustion and apprehension for the future made an uneasy cocktail. An assault, like the day's drive on the island, slated for dawn, meant that the troops had to be up well before that, throwing down an uncooked K-ration meal out of a waxy box container, and marching to the front to ready for the attack—shaking off the raw morning fog, waiting for the order to go. And then they went into battle—wet from sweat, swamp, and stream, and on their feet for 18 hours before the day's battle came to an end with little prospect for much sleep before the next dawn.

After gaining its foothold on the high ground, cold, wet, exhausted, and muddied, the infantry shivered in the dark. Some balled up in the bottom of a foxhole for a spate of fretful sleep. Others stood watch—blinking, straining to look deep into the black for signs of a moving shadow, or listening for the crack of a twig, the creaky turn of an armored track, or the howl of an incoming mortar round that might signal the enemy's advance. This twilight time, the battle at the end of a day of battle, was the greatest measure of a unit's discipline and skill. Despite all the privations and miseries, there was still work to do: weapons cleaned, fields of fire cleared, and plans coordinated. There were no time-outs in war. All these things happened only if troops were exceptionally well prepared or driven by iron-willed leaders. That night, there were few signs of either.

At the battalion command post, Colonel Seeger anxiously counted the hours till sunrise and did little else. There was a reason why as a leader, one military historian rated him as a "nice guy, but no drive, spirit, courage, or leadership."[23]

Meanwhile, during the night, the fog rolled in and stayed. In the morning there would be no aerial observers. And the river swelled two feet. Now, without a bridge, no one could cross. Major Knouf, who had delivered his last load of supplies, found himself on the wrong side of the river. He looked back across the rising waters to the regimental lines. There would be no return. Knouf was an infantryman now and was there for the duration.

## DAWN'S EARLY LIGHT

While the GIs wearily waited for daylight, in the warmth of a farmhouse not far distant, the Germans plotted.

Perhaps the most unfortunate turn of events for the men of the 90th on the night of July 22, 1944, is that the Germans they faced were led by Lieutenant Colonel Friedrich August Freiherr von Heydte, commander of the 6th Parachute Regiment. Many of the German soldiers fighting under him had no more combat experience than the American infantry. As a leader, however, Heydte was nothing like his American counterparts. He was a combat veteran of North Africa, Sicily, and the Russian front. He was used to fighting with nothing. He depended on personal leadership and creative, innovative tactics to make up for want of everything: men, ammunition, and supplies. And he was good at his job.

Heydte did one thing during the battle that Landrum and Clarke never did. He made a decision that made a difference.

The German lieutenant colonel knew the Americans at St. Germain would stop their attack at dark. They always did. He had until morning to assess the situation and launch a counterstrike. He also knew that without armor, air support, or accurate artillery fire, the GIs were vulnerable. The sooner a counterattack was launched, regardless of its strength, the better chance it had of pushing back the Americans. He would send all he had—three tanks, about 50 men, and a top sergeant to lead them. All they had to do was overcome about 300 dug-in infantrymen.

Sergeant Walter Uhlig never questioned his commander's judgment, even when tasked to take back the island in the face of overwhelming force. If they had followed American doctrine, they would now be retreating, not advancing. But they did not play by American rules. The Germans moved at night when they could not be seen by the American fighter planes or the aerial artillery observers. They would have another advantage as well. When the GIs attacked, they battled against well-prepared and organized defense positions. When Uhlig counterattacked, he would be going up against an exhausted and hastily organized enemy.

Without the threat of air attack or artillery, Uhlig's task force made its way to the front. His only loss—one of the tanks. It got stuck in the mud. That was an unfortunate loss. He would be short a third of his armor before the battle had even begun—but at least he would have two more tanks than the Americans.

They reached the island by dawn. Fortunately, it was still overcast. There would be no American planes. At 7:00 A.M., Uhlig struck.

The attack did not go well. Once in the open, in daylight, the Germans had the same problem as the Americans. Tanks and infantry on the far bank, unable to cross the river, could still see the advance on the horseshoe, and they poured fire onto the island driving the enemy soldiers back as soon as they appeared.

Orders also went out to the American artillery to fire in support, but lacking contact with the last artillery observer alive on the White Witch, the gunners could only guess at the best place to shoot. The Americans shot at the same place as they did the day before—on empty, unoccupied ground.

When Sergeant Uhlig withdrew to regroup, gathering his men and organizing them for another assault on the enemy lines, the American projectiles landed harmlessly behind them in thunderous cracks and billows of flying dirt and acrid smoke. He turned to his men and told them they had no choice, they could either try to retreat and be killed by the U.S. artillery or charge the enemy, knowing that the Americans would never shoot any closer to their own lines out of fear of hitting the GIs.

## SOUNDS OF SILENCE

A final German counterattack at 9:30 A.M. plunged straight through the hole in the horseshoe. The defenders panicked. The defense was leaderless. Most of the American troops abandoned their positions and raced back to the stream, where they were cornered by the water's edge and a steady treatment of German fire.

Nothing is more frightening in a desperate moment of battle than the realization that no one is in charge, that there is no safe haven of leadership that offers the comfort of a confident leader or the promise of survival. In war, numbers without leadership is nothing.

Little could be done from the far shore. The tanks and artillery held their fire out of fear of hitting friendly troops.

With his command dissolving around him and no means to fight off the German tanks, Seeger ordered the men to lay down their weapons. Some had not even waited for the word—throwing down their arms and throwing up their hands. Others waived white handkerchiefs.

Knouf was near the battalion command post when the surrender started. Defiantly, he ignored Seeger's order and decided to lead a charge back toward the American lines. He was wounded almost immediately.

On the far side of the stream, Clarke listened as the battlefield fell silent. The sound of shooting melted away. The report of the surrender—and the losses—drifted back to the command post. One officer and 68 men were killed. Five officers and 99 men were wounded (including Knouf; a soldier saved his life by carrying him to a German aid station after the surrender). Eleven officers and 254 men just gave up.

Over 400 were lost, to gain—nothing.

That afternoon, Clarke was replaced as regimental commander.

Once the corps commander learned the extent of the disaster, Landrum's job was in serious doubt. There was little question but that the attack demonstrated that he had failed to turn the division around. "Short, fat, uninspiring," one combat historian concluded, he "[c]ommanded the division from an arm chair in a cellar."[24] In retrospect, Landrum's effort to shake up the division seemed obviously wrongheaded. He fired the assistant division commander, Sam Williams, not because he was not one of the command's few good combat leaders, but because Williams disagreed with him. After one battle when Landrum failed to commit the division reserves, "Hanging Sam" grilled him for his "god damn stupidness."[25] Williams was right, Landrum was just not a first-class combat leader. This time it was Landrum who got relieved.

Meanwhile, at his command post, Heydte hosted some of the captured American officers. He offered them tea. It was not an empty gesture. Heydte was a professional soldier. He was extending a courtesy to brother officers. The lieutenant colonel was also curious to meet the Americans. What kind of men led soldiers into battle in this manner?

## TAKING THE HIGH GROUND

In contrast to the 90th, the infantry of the 2nd Division, another rookie command, knew a different kind of war.

Like the 90th, the 2nd Infantry Division had piled ashore after D-Day in its first campaign of the Second World War. It also had the mission of pressing inland to advance the expanse of the Allied lodgment area. The division was on the other side of St.-Lô, the city that marked the pivot point for Bradley's planned breakout battle. Its job, like the 90th Division, was also to hold the enemy in place until U.S. forces broke through into the German rear. Its mission was also the same: secure a piece of high ground that would dominate the enemy lines. The objective had a simple, uninspiring name—Hill 192, the elevation marked on the topographic maps handed out to the troops. But like the assault on the White Witch, taking the high ground would prove a daunting, almost impossible task.

The sunken dirt lanes that linked the Norman farmers to their fields laced the hedgerows, but all roads led to St.-Lô. That was the way it was in the medieval countryside. Roads converged on the great towns. The great medieval towns also shared two other things in common: defensible terrain (to protect against invading armies) and access to a river (a lifeline for trade and commerce). St.-Lô was no exception. Roads spidered out of the city like spokes on the hub of a wheel, and St.-Lô sat on high ground above the banks of the Vire River. These attributes made the city a natural turning point for the breakout. Once the Americans pierced the German lines and turned to encircle the enemy in front of the 90th, the river would protect the rear of the encircling forces from German counterattacks. The highway running out of St.-Lô straight west toward the coast also made for an easily identifiable feature to mark to starting line for the First Army offensive.

Controlling St.-Lô was a virtual prerequisite for the breakout. And that meant controlling the high ground around the town, the roads, and the river crossings. The Americans considered Hill 192 particularly important. From its heights, the Germans had erected an observation tower from which they could see the Allies unload supplies on Omaha Beach and virtually everything the Americans were doing across the front of two U.S. corps, a distance of several miles.[26] It was as good as having an air observer circulating permanently over the American lines. The Germans had no intention of giving up this advantage. Troops in heavily defended strongpoints ringed the hill like a medieval fortress.

The 2nd Division first tried to take the hill on June 12, 1944, less than a week after the landings. Four days and over 1,200 casualties later, it gave up.[27] Before there could be a breakout, it would have to try again.

For weeks, the division stared up the heights of Hill 192. The troops did not like what there was to see. It was not a particularly steep hill, only 1,000 yards in distance and a 150 feet in altitude from the American lines to the flat spot on the top. On a warm Sunday afternoon, picnickers could hike to the summit in short order and never lose their breath—if it were not for the German defenses. The hill (except for a large diamond-shaped woods on the southeast side near the crest that the Americans could not see) was covered with hedgrows and orchards, infested with dug-in German positions supported by interlocking fields of fire. That meant that from one strongpoint the enemy could observe and fire on infantry attacking the strongpoints on either side of the position. For a month the Germans had been digging in. Some of the dugouts were 12 feet deep with firing platforms to stand on and firing slits covered by foliage that made the positions indistinguishable from the surrounding countryside.[28]

In addition to the hedgerows, three small villages—Cloville, le Soulaire, and la Croix-Rouge—blocked the slopes of the hill, while farther down the road leading to the Bayeux-St.-Lô highway, there were some farmhouses. All these could be and probably were fortified by the Germans as well. And all of these, the farmhouses, villages, bunkers, and machine-gun nests had been linked with a network of tunnels, trenches, and sunken country lanes that allowed the enemy to shift supplies and reinforcements around out of sight of the Americans. The Germans had been busy while they waited for the GIs to come again.

The layout of enemy defenses made them especially troublesome. The Germans had adapted a scheme that had been perfected on the Russian front. There they found there was never enough troops to cover the vast expanse of open ground on the Russian steppes. The Germans covered these gaps not with troops, but with fire—fire from well-prepared and fortified positions that could not be easily bypassed because they were covered by fire from other strongpoints. Fighting through such a network was a costly, time-consuming process.[29]

As a matter of comparison, the German strongpoint system was nothing like the defenses thrown up over the night at the White Witch. On the island, the GIs set up a "linear" defense. Once the line was breached and the enemy was behind the U.S. troops, the Americans were "outflanked." In other words, Sergeant Uhlig and his men were in a position to cut them off from retreat or support from the friendly troops in the rear. In addition, once troops were flanked, they could well find themselves being shot at from two directions, the enemy ahead of them and behind. Since defensive positions were normally built to guard against attacks only from the front, the danger of being outflanked was particularly harrowing. The U.S. troops were not prepared to shoot at or protect themselves from an enemy that was behind them. In contrast, strongpoint defenses were built on the assumption that the enemy would find gaps in the line and could attack from any direction. But since the strongpoints were constructed for all-around defense and since they could fire in support of one another, they were far more difficult to outflank.

The Russians threw thousands of men and tanks at the strongpoint defenses on the Eastern Front, grinding them down by a process of attrition. That, however, would not work in Normandy. The 2nd Division had neither the time, men, nor material to batter its way up Hill 192.

## HOMEWORK

To get ready to take Hill 192, the division went back to school. In the middle of a war zone, Major General Walter M. Robertson, commander of the "Indian Head" Division (so-called because of its shoulder patch sporting the profile of an Indian chief), decided to stop in the middle of the war and start training again. He proposed the task: throw out the doctrine and figure out how to fire and maneuver through the hedgerows without piling up U.S. dead in the temporary cemetery near the Graves Registration Point at St. Mère Église.

In terms of weapons and technology, the Americans had three real operational advantages over the Germans: armor, airpower, and artillery. While tank for tank, the German armor had many advantages, it just did not have near the numbers as the American forces. Likewise the Americans had virtual air superiority. Weather permitting, they could fly where they wanted, when they wanted, and shoot at what they wanted. The GIs also had much more artillery and, unlike the other armies in Normandy, the means to effectively "mass" its fires, the ability to have all the artillery tubes within range fire on a single area. What Robertson ordered, before the word came to climb Hill 192 again, was to figure out how to overcome the test of terrain and use all these assets to the best advantage.

Several divisions, including the soldiers of the Indian Head, joined in developing solutions for busting the bocage. What they were looking for was a way to get an observer to a point where he could see the enemy without getting shot and then direct armor, artillery, and airpower to do the killing without putting the lives of the infantry at risk. The greatest obstacle to that goal was the German MG 42 machine gun, the mainstay of the enemy's defenses. Lightweight, dependable, rugged, simple to operate, and with a high rate of fire, this crew-served weapon was ideal for hedgerow fighting. And the Germans had lots of them and plenty of ammunition.[30]

An MG 42 dug in behind the corner of a hedgerow and camouflaged could command the length of the entire field, making passage simply impossible. To make the machine guns even more effective, the Germans would plan mortar and artillery targets right on the other side of the hedgerow on the opposite end of the field where the Americans would be attacking from. When the GIs attacked, the machine gun would drive them back behind the hedgerow for cover, and then the Germans would call a short, sharp rain of supporting fire right down on top of them.

While an infantryman's shirt could not stop a machine-gun bullet or a fragment from a mortar round, the armor on a tank could. The problem was getting the tank into the fight. That required busting through hedgerows, and a solid hedgerow could block a tank.

A few tanks had been shipped to Normandy with blades on their fronts similar to commercial bulldozers. The idea was to provide the means to clear rubble off the beach exits and roadways that might block an advance when military engineer units were not at hand.[31] For example, a tank with a blade could push a pile of rubble into a shell hole in a road, making it passable for trucks and tanks. The blades proved useful for a number of tasks and, unexpectedly, seemed perfect for bocage fighting. The Americans found that a dozer tank was powerful enough to push its way right through a hedgerow. Going straight through the hedgerow, it could keep its main body and machine guns level and firing, suppressing the enemy machine guns.

There were, however, only a handful of "dozer" tanks in the theater. A typical battalion had about 70 tanks, but, on average, only four had dozer blades—not nearly enough to meet the needs of all the infantry. In July 1944, Bradley's headquarters ordered 278 additional dozer tanks, but commanders feared the summer would be over before they could be shipped from the States.[32] The Germans also were not stupid. When the Americans attacked, the word went out, "kill the tank with the blade first." Some other method of busting hedgerows would have to be improvised.

The divisions then turned to the Army engineers. After a little experimentation, combat engineers found that two charges of about 25 to 50 pounds, placed several feet apart, would blow a big enough hole to drive a tank through. But it was not that simple. One engineer battalion calculated that in a typical battle an armor battalion over the course of an average attack (about a mile and a half) would have to cross upward of 34 hedgerows. That would require 17 tons of explosives. There probably were not enough demolition packs in the theater to meet the needs of all the divisions, and even if there were, there was no practical way to carry them, nor enough engineers to emplace them.[33]

GIs in the division on the flank of the 2nd, the 29th Infantry Division, hit on a more effective solution. If the charges could be buried inside the hedgerow, far less explosives were needed. There was, however, still a problem. A noisy engineer squad digging holes on the back side of a hedgerow would get the attention of the German defenders who would then call down pre-planned artillery or mortar fires. The Germans knew they would not be able to see the Americans hiding in the hedgerows in front of their positions, but they would probably be able to hear them, so they sighted in the targets ahead of time, accurately recording the locations and reporting them to their artillery or mortar support. Then, when they heard the Americans approach, they could just call for fire on the locations where they assumed they would be. Usually, they were right.

The German habit of peppering the hedgerows with fire at the first sign of an American advance made sending in engineers laden with picks and shovels and high explosives first a dubious idea. There had to be a better way.

Leaders in the 29th figured it out. It was the genius of two commanders and their men from the 747th Tank Battalion and the 121st Engineer Combat Battalion who experimented with various ways to work together. The method they derived that seemed best was to weld metal pipes onto the front side of the tanks' final drive assemblies, reinforced with angle irons. The tanks, virtually immune to machine gun and mortar fire, would drive headlong into the hedgerow punching holes (about four feet deep and six-and-a-half inches in diameter) and then pull back. Engineers would rush forward, throwing 105-mm shell casings packed with only 15 pounds of explosives into the breech. The hole and the casing created a shaped charge that pushed most of the force of the explosion into the back of the hedgerow blowing a space large enough for the tanks to rush forward and drive across the field and over the German defenses.[34]

Even these initiatives, however, were not good enough. They still needed infantry to protect the tanks from German *panzerfausts* (shoulder-fired anti-tank rockets) and to safeguard engineers against snipers and ambushes. And the infantry still needed to be protected from the MG 42.

## WORLD WAR I REPRISE

The 2nd Division knew that hedgerow busting tactics were not enough to tackle the web of defenses on Hill 192. They added their own refinements. The engineer team (three or four men) and an infantry squad (about a dozen soldiers) were assigned to accompany each tank. The infantry squad secured the hedgerow. Then according to an Army historical summary,

> When the engineers had blown a hole for the tanks to pass through, the tanks would enter the field, fire their 75-mm guns into the corners, and spray the lateral hedgerow ahead to cover the infantry scouts advancing (in this case) along the axial hedges. These scouts would also be covered by BAR [Browning Automatic Rifle] men.[35] Two of the four demolitions men followed behind, and the engineers and the leader of the infantry squad would choose the best place for the tank to go through the next barrier. Special EE-8 phones were installed on the rear of the tanks and connected with the tank's interphone system for tank-infantry communication during action. Two engineers would stay with the vehicle to protect it during advance, scanning and firing at side hedgerows to keep down enemy bazooka [shoulder-fired rocket] teams.[36]

As the infantry squad moved forward in a wedge formation, spread out on either side behind the tank, follow-on troops scoured the hedgerows looking for any bypassed enemy or snipers.[37]

Finally, to make easier the task of lugging the explosive packs they would need to blow the hedgerows, the engineers planned to tie them on the backs of the tanks. In this manner, they would be readily available and also spare the infantry the task of humping the explosives up the hill.

The real genius of the 2nd Division attack on the Hill, however, was the artillery plan, an idea borrowed from a tactic that was no longer in the army field manuals—a World War I style rolling artillery barrage.

During the First World War, the assaulting troops frequently found that after days and weeks of bombardment, they would attack only to find the enemy defenses completely intact. The enemy would hide in bunkers deep underground until the preparatory fires lifted, and only then would they man their positions. And so, the assaulting force added additional fires they called "the rolling barrage." These would be artillery fires that would essentially walk in front of the infantry all the way to the objective. After firing a salvo of fire at a line of terrain, the artillerymen would shift to another line of targets slightly farther forward. In theory the attacking infantrymen would march behind the fire wall all the way to the objective, as the exploding artillery shells obscured observation of their advance and forced the enemy to take cover.

The only difficulty was that in practice, rolling barrages almost never worked. The infantry would usually get hung up trying to cut its way through barbed wire and other obstacles and slowed negotiating the shell holes churned up by the exploding artillery. Communicating these problems to the guns, however, was a problem. Most communication was done by phone over wires laid above ground by hand. These were often cut by enemy artillery fire. There was no way to tell the artillery to wait for the infantry, and so fire from the guns marched over the objective and the enemy took position and waited, while the attackers anxiously watched their covering fire disappear into the distance. The tactic hardly proved its worth and was largely abandoned by modern armies—until the day came to attack Hill 192.

The American artillerymen had several advantages that their World War I predecessors lacked—forward observers (both on the ground and airborne) to spot the fires and send corrections to the artillery, radio communications to supplement the wire and phone lines usually used to call for fire, and the fire direction center (FDC). The advent of the FDC was particularly important. The FDC could do what could never be done with First World War artillery units—have everyone fire on the same place. During World War I, when the call came to fire, a command would pick out an identifiable terrain feature or map location and ask all units to shoot somewhere in that area. The FDC used a much more sophisticated method that enabled one field artillery headquarters to direct the fire of all artillery pieces within range and accurately place the exploding rounds to within 50 yards of a specific point on the ground.

Artillery fire plans were based on numbered grid squares drawn over a map of Hill 192. The grid was divided into four zones, each assigned a color. Using the system to designate where to fire, the infantry could march the fire up the hill in 50-yard increments.[38]

Of course to provide such a density and duration of fire, a lot of artillery would be needed. In a normal battle, a regiment would have one or two field artillery battalions, each containing three batteries of four guns each, backing it up. For the assault on Hill 192, eight battalions, over 100 tubes of artillery, would be available to support the attack.

The World War I style assault might have seemed an anachronism, but for the commanders there appeared to be little option. While the GIs knew the hill was heavily defended, they had absolutely no idea where the enemy was. They had taken aerial photographs, which showed nothing. They flew some of the ground commanders over the position in the planes of the aerial artillery observers; they saw nothing. At night, they launched patrol after patrol at the enemy lines. They got shot to pieces. "Led by lieutenants until expended," one officer recalled, "and then by sergeants, reduced to near nothing life expectancy of all who took part."[39] It was futile.

On the other hand, the promise of paving the way to the objective with a rolling wall of protective fire seemed like a great idea to the infantry. "After hearing of all the fire support I was to receive," remembered Lieutenant Colonel Frank T. Mildren whose command was to lead the way up the hill, "I figured the battalion could almost walk up the hill without too much effort."[40] At least that was what he hoped.

## AMERICAN FORCES IN ACTION

From the division command post at Cerisy-la-Forêt, General Robertson waited for daylight and the coming attack. He was hopeful, too. The troops had trained their hedgerow busting tactics for two weeks. The artillery had carefully planned an ingenious way to cover the advance, and there was even a promise of air support, fighters that would be available to bomb and strafe the enemy lines. The plan called for four groups of fighters, each with 48 planes that would arrive over the battlefield in waves every 15 minutes starting at the beginning of the attack.[41]

Robertson's assault on Hill 192 involved all three of his infantry regiments. The 9th Infantry Regiment, whose sector bordered the hill, remained in place, but from its position would fire on the enemy lines. The 23rd Infantry Regiment would attack with two battalions in column up the eastern slope and over the top to secure high ground south along the Bayeux-St.-Lô highway. The main effort, however, would be made by the 38th Infantry Regiment commanded by Colonel Ralph W. Zwicker. Zwicker's scheme of maneuver called for the same advance as the attack at the Séves, two battalions abreast, side by side. Their task was to fight up the western slope of Hill 192 through the heart of the German defenses. In addition to the attack of the 23rd Regiment, two other divisions were conducting supporting operations, but all that mattered little if the 38th failed to take its objective. It all depended on the 38th.

And Zwicker believed the 38th was ready. For days the battalions had taken turns coming off the line to rehearse their attacks. All the squad leaders in the lead assault units had been given a map or sketch showing them the location of every hedgerow in their path and the route the squad and the supporting tank team would follow.[42] The regimental supply officer even counted the number of hedgerows, calculated how much ammunition would be needed to take them, and then ensured that each unit had been issued enough rounds to see it through the day. The tanks for the hedgerow busting teams were infiltrated into the fronts in ones and twos over the course of the night before the attack so that the Germans would not suspect that the Americans were massing their armor for a big attack. They had thought of everything, he hoped.

At 5:30 A.M., an hour before dawn when the main attack was scheduled to start, Zwicker heard a rumbling thunder in the distance. It was not rain. He knew that, though there was a heavy morning fog that would force canceling the planned air strikes. The rumbling was artillery, part of the planned fires on the hill. For 50 minutes the artillerymen struck any known or suspected enemy position and also where they thought, from studying maps, the location of the enemy reserves and artillery might be.

The goal of these fires was modest, hopefully to disrupt the enemy defenses enough to get the attack off to a successful start, sow confusion, and perhaps catch some of the enemy behind the lines unprotected in the open. For the last 10 minutes before the regiment's main advance, all the battalions shifted their fires onto the first line of enemy-held hedgerows, trying to cripple the first line of the German defense right before the battle began. It was time to attack.

From the artillerymen's standpoint, from the start everything seemed to go exceedingly well. The records of the 65th Field Artillery Battalion, one of the units that fired throughout the day, reported that at the start they were called upon to shift fires 100 yards every 5 minutes and then at 100- and 200-yard jumps every 10 minutes for most of the remainder of the barrage, although at one point the guns fired at one grid for an hour. By the end of the day the gunners fired over 5,000 rounds.[43] Altogether, the artillery fired over 25,000 rounds. On the average, each tube fired over 300 times.

In fact, the Americans were so proud of their innovative plan that they featured the attack on Hill 192 in their *American Forces in Action Series* produced right after the war to highlight the genius and determination of the GI. "In a nation at war, teamwork by the whole people is necessary for victory," Dwight Eisenhower, serving as the Army's postwar Chief of Staff, wrote in the 1946 forward to the pamphlet, "But the issue is decided on the battlefield, toward which all national effort leads. The country's fate lies in the hands of its soldier citizens; in the clash of battle is found the final test of plans, training, equipment, and—above all—the fighting spirit of units and individuals."[44] Hill 192 was enshrined as a classic example of what the American soldier accomplished in battle. The attack was remembered as a real triumph in GI ingenuity.

## THE WAR THE INFANTRY KNEW

On the ground, at first light on the morning of the charge up the 1,000 yards of Hill 192, the course of events did not seem as worthy of deification.

Frank Mildren was anxious. The commander of the 1st Battalion, 38th Regiment, spearhead of the attack, found very little cause for optimism. His task was to drive up the right flank of the battalion zone, the most strongly defended ground on the hill. And it was strongly defended for a reason, because it led straight to the highest point on the hill. It was the one piece of real estate that Germans really did not want to give up, as Mildren found when his two companies leading the charge began the attack. They took very, very heavy casualties.

Nothing went right. The opening artillery preparation had no effect on the enemy mainly because the preparatory fires started the hour before the attack, hammering the suspected enemy positions in the rear, alerted the Germans manning the forward hedgerows. Knowing an American attack was coming, the troops at the front, rather than stay in place, left their positions and moved into hedgerows closer to the American lines. They could do that because they knew artillery fire was accurate only to within 50 yards and that before an artillery barrage, the GIs would leave a space of uncovered ground between them and the enemy to avoid hitting friendly troops with projectiles made in the United States.

The Americans found themselves attacking through enemy infantry at 6:20 A.M. just to get to the designated start line of the assault. And they came under German mortar fire as well. The Germans understood the key advantage of mortars in a close fight. It was something called "range probable" error. And they knew how to use that advantage to good effect.

Mortars were the infantry's artillery, a short metal tube and a base plate to rest the tube on. They could be carried by a few men. The trade-off was that they fired small projectiles lofted out of the tube by very little propellant at very low velocity. The way they achieved any range (perhaps at most a mile or two) at all was to aim the tubes at very high angles, using the oblique trajectory and the force of gravity to get the round to the target, much like lobbing a softball over the plate. In contrast, artillery pieces weighed much more because they had to withstand the explosion of larger propellants that could throw larger projectiles with much greater velocity at longer ranges (upward of nine miles). On the other hand, the angle and slow rate of descent did give the mortar a unique advantage. The mean point of impact of mortar rounds fired at one spot was a fraction of the dispersion of artillery. In the best of all possible worlds, the artillery could count, on average, that two rounds fired at the same spot would fall within 50 yards of each other. Mortars, because they were fired at shorter ranges, higher angles, and slower speeds, could be much more accurate. While commanders always worried about hitting their own troops with artillery in close combat, they were less worried about mortars. And so, when the Germans snuck forward to attack the Americans, they used mortars to cover the advance and call fires to within a few yards of their position.

The mortars also achieved an unexpected bonus. One round knocked out a tank supporting the battalion's hedgerow busting teams. "American tanks in the first assault wave were disabled or forced to withdraw," recounted the *American Forces in Action* pamphlet, as the tank company commander "recommended that they be committed elsewhere."[45] Mildren passed the bad news to Zwicker, who ordered the armor to shift in support of other units.

What the *American Forces in Action* pamphlet did not mention was that killing a tank with a mortar round was not supposed to happen. Something in the combat narrative was left out. A U.S. medium tank should have been able to take a direct hit from a mortar round without greatly disturbing the crew inside, let alone demolishing the tank. Normally, that would have been true, except for the demolition packs stacked on the back of the tanks for blowing holes in the hedgerows. When the mortar rounds hit the packs, the force of the explosion ripped the turrets off.

And the mortars were not the only problem. One tank laden with explosives got hit by a *panzerfaust* and exploded. Another struck an antitank mine and suffered the same fate. No wonder the armor company commander wanted to withdraw his tanks and find a different route up the hill. Using the tanks to carry the explosives was one innovation that in hindsight did not seem like such a great idea.

And it got worse. By 9:00 A.M., one of the attacking companies had lost so many men it was "combat ineffective." In other words, the commander did not think he had enough men left uninjured to continue to carry on. That meant that probably over half of the attacking force had been killed or wounded.

Meanwhile, the other attacking company continued to press forward. But that was not necessarily good news either. It got at least 200 yards ahead of the stalled company and then it too had problems. The company was taking fire from its flank, the area where the attack had stopped. This was the classic problem of combating a strongpoint defense; even successes could turn to failure because attacking troops could be held up by being fired upon from passed enemy positions from behind them. And the strongpoint holding up the battalion seemed especially large and well prepared, spread over four fields, and manned by at least two platoons of enemy defenders armed with rifles, machine guns, and *panzerfausts,* and apparently an ample supply of ammunition.

And it got worse still. By midmorning, the fog had burned off and the sky began to clear. A few American planes made a run at strafing and bombing the enemy lines. Some missed and bombed the troops of Mildren's battalion. One bomb destroyed the battalion aid station. Another landed on attacking infantry.

Mildren had to do something.

And he did. The battalion had kept one company in reserve. Reserves were troops that commanders did not commit immediately in a battle plan. They were held in "reserve." As events unfolded, commanders sent them where they were needed most, either to exploit success or avoid disaster. It was one of the few means by which leaders could influence the course of combat after the shooting got under way. And it was a vital decision. A commander probably got to make the choice only once. Once the reserve unit was sent in, there was not much else that could be done. The timely launching of reserves had made all the difference in the German counterattack on the Séves River. It could make all the difference here as well. And it did. Mildren ordered his reserve company to move up into the gap between the two companies on the line. With this addition, despite losing its tank support, the battalion continued to advance.

The major challenge that remained was busting the hedgerows without the tanks. Elsewhere on the battlefield, hedgerow-busting teams were making quick work of the obstacles blocking their advance, but Mildren's teams had lost a good chunk of their tank support at the outset. Mildren's men improvised with what they had. The walking wall of artillery proved helpful in keeping the enemies' heads down and allowing the infantry to advance. They set up machine guns behind each hedgerow to spray the one ahead, while scouts went out the hedgerows on the flanks of the field to check the hedgerows ahead. Following the scouts, squads would advance backed by BAR fire.

## THE LONGEST AFTERNOON

Unlike Landrum, General Robertson was anything but detached from the course of the day's combat. He understood what was happening on the other side of the hedgerows. "We have a battle on our hands," Robertson reported, "[but] things are breaking a little a hundred yards and a hundred yards there."[46] It did not seem like much, but Robertson knew that gaining

100 yards on Hill 192 was a real achievement. It meant they had found a way to fire and maneuver at last.

Still, even with the artillery support and the reinforcements on the way, it was a long, trying day for the troops fighting up Hill 192, particularly for the men of the 2nd Battalion, 38th Infantry Regiment. The confusion and the accidental bombing by the American planes delayed Mildren's reserve company by two hours, and instead of attacking into the gap between the two assault companies, the reserve company plunged headlong into the German strongpoint that had held up the advance.

The average battle in the hedgerow was bewildering and disorienting. Troops were never clear where the enemy was firing from, what was going on with friendly forces the next field over, or when they might stumble head long into a vicious German counterattack. Hedgerow battles were wars in isolation. Soldiers felt alone, naked, on their own, ears wringing and flinching at the crack of an explosion, jerking at the whine of ricocheting shrapnel. It could be difficult to see, wiping stinging sweat and grit from flying dirt with the back of a dirty hand. It could be difficult to hear, distinguishing the cries for help from the orders barked with a rush of adrenaline, and the curses in fear and anger. There was no promise of an easy advance in a hedgerow fight.

Mildren's reserves found when they got to the front, however, that the walking wall of artillery appeared to make a difference. The ability to move a curtain of fire almost at will gave the infantry some control over their fate. Artillery fires could keep the enemy at bay until the infantry was ready to go. Running into the teeth of a well-prepared strongpoint, the reserve company found to the surprise of both the Germans and the Americans, the enemy defenses gave way.

After clearing the strongpoint, Mildren's companies pushed ahead, more or less, side by side up the hill. By 1:30 P.M. the battalion's lead company reached the diamond-shaped woods to the south just beyond the crest of the hill. This was really unknown territory. The Americans had no idea what would be waiting for them in the dense woods. From the aerial photographs all they had been able to make out was the dark blotches of thick tree cover. It seemed an ideal spot to build a reverse slope defense from which the Germans could pick off the attackers as they topped the hill and tried to come down the other side. The GIs expected a tough fight, an infantry fight, at close quarters.

When two companies of the battalion crested the hill and headed down into the dark woods in a long skirmish line, they found something they had not expected—very little enemy. Artillery fire had burned out most of the foliage and the troops advanced through skeletons of blackened trees. Before nightfall, the entire battalion was over the top and advancing down the southern side of the hill toward the highway.

The division now owned the best real estate on Hill 192. It cost 69 killed, 328 wounded, and eight missing. A horrific price, but the 90th had lost almost the same number of boys at the battle on the Séves River, and all it had achieved was a humiliating defeat. At least the Indian Head had taken the high ground.

## LESSONS LEARNED

Two weeks after the assault on Hill 192 an unfinished letter was found on the body of a German soldier. On the day of the battle he had defended one of the forward hedgerows until the noontime push of the 38th Regiment forced a retreat. "I left the platoon sector as last man," he wrote, "crept back again with another to get back to the wounded. On our way back we were covered with terrific artillery fire … . Every moment I expected deadly shrapnel. At that moment I lost my nerve. The others acted just like me. When one hears for hours the whining, whistling and bursts of shells, and moaning and groaning of the wounded one does not feel too well … . Our company had only thirty men left."[47] The creative combination of hedgerow busting and marching artillery had proved too much. The dead hand of a German infantrymen explained why the Americans had bested Hill 192.

Perhaps the most remarkable feature of the 2nd Infantry Division's attack was that it occurred on July 11, 1944, over a week before the 90th Infantry Division's drive on the White Witch. What was remarkable was that the 90th applied none of the lessons of the 2nd's attack. Landrum's assault had been by the book: dogmatic, uninspiring, and lacking any hit of innovation. It was nothing like the Indian Head attack on Hill 192.

Nor was the 2nd Division's achievement singular. A number of commanders had experimented with hedgerow-cracking tactics, figuring out what the Army field manuals could not tell them. "In Normandy," as historian Michael Doubler wrote in his study of busting the bocage, "commanders were held responsible for developing and implementing solutions to tactical problems and were often given wide latitude in finding answers. Commanders within each division listened to ideas from their units, learned from the experiences of other divisions and then developed their own tactics."[48] Senior leaders depended on their subordinate commanders figuring out how to fight.

There were two reasons why the generals relied heavily on the creativity of their officers. The first was that "field-grade" officers (colonels, lieutenant colonels, and majors), the regimental and battalion commanders and their staffs, were often in the best position to win or lose a day's battle. Generals were most important before the battle: assigning missions, allocating forces, and approving plans. Once combat was joined, it was too late and too difficult to make major changes, and the resources they could bring to bear were usually too far from the front to be able to influence the course of a battle in the hours between dawn and dusk. On the other hand, while the troops at the front (company commanders, platoon leaders, sergeants, and foot soldiers) might take a hedgerow or two, they could not advance farther without the support provided by the battalion and the regiment who controlled the reserves, tanks, and fire support that could be thrown into a battle at the right time and place to sustain an attack or turn back the tide of defeat (as when Mildren launched his reserves restoring momentum to the drive up Hill 192). The field-grade officers were the independent decision makers on the battlefield who could, over the course of a day, turn a general's desires and an infantryman's sacrifice into victory.[49]

The second reason why generals depended on creative colonels was that their officers were well suited to the task. They were the core of an industrial-age generation, comfortable enough with technology to experiment and innovate on the battlefield. Normandy fighting, the success of the 2nd Division, and the failure of the 90th illustrate why this particular genius for war was so important. The same men, the same equipment, and the same mission, but with very different outcomes—genius was the difference between victory and defeat.

Clausewitz, the great military theorist, cautioned that simplicity in war was critical for a very important reason. Combat, Clausewitz emphasized, was always influenced by "friction," accidents, chance, and unpredictable events that always happen on the battlefield. Both the battles on the Séves River and Hill 192 demonstrated that. Landrum never predicted the river would rise, cutting off his troops on the island. Robertson's men also had ill luck, including tanks destroyed by mortars and troops bombed by their own planes. These were setbacks that field manuals, set-piece training, and elaborate plans could not predict. No commander could prepare his men for every possible contingency on the field of battle, as the Americans discovered when they encountered the hedgerow defenses. Friction, Clausewitz warned, eschewed the notion that war could be fought by the numbers. There was no rule book.

Since events on the battlefield could get very complicated, it was important that plans be simple. But in practice, executing the simple, as Clausewitz reminded, would be difficult. The Americans knew that before they went into the battles of Normandy. Marshall's study of combat lessons from World War I concluded, "it is fallacy to preach simplicity as a battle cure all … . a simple maneuver, though decreasing the likelihood of serious error, may fail to meet the situation."[50] Both the 90th and the 2nd relearned that lesson firsthand. In battle disaster happens. That is why overcoming friction required genius—innovation and adaptation. The 2nd could. The 90th could not.

During the war the 90th got better. DePuy saw the difference in the division as inept officers were relieved or killed and experienced young officers were elevated into command. By the end of the campaign in Northern France the 90th was a different division, as solid as the 2nd or any other unit on the Western Front. And it was all because of changes in leadership.

In World War II, America sent its army off to war with lots of technology but little combat experience. What made the difference between "right war" and "wrong war" was GI ingenuity. And the Americans would need a lot more of it before they battled beyond the beachhead and drove the Germans back toward Paris.

GI genius alone, however, would not be enough. They would also need the genius of their fathers—the fathers of GI genius. And that was another thing altogether.

# CHAPTER 2

# Day of the Doughboys

## THE TROGLODYTE WORLD

AMERICANS HAD BEEN THERE before. Writer and World War II veteran Paul Fussell described the place as "wet, cold, smelly thoroughly squalid."[1] The place called the battlefields of France, battlefields dug deep into the dark soil of mother earth—the troglodyte world. "To be in the trenches," Fussell wrote of combat during the Great War, "was to experience the unreal, the unforgettable enclosure and constraint, as well as a sense of being unoriented and lost. One saw two things only: the walls of the unlocalized and undifferentiated earth and the sky above."[2] When the American parachutists jumped into the black night on June 5, 1944, stormed ashore on the beaches of Normandy on D-Day, June 6, and plunged into the hedgerows, they were returning to the battleground of their fathers, France. It was a place of battle similar in character as well as location.

The war diary of General Bradley, who commanded American troops in Normandy during World War II, bore witness to the fear that the GIs had inherited the doughboys' days. Hedgerow fighting seemed eerily like World War I trench combat. It was something the First Army commander was desperate to avoid. While planning the breakout Bradley affirmed (in thoughts written down by his aide Chester Hansen and later used as the basis for his memoirs, *A Soldier's Story*) that he "was determined that we must avoid at all costs those pitfalls that might bog down our advance and lead us into the trench warfare of World War I."[3] The war could not be won one hedgerow at a time.

The doughboy generation had found a way to break out of the static warfare against a dug-in enemy rooted deep into the earth. Bradley was determined his GIs would do no less. For starters, they had the genius of the doughboy way of war to build on.

## SCHOOL FOR SOLDIERS

Ben Lear, one of the oldest generals on active service during World War II, remembered the doughboys' days. He was a colonel in the Great War. During the Second World War, as commander of the Second Army in the United States, Lear trained many of the troops that fought in Normandy. He might have commanded them himself if not for a bad run of luck.

Lear's first bad break came during the Louisiana Maneuvers in 1941. The maneuvers were ordered by General McNair to test the Army's men and machines. Lear commanded one of the forces; Walter Krueger commanded the other, aided by an energetic, innovative, and resourceful chief of staff, named Lieutenant Colonel Dwight Eisenhower.[4] Lear lost. Eisenhower and Krueger went off to war. Lear did not.

Lear's second bad break came shortly after. During a training exercise, he found a truck column stopped by a golf course in Memphis, Alabama. At the sight of a group of women golfers teeing off, the GIs forgot about practicing war, erupting in cat calls and wolf whistles. Little wonder, many were little more than newly minted soldiers, civilians clothed in uniform. When Lear intervened, rather than snapping to attention, they became belligerent. One cried, "Hey buddy. Need a caddy?" The general was not amused, punishing the troops by ordering them on a 15-mile road march in record-breaking heat. The story of "Yoo-Hoo" Ben Lear made the front pages, which might have not been so bad if one of them had not been read by Bennett Clark from Missouri, the state from which many of the troops had come. Clark was a U.S. Senator. Lear was accused of being petty and vengeful. Clark even tried to block Lear's promotion.[5] The general never received an overseas command.

Both the defeat in Louisiana and the embarrassment on the Alabama golf course are instructive. They typified Lear's character. He lost the Louisiana Maneuvers because his approach to war was old-fashioned, dogmatic, and conventional. Lear had difficulty adapting to the new ways of combat. On the other hand, he understood well the fundamentals from the old ways of war that were a prerequisite for success: discipline, professionalism, solid organization, and respect. He would not stand for "loose conduct and rowdyism." Modern wars could not be fought by ignorant, ill-disciplined mobs of farm boys. This was what the Great War had taught him.

Months before the Japanese sneak attack on Pearl Harbor on December 7, 1941, Lear insisted that the GI citizen soldiers of World War II start their preparation for battle by learning the lessons of their fathers. Lear ordered that all soldiers undergo a course of educational lectures. He determined there was a "general lack of comprehension among many soldiers—similar to that among much of the civilian population … the necessity for diligent and arduous training in preparation for our probable entry into the war."[6] War was serious business. Lear's GIs got a good dose of red-blooded American history and world politics. After Pearl Harbor and the American declaration of war, the lectures were reproduced in a book-length, civil defense edition—*School of the Citizen Soldier*.

Featuring prominently in the Lear program was instruction on "The Rise of American Industrial Civilization." It included lessons that celebrated the American knack for harnessing science and technology, the Americans' "particular genius."[7] Between 1865 and 1917 American civilization was transformed by an industrial revolution, informed the *School of the Citizen Soldier*. The result was that "the great corporation appeared, making possible the organization of men, materials, and financial power into gigantic production units." This was all made possible because of the American skill at machining standardized parts on the assembly line. "The principle of standardization and interchangeable parts started American industry on the road to mass production which in the twentieth century has put American plants in the forefront of world manufacturing. After December 7, 1941, Americans turned to their assembly lines to save the nation." Organizational innovations, the American skill at machine tooling parts, and "outstanding achievements in electrical engineering [radio and telephony], and the perfection of the internal combustion engine has changed the world," concluded the *School of the Citizen Soldier*.[8] Lear wanted GIs to understand that mastering this genius, the genius that could create disciplined mass armies, tanks, artillery, and airpower was a prerequisite for modern war.

Lear knew that genius was not an American invention. But he and other military men had been well schooled in understanding its importance in fighting and winning wars.

## A SHORT HISTORY OF GENIUS

There are constants in war. The need for genius is one. The enduring interest in General Carl von Clausewitz's *On War* is another. It was first printed in 1832 (110 years before the publication of *School of the Citizen Soldier*); few discussions of the theory and practice of warfare did not invoke the classic treatise *On War* or the name of its author, a veteran of the Napoleonic wars at the turn of the nineteenth century. The book's enduring attraction to students of the military art suggests that indeed there must be some timeless continuity in the practice of war; otherwise why would soldiers in an age of machines pour over pages written in days of combat fought with musket and bayonet.

In the United States, by 1914, as one leading historian studying the great Prussian author concluded, *On War* had become "ensconced as military classic."[9] Lear read Clausewitz. A young Eisenhower had been directed to read *On War* three times. George Patton, one of "Ike's" most famous generals during World War II, wrote in his war diary that when he had tried to convince the Allied commander of a plan for Normandy, he invoked Clausewitz's name several times. He knew that would get Eisenhower's attention.

American soldiers read Clausewitz and Clausewitz spoke of genius.

Clausewitz devoted a whole chapter of *On War* to military genius and with good reason. He had to explain Napoleon. Napoleon had been the dominant military figure of the age. The emperor of France had conquered Clausewitz's Prussia and destroyed its armies in humiliating routs at the twin battles of Jena and Auerstadt in 1806. If armies in war were (as Clausewitz described them) like ships tossed on a stormy sea by friction, buffeted by uncertainty and chance, then how had Napoleon managed to consistently over the course of decades to best his opponents often regardless of the odds—this was something that a sound theory of war would have to explain.

The answer was genius. Genius became one of the pivotal operational concepts in the Prussian's cosmology of war, one of the few dependable means that gave humans command over what is perhaps man's most ungovernable activity. There were so many intangible factors that controlled the course of a campaign: the will of the people, the wisdom of political leaders, the quality of the military, the variables of terrain and weather, the chance turn of events on the battlefield; commanders had to rely on a few key concepts to see them through. Genius was one of them.

Genius was instinctively knowing how to do the right thing, at the right time, at the right place.[10] This genius, as far as Clausewitz was concerned, had very little to do with mastering technology. "Today armies are so much alike in weapons, training, and equipment," he wrote in *On War*, "there is little difference in such matters between the best and the worst of them."[11] In a text that runs over 550 pages in the modern English edition, technology hardly rates a mention and merits no listing in the index.

Clausewitz's indifference to technology was understandable given that over the course of the many years and wars of the Napoleonic era, there was actually little groundbreaking technological innovation in military affairs.[12] All the wars were fought and won with sword and cannon, ships and sail, beans and hay, generals on horseback, and admirals on the quarterdeck. It is not surprising that the veteran of many horse-drawn campaigns simply did not think a facile understanding and manipulation of science and technology was essential for military genius. Instead, Clausewitz chose to emphasize nonmaterial factors. Genius was a combination of intuition, determination, and quick thinking.[13]

*On War*'s author also viewed genius as essential to the province of the commander alone. "If every soldier needed some degree of military genius," he argued, "our armies would be very weak."[14] It was too much to expect a society to produce a generation of men with special mental and moral powers. Genius was for generals.

The intellectual elitism of *On War* also makes sense given the character of wars in the Napoleonic Age. A hallmark of the emergence of the nation-state was the capacity of the state to harness the capacity to wage war, and Napoleon ruled at the zenith of this era.[15] The leader of France, one individual, was able to harness the political economy, mobilize the population, and command armies in the field. Napoleon's competitors adopted similar practices. Understanding both the real power and the romanticized vision of the place the great commanders played in nineteenth-century warfare, it was not remarkable that thinkers like Clausewitz placed such a premium on the genius of elite leaders.

Genius, however, could not remain static. The character of war changed considerably over the next century: technology evolved and societies became more sophisticated and complex. To keep up, the character of genius would have to change with them. Clausewitz would have understood and appreciated that. So did the doughboys as they prepared for World War I.

## TURNING THE TIDE

The author of *On War* would not have recognized war in 1918. He had lived during an age when a general might well be able to see the entire battlefield, with armies marching forward in rows of brightly colored uniforms, under banners, to the beat of drummers, marching to within a few hundred yards of the enemy. Generals fought armies that could distinguish the features on the faces in an opposing column before the battle became lost in billowing clouds of smoke from cannon and musket. America's doughboys arrived in France to find a battlefield where a day's casualties might be in the tens of thousands, numbers equal to the entire ranks of both sides in a Napoleonic battle; where the front lines stretched farther than an army of Napoleon might march in an entire campaign season; where battles might be fought without ever seeing the face of the enemy; battles that could last for weeks and months, not hours, over ground where armies measured progress in yards. Turning the tide in this kind of war required a genius undreamed of in the days of Clausewitz.

When America's army joined the fight, it found the British and French allies on the edge of exhaustion, unable to break the stalemate on the Western Front. To make matters worse, Russia had withdrawn from the conflict making a separate peace with Germany. In turn, the Germans had been able to turn all their attention to the war in the West. In the summer of 1918 they struck. The summer offensive drove a wedge deep into the French lines, threatening Paris before the attack stalled. While the drive for final victory failed, the news was not all bad. The Germans held a commanding position, called the Marne Salient (named after the river that formed the last natural barrier between the enemy and the capital of France). And they held it with 40 divisions.

The Germans stubbornly clung to their ground thanks to the rail line through the logistical center at Soissons that ferried troops and supplies in 22 trains per day. Cutting the German rail line meant everything. To take out Soissons, American forces were needed for the counterattack. If the Allies could pierce the shoulder of the salient and threaten the rail center, it could force a devastating withdrawal of the German Army that might end the war. At least, that was the plan. The only problem was that the objective was six miles from the Allied lines, an impossible stretch of distance in the days of trench warfare.

Slicing through the German salient was a formidable mission. The task the Americans faced would prove not dissimilar to the challenge faced by the First Army in Normandy in 1944. It required breaking through well-established forward defenses to reach the terrain beyond where forces could maneuver more quickly and freely.

## ENGINEERS AND ENTREPRENEURS

While the breakthrough battles at Soissons and St.-Lô bore many similarities, the men who fought them were very different. The doughboys were a breed apart from the GI generation, as different as the doughboys were from Napoleon's Imperial Guard.

Doughboys and GIs grew up in different Americas. Doughboys were the generation that created industrial production on a grand scale. They were born in the age when American engineers and entrepreneurs recorded unprecedented achievements in harnessing advances in science and technology in the service of industry.

Nothing illustrated the blooming of the U.S. industrial age better than the rise of the American steel company. By 1901, J.P. Morgan had established the world's largest company, U.S. Steel, with assets worth $1.4 billion, almost three times the annual revenue Washington took in that year. "God made the world in 4004 B.C.," one popular joke went, "and in 1901 it was reorganized by J.P. Morgan."[16] Men like Morgan put the "big" in big business.

U.S. factories proved they had arrived as a global industrial force when it came time to feed the dogs of global war. Steel was, of course, one commodity that American industry turned out in breathtaking volume, but there were other vital contributions as well. The U.S. chemical company DuPont supplied 40 percent of the Allies munitions. Britain alone purchased over $3 billion in goods from the United States during the war, an amount equal to quadruple what the U.S. government collected in taxes the year before America entered the war.[17]

Concomitant with the rise of industry came knowledge and skills that proved essential for undertaking industrial-strength warfare. By 1918, the United States had become a nation that knew how to harness more than horses. By the turn of the century engineers were everywhere in America. They permeated the ranks of middle management in companies such as U.S. Steel, Bell Telephone, and General Electric. They were men skilled at designing, planning, and implementing big projects—like organizing for war.

America's engineering culture also gave rise to scientific management—redesigning business practices to gain greater productivity and efficiency. The 1911 publication of Frederick W. Taylor's *Principles of Scientific Management* marked the outbreak of a management craze. Industrial engineers armed with clipboards and stopwatches fanned out across shop room floors measuring every action, turn of machine, and item consumed to determine the most efficient way to increase worker productivity. One of the by-products of the new efficiencies was a call for creating "middle management," an additional layer of leadership for overseeing vast industrial enterprises. The ranks of middle management provided a cadre of men trained and disciplined in the art of organizing and supervising complex business activities. In 1917 they would be asked to turn their skills to organizing men in preparing for battle.[18]

Likewise, as industries became corporate enterprises, the turn of the century became the Age of Accountants. They were so important to industrial activity that governments, for the first time, set standards for their practices. New York legislators even created a new term, "certified" public accountant. Others copied the New York practice of accrediting accounting professionals. "By the beginning of the First World War," concluded economic historian John Steele Gordon, "the system was universal throughout the capitalist economy."[19] Accountants became the principal tool for tracking a vast number of activities and providing data to managers who could then make informed decisions on how to best organize and allocate resources. These

were talents that would prove quite useful in preparing to mobilize millions
for war.

## THE GENERAL

Few understood better what was happening to America than Robert Lee
Bullard. Bullard's views are important because when the doughboys went into
their first major combat during World War I at the Battle of Cantigny on
May 28, 1918, they were under the command of General Robert Lee Bullard.
And no officer, more than Bullard, comprehended the intellectual transfor-
mation required to accommodate the emergence of doughboy genius.

Bullard's career and thinking, as his biographer, acclaimed military historian Allan Millett, wrote, "reveals the fundamental changes in officership
which accompanied America's emergence as a self-conscious world power,
industrial nation, and an occupationally specialized society."[20] Graduating
from the military academy at West Point in 1885, Bullard spent his professional adult life as an Army officer witnessing the rise of American industry
from the sidelines at dusty stateside camps and exotic overseas posts. What
he saw and read worried him. The nation's small peacetime military at the
turn of the century was largely out of touch with the rest of America. The general was concerned both about the challenge of turning a mass of civilians
into a disciplined army of soldiers and how to tap the vast reservoir of civilian
skills and knowledge that citizen soldiers would bring to the fight.

The military, Bullard feared, was simply not mentally prepared for industrial-strength warfare. He believed there was, for example, insufficient intellectual capacity to deal with the gargantuan logistical obstacles to raising,
organizing, shipping, and employing a mass military. To win, America's army
would simply have to learn how to bridge the gap between the civilian world
and martial order.[21]

On May 29, 1917, Bullard began to discover how accurate his assessment
of the need for something like doughboy genius really was. A terse telegram
from the War Department ordered him to report to Washington, D.C.,
"equipped for extended foreign service." Bullard soon found himself
commanding the First Division in France and preparing the doughboys
for war.

## THE FIGHTING MACHINE

That Bullard had a division at all to command was pretty remarkable. As
in World War II, the doughboys had little time to muster, train, equip, and
deploy a mass army of men in the millions to fight a modern, industrial-

age war. The U.S. Army before World War I was largely a constabulary force deployed throughout the American West and overseas in small units. From 1902 to 1911, the active Army averaged about 75,000 men. Considering British losses at the Battle of Arras (April 9–15, 1917) were 84,000 and Arras was considered a victory, it was obvious that America needed a much larger force to meet the demands of trench warfare in Europe.

When America declared war in April 1917, there were still only about 260,000 doughboys in uniform, including both the active force and the men in the National Guard, troops that normally trained only two weeks each summer. They had a long way to go to get ready for France.

And they got there in record time. By November 1918, the United States had 2 million men and 40,000 vehicles in France—not bad. In part, the Americans met the challenge because of their ability to apply industrial-age skills to modern war, the capacity to organize large, complex activities.

Before the war, the military had some officers skilled in the ways of science and engineering that would be needed to run industrial-size warfare. The geniuses among the American captains of industry and science included not a few men in uniform.

America's most famous engineer at the turn of the century was George Washington Goethals, an Army officer. An 1880 graduate of West Point, in 1907 President Teddy Roosevelt appointed Goethals as the Chief Engineer of the Panama Canal Company. It was a task equivalent of war: managing tens of thousands of workers, millions of dollars in equipment and supplies, brutal conditions, and a multitude of unprecedented engineering challenges. Thanks to his administrative abilities, the canal long plagued by problems was finished years ahead of schedule, a feat considered one of the greatest achievements of the age. Goethals supervised army logistics for the war.

Goethals's medical officer, William Crawford Gorgas, was a scientist of the first order. Before he arrived in Panama, disease claimed thousands of lives. He purged the Isthmus of Yellow Fever. During the Great War, he served as the Army Surgeon General.

And the Army began training a generation of officers for industrial-strength warfare. "Constabulary armies," wrote historians Douglas V. Johnson and Rolfe L. Hillman, "do not expand to handle world wars without great difficulty."[22] They were exactly right. Even though the United States won the Spanish-American War of 1898, its ability to mobilize men and equipment proved a near disaster. In the wake of the war, Secretary of War Elihu Root instituted a series of reforms including establishing a general staff, a group of officers who would spend all their time working on long-term planning for large-scale warfare. He also created a war college to educate them in managing high command and mobilization tasks.

Despite these efforts, as Bullard had feared, the Army was far from ready for industrial-strength warfare. The logistical system almost collapsed. Not surprisingly, as a prescient student of future combat, Colonel George C. Thorpe wrote in his classic 1916 study, *Pure Logistics: The Science of War Preparation*, "Napoleon never mentioned logistics," and so neither did Clausewitz, and neither did subsequent military studies; "if we may judge of the matter from the silence of books on the Science and Art of War, the conclusion is irresistible, the military themselves know next to nothing … ."[23] That was a problem, Thorpe concluded, since modern war was nothing like it was in the Napoleonic Age. "At the same rate in which we find modern war losing its mystery and chivalry, we find it ranging itself in close alliance with industry of the commercial kind," Thorpe suggested, "from which war is acquiring 'business methods.'"[24] War had become big business and the American military just was not prepared for that. Thorpe shared Bullard's fear that the military was not ready for the logistical challenge of large-scale operations. The Army would need industrial genius.

When war came, the War Department sorted out its logistical nightmares, railroad traffic jams, and clogged shipping lanes by calling in civilian business experts.[25] The Americans faced similar challenges in commanding their armies in the field. They met them largely by learning the skills of managing large organizations and complex problems on the job.

Ironically, the genius of American industry which led the world in pioneering new technology and business practices proved of little help in generating the machines of modern war for the Doughboy Army. The demand for arms was so immense and immediate, American industry could not reorganize fast enough to provide the three greatest technological innovations in modern war: artillery, airpower, and armor.

## GUNNERS AT WAR

By the advent of the First World War, artillery had become the greatest killer on the battlefield. And it was all because of changes in technology. That, however, is a story that requires a bit of telling.

Before the age of World War I quick-firing artillery, the guns could never be out of site of the infantry. The artillerymen had to see their targets in order to bring fire upon them. That was not a problem in the Napoleonic Age when infantrymen carried smoothbore muskets.[26] The infantry musket had a smoothbore so it could be quickly loaded. The diameter of the musket ball was smaller than the barrel so that it would slip easily down. That meant, however, that when the musket was fired, some of the gases that propelled the ball forward would escape and the ball would rattle down the tube as it exited. The result was limited range and accuracy. That was good news for the artillery which could set up out of the effective range of musket fire and blast away at the enemy's horse-mounted cavalry and foot-borne infantry.

In 1855, the Minié ball changed everything. It was a projectile with a soft-lead base that expanded when it was fired sealing in the gases. The Minié could be fired effectively by a rifled gun, a barrel with groves cut into it that would impart a spin to the bullet, making it fly much straighter. As a result, a rifle firing Minié bullets could be loaded and fired three times faster and be accurate to three times the range of a musket, upward of 600 yards—and that put the artillery within range of the infantry.

Getting the artillery back into the fight required moving behind a terrain feature where the guns could shoot without being harassed by infantry fire, but that required knowing where the artillery shells landed when they were fired without seeing the target. And that required several advances in technology. The first was finding targets. In direct-fire battles the artillery picked its own targets. When the artillerymen moved out of sight of the infantry, someone would have to pick their targets for them. That was an electrical engineering problem, a field telephone and a wire to provide communication with the infantry, and that required adapting commercial telephony.

The second innovation required adapting advances in commercial metallurgy and machine tooling. Every time an artillery tube fired, it moved. Hence, two rounds fired from the same tube never landed in the same place. Artillery made of steel tubes mounted on carriages with pneumatic or hydraulic recoil systems changed that. The recoil systems absorbed the force of the firing so that the tube did not move, making the location of the artillery tube constant from firing to firing. Maintaining a constant firing position was a prerequisite for accurately determining how to predict exactly where artillery rounds would land on the battlefield. Additionally, rifled steel tubes could withstand more powerful powder charges resulting in more accurate, longer-range fires.[27]

In World War I, quick-firing artillery provided long-range indirect fire support out of sight of the enemy machine guns and churned the no-man's-lands between the lines into an impenetrable moonscape. The only problem was the Americans invested almost nothing in these weapons before the outbreak of the war. In the summer of 1917 when General William Snow was called to Washington to take over the newly established position of Chief Artillery of the Army, he had almost nothing to command; he had not even a desk. When he asked the Secretary of the General Staff to have some stationary printed with an office letterhead, the secretary balked at the expense and offered to buy him a rubber stamp.[28] There was not much more to the American artillery force.

Nor was there much success in harnessing American industry in manufacturing guns, even after the federal government opened its coffers and started buying machines for its new army. The Americans tried to develop their own modern quick-firing howitzer. It had a unique split-trail carriage design. The artillery tube sat on the trail and could pivot to shift the direction of fire without moving the gun and changing its location. The trail also absorbed the shock of firing along with the tube recoil mechanism. Again, this was important because it kept the artillery piece from moving, maintaining a constant location. Traditionally, guns had a single trail. That limited how far the tube could move to either side before the angle became so severe that the gun was unstable. A split trail looked like a fork. It could keep the gun more balanced, allowing the tube to shift farther to the right and the left. The split trail could also allow the gun to fire at higher angles, since the tube could be elevated without its base hitting the trail. Higher-angle firing could mean greater range and the ability to shoot over higher-terrain features.

The only problem with the inventive American design was that the split trail and the recoil system to support it were experimental. By the time the split-trial design was perfected and factories retooled, the war was almost over. Of the some 2,500 artillery pieces the doughboys fired in France, only about 100 were manufactured in the United States. The rest, including virtually every gun firing in support of the Allies at Soissons, the Americans bought from their allies.[29]

The United States had better luck developing a communications system that could link the guns to the infantry. America was the world leader in telephone technology. The Army borrowed technical expertise from the private sector, principally Bell System. The Army commissioned John J. Carty, the chief engineer of the American Telephone & Telegraph Company, who played a pivotal roll in recruiting volunteers from industry and establishing the military communications system.[30]

## FLIGHT OF FANCY

America's experience in fielding its air arm for the Great War paralleled its failure in mass producing field artillery. The combustion engine made controlled powered flight possible, and the United States was a global leader in engine technology. Before the start of the war, the fledgling U.S. aviation industry was on par with those of other nations. In 1909, the Wright brothers' company sold the first military aircraft in the world, the Wright Military Flyer, to the U.S. government. Other nations, however, sprang ahead as their countries built factories to churn out planes for battle. Meanwhile, up to the outbreak of the war, the American aviation industry remained a small collection of mom and pop outfits. In 1911 there were about a dozen U.S. firms manufacturing planes. None of them made much money. Even their biggest customer, the U.S. government, had bought only a handful of aircraft and they were obsolete before America entered the war. When the United States joined the fight, the entire Army Air Service consisted of 12,000 people, 65 pilots, and no combat-ready planes.

In one of its first acts of war, Congress appropriated $640 million, an unbelievable sum at the time, to mass-produce an American air armada. Three decisions, however, doomed the American effort to field its own air fleet. (1) The government awarded contracts to the large automobile manufacturers rather than to the aviation companies. The idea was that making the conversion from cars to planes would not be too difficult. That assumption proved to be wrong. Automotive manufacturers lacked the expertise and skill to become aviation companies overnight. (2) As with field artillery production, the government opted for standardized U.S. engines and planes based on untested American designs rather than adopting the battle-proven blueprints used by the Allies. (3) The Army kept changing its mind over how many and what kinds of planes it wanted.

In the end, industry produced somewhere between 200 and 400 planes for about $1 billion. The whole affair became a scandal of the first order.[31] Meanwhile, the U.S. Commander in Europe (in a real stroke of doughboy initiative) arranged to buy 5,000 planes and 8,500 engines from the French for $60 million. America's air force (to borrow a line from the popular World War I song) was made "over there."

## THE INFANCY OF ARMOR

The U.S. automobile industry also did not contribute to the U.S. armor force in any significant way. Again the American appetite for war machinery was impressive. In 1917, the commanders in France requested a tank force of 350 heavy tanks and 1,200 light tanks. Again the issue was how to create an industry to meet the demand starting from scratch.

Again the Americans tried to introduce a new, untried system, this time the joint U.S.–British Mark VIII "heavy" tank. Design changes and disagreements slowed production. The U.S.–built "Liberty" combustion engine intended to power the tanks was the same one planned to be installed in the American-built war planes. Engines were diverted to airplane production as soon as they came off the assembly line.

By the summer of 1918, while the doughboys prepared for the attack on Soissons, there was not one American tank in France. The war ended before the assembly line for the Mark VIII had even been completed. Eventually

100 of the tanks were assembled—in 1920. The Army also ordered 15,015 tanks based on the French light tank design from the vaunted assembly lines of the Ford Motor Company. Ford produced 15 before the contract was canceled. The first two arrived in France nine days after Germany surrendered.[32]

The first American officer was not appointed to the tank corps until November 1917. He was an ambitious cavalry officer—George Patton. Patton had to establish a training school, recruit the men, write the doctrine, beg for tanks, and learn mechanics.[33] Thanks to his determination and organizational skills, after months of training his fledgling cadre of armored warriors was ready for battle. All they needed were tanks to fight with.

By the time for the summer counteroffensive, the Americans fielded three battalions. Patton would lead them into battle. Combined with support from Allied armor units, they had a total of 419 tanks. These forces were not "made in America." Doughboys fought mostly in French tanks and some borrowed from the British or were supported by French or British armored units.

## OVER THE TOP

In the end, it was not the material forces that the Americans brought to France that made the difference in battle. Rapidly figuring out how to organize and manage for industrial-strength warfare marked the character of doughboy genius. In fact, the drive on Soissons would not have even been possible if the American Army had not been able to organize, equip, and deploy in time to help blunt the German summer offensive of 1918. By the time the Germans made their last desperate drive to win the war, the Americans already had a million men in France organized in 19 infantry divisions, each one twice the size of the divisions commanded by any other nation in Europe.

For the drive on Soissons, two of the most experienced and well-trained American units were to lead the attack. The Second Division (whose lineage would extend to the 2nd Infantry Division that took Hill 192 overlooking St.-Lô) and Bullard's First Division, which had already garnered honors by helping blunt the German Marne Salient at the Battle of Cantigny.[34]

Soissons was a different kind of battle. As a result of the German advance, the Americans would not confront the maze of concrete fortresses, tunnels, bunkers, corn rows of barbed wire, and elaborate trenches that still lined the stationary portions of the front. Instead the doughboys faced a rolling plateau of wheat fields cut by ravines, rocky slopes, small villages, woods, and marshes. The Germans used these natural obstacles as their defense lines and guarded them with machine-gun nests.

George Patton Instructing at the U.S. Tank School in France, 1918. (Courtesy, George S. Patton Collection, Military History Institute)

The plan for overcoming these defenses called for the two U.S. divisions and a Moroccan division to lead the assault with two French divisions in reserve driving east toward the town of Soissons six miles away. The First Division would attack on the northern flank, with regiments abreast (side by side), preceded by a rolling barrage of artillery. The Americans would forgo the usual days of preparatory artillery fire that would normally precede attacks, since it had proven largely ineffective except for turning the ground dividing the two armies into an impassable moonscape.

The armor and air support would be—French. The doughboys would be accompanied by several battalions of tanks under *Groupment XI*. Overhead, aircraft from *Ecadrille Spad 42* would support the ground assault.

Merely getting the division on the road and headed to the front for the attack proved a significant achievement. Tens of thousands of men and thousands of horses and vehicles all managed to move up on the night of July 16, 1918. The division movement did not look anything like the smooth operation of an assembly line on a factory shop floor. In fact, it was a mess of mud, men, machines, and horses all stumbling in the dark. Nevertheless, it did succeed in positioning the troops in the staging area in time for the offensive to begin.

On July 17, 1918, the division headquarters issued a terse command, "the attack orders in Field Order No. 27, G-3, 694, will take place July 18 at 4:35 A.M."[35] It was not signed by Robert Lee Bullard. The day before the order for the big attack, Bullard was promoted and assigned to command of an American corps. The division attack order was signed "by command of Major General [Charles Pelot] Summerall." Summerall had commanded the division's artillery brigade, so he knew the division and its leaders well. That was good; after taking over he would have time to do little more than sign the attack order and wait for the appointed hour to go over the top.

J-day, H-Hour, on the morning of July 18, 1918, the division's assault began. Almost immediately the reports filtering back to Summerall's command post suggested reaching Soissons would not be as simple as the one-line attack order might suggest. In particular, the division commander was concerned about his Second Infantry Brigade.

The second brigade seemed to be attacking in the wrong direction.

## STRENGTH FOR THE FIGHT

Explaining the fate of the Second Brigade requires some knowledge of how Americans organized their divisions for World War I. The doughboy division bore little in common with the GI division that fought in France a quarter of a century later. In World War II, the American division was organized for fire and maneuver. The organization was based on the "threes." At every level from squad to division there were three maneuver elements: one to establish a "base of fire," shooting at the enemy soldiers to keep their head downs; a second to maneuver to the objective; and a third to serve as a reserve, exploiting success and reinforcing the main effort. The many means that the World War II division had to bring fire on the enemy also meant that firepower could be substituted for manpower. A division in the Second World War was about half the size of its doughboy counterpart.

In contrast, the World War I division was built on the rule of "fours." Where a GI division had three infantry regiments, a doughboy division had four. And it had four regiments for a very good reason. The Americans studied the battle experiences of their allies to determine how best to organize their own forces, using principles not totally dissimilar from the scientific management methods advocated by Frederick W. Taylor.

Taylor's most famous experiment, discussed in his path-breaking book, *Principles of Scientific Management,* explained that by studying the manner in which workers moved heavy loads of pig-iron ingots, then reorganizing the process, implementing rest breaks, and eliminating unnecessary steps the out-load rate could be increased from 12.5 tons to 47 tons a day, almost a quadruple rise in productivity with the same number of employees.[36] War in the trenches raised similar work-flow challenges. The problem was how to get the most combat power at the front for the longest period possible given the number of troops available.

In a typical World War I battle, generals ran out of manpower before they could break through the enemy's defenses as their troops were cut down by barbed wire, artillery, and machine-gun fire going "over the top" of friendly trenches and across the "no-man's-land" that separated them from the opposing trench lines. And if they did break through, as the Germans had done in the Marne Salient, the breakthrough forces lacked the manpower to continue to advance in the face of an enemy counterattack. As the Allies' human reserves dwindled over the course of the war, they attempted to keep up combat power at the front by being able to rotate units into action quickly. The main operating principle was to design small easy-to-replace units that could be swapped out fast like standardized parts on an assembly line. The American Army put some of its best minds on the problem to see if they could figure out a more efficient solution.

The General Organization Project described the result of the Army's various studies on combat work flow. Rather then emulate the Allies' practice of using up units and then replacing them, the Army wanted, according to military historian John B. Wilson (who has written the authoritative history of the evolution of the American infantry division), "a unit with sufficient overhead (staff, communications, and supply units) and enough infantry and artillery to permit continuous fighting over extended periods."[37] The Army wanted staying power. The project recommended a massive division of about 25,000 men, organized in four regiments—the square division.

The designers also recognized that it would be too difficult for Summerall and his fellow division commanders to be able to manage such a vast mass of men in battle. So they followed another of Taylor's prescriptions for effective organization and created a level of middle management to control the infantry regiments in battle, infantry brigade headquarters that would each direct the operations of two regiments.

## WRONG TURN AT SOISSONS

Even with a middle layer of management, in practice it proved very problematic to control all the manpower in the American division. The Second Brigade headquarters experienced the difficulty firsthand. The division's advance looked nothing like regiments and battalions moving as if on parade over the rolling French countryside. A huge ravine bisected the brigade's front; a ravine a half mile wide at its base with steep, rocky, and heavily wooded slopes; a ravine far too prominent to be simply marched around. And the ravine cut to the northeast out of the division's sector. The brigade had little choice but to follow its course, using the low ground as the main approach to their first objective—the Paris-Soissons road.

Troops from the brigade's 2nd Battalion, 28th Infantry Regiment led the advance. The floor of the ravine was flat, marshy ground, lined with belts of trees and dotted with villages of sturdy stone houses. The enemy could not have asked for better ground to establish a network of machine-gun nests or more difficult terrain to slow the American advance and trap the dough-boys under the fire of German artillery.

As the doughboys in brown trudged into the valley of death, Major Clarence Huebner commanded the 2nd Battalion. Huebner joined the army as a soldier. After seven years as an enlisted man, he received a commission in 1916 and began working his way up through the ranks. At the Battle of Cantigny he took over after the battalion commander had been killed. And he earned a Distinguished Service Cross, one the service's most prestigious medals for bravery.

At Cantigny, for three days Huebner had to rush back and forth braving artillery and machine-gun fire to maintain effective command of his battalion. Now he had to repeat the effort all over again. His first attempt was to order two companies to advance through the flat ground in the base of the regime. That did not work. The troops got barely 100 yards before they came under machine-gun fire and an artillery barrage directed by German observers from the high ground above.

Huebner was undaunted, but more forces were needed to press the advance. He decided to combine his troops with infantrymen from the 3rd Battalion and together they waded through the swampy ground and seized one of the villages that had held a German machine-gun nest. By effectively maintaining control of his infantry, continually exposing himself to fire, moving back and forth, assessing the situation, making spot decisions, Huebner managed to achieve some real progress. By 9:30 A.M. his men had advanced the division's Northern Front several hundred yards up one side of the ravine.

The success of Huebner's battalion was good, but not good enough. By the end of the day, the brigade was a still a half mile short of its objective, the Paris-Soissons road and its slow advance meant that the First Infantry Brigade would also have to hold back its attack so that there was not a gap between the two units that might invite a German counterattack. To make matters worse, the division on the Second Brigade's other flank had lagged even farther in its attack as well. If Summerall pressed the division advance he might expose the Second Brigade to a counterattack from that direction as well.

Prospects for the advance on July 18, 1918, seemed little more promising. First, the doughboys would have to reach the Paris-Soissons road and then attack down the other side into another substantial ravine. It was an imposing and terrifying task, one that would have been impossible for any other Allied division to even consider. An Allied division would have been a spent force after the first day's offensive, lacking sufficient troops to attack another day.

Manpower was particularly important, given that the artillery, armor, and aviation support for the advance had proved to be of little help. Most of the tanks broke down, were knocked out of action, or could not negotiate the ground. To support the entire attack only 324 tanks were allocated. Only 225 made it to the battlefield by July 18, 1918. Before dusk, 102 were lost, 62 to artillery fire. The artillery support was relatively meager, and it was difficult to coordinate the use of the fires with the advance of the infantry. As for air support, the doughboys claimed they saw more German than Allied planes during the battle.

Soissons, however, justified the Army's decision to create the square division. If it had adopted the Allies' organization, the battle would have had to stop while a replacement division was brought up after the first day's attack. The First Division, however, while bloodied and bruised, still had strength for the fight. It could attack another day. And leading the way would be the remnants of Huebner's 2nd Battalion. Huebner, however, was not with them. He had been wounded in action.

In the end, however, it was Huebner and others like him who made the difference at the sharp end of battle. This was an age when the genius of generals, the solution advanced by Clausewitz as the answer to the trials of the battlefield, was no longer adequate. The guts of the battle at Soissons happened out of the sight and influence of the generals. On the other hand, the time for GI genius (the ability of combat leaders during World War II to improvise in combat with technology to gain a decisive edge) had not yet come. Technology and methods of industrial management (the stuff of doughboy genius) had helped get the American Army to the battlefield. Once the doughboys were there, however, technology, by and large, failed them. The three great tools of modern war, armor, artillery, and airpower, were still relatively immature instruments not easily adapted to the challenges of trench warfare and managed by men who were still trying to master the wonders of the new technological era in which they lived. No, it was leaders and manpower that made the difference in the advance, decisions and bravery in the face of death— skills and talent as ancient and timeless as war itself. In World War I, while doughboy genius helped get the soldiers to the fight, it was gutsy men like Clarence Huebner who won battles.

The doughboys continued to push forward on July 19, 1918, and the next day, and the next. The attack concluded on July 22 with the First Division holding key terrain threatening the German's main supply route. In the end, the square division had proved its worth and carried through, but at some cost. On the afternoon of July 22, a lieutenant from one of the infantry regiments rang through to the command post only to find General Summerall answering the phone.

> "Hello," the general bellowed, "this is General Summerall. Who is this?"
> "Lieutenant Thomas, sir, 26th Infantry."
> "Well how are things?"
> "I have to report that we have broken through as far as we can. Our colonel is dead, our lieutenant colonel is dead, and all the majors are dead or wounded. And God knows how many lieutenants and captains. And the situation with the men is just bad."
> "Great God, Mr. Thomas! Who is commanding the regiment?"
> "Captain Barney Legge."
> "How's he doing?"
> "Fine, sir, with what he has left."
> "Well, who is his executive officer?'
> "I guess I am ... ."[38]

The division's battle had come to an end. The First Division was relieved from the line.

The Allied attack continued. Soissons fell on August 2, 1918. The Germans began to withdraw from the Marne Salient. It was a victory, attributable in no small way to the contribution of American manpower.

What the battle at Soissons did not do was break the will of the enemy. The German withdrawal from the Marne proceeded in a deliberate and organized manner. Elsewhere on the front the enemy held its own as tenaciously as ever. There would be more battles before the doughboys could, as they sang in the song's refrain, "come back till its over, over there."

## AGONY IN THE MEUSE-ARGONNE

Not every American effort in the Great War was as successful as Soissons. As in case of the 90th Infantry Division at the Battle of the White Witch during World War II, the failures of doughboys in battle is as instructive in appreciating the nature of the genius of U.S. soldiers as are their triumphs. A case in point was the performance of the Thirty-Fifth Division in the Meuse-Argonne. The division's fate was very different from that of the First Division at Soissons, but it is equally important for understanding the role doughboy genius played in turning the tide in the Great War.

After Soissons, the next major combat operations for the American forces saw U.S. forces attacking the St. Mihiel Salient. Both the First and Second Divisions, veterans of Soissons and now the Americans' most well-trained and battle-tested units, participated. The Thirty-Fifth, as yet untried in combat, was assigned to the reserve. Operations at St. Mihiel began on September 12, 1918, and went well. The engagement garnered 15,000 German prisoners and regained a substantial amount of French real estate. The campaign concluded without the Thirty-Fifth seeing any action. That would change soon.

Helping reduce salients at the Marne and St. Mihiel were notable achievements, but not enough to win the war. Defeating the German Army once and for all would require taking the offensive. With the arrival of the Americans in strength the Allies hoped to secure that end before the year came to a close. The French command proposed shifting the U.S. forces from St. Mihiel over 50 miles to the Meuse-Argonne region west of the city of Verdun for a major attack aimed at breaking through the German lines in depth. The plan called for throwing nine doughboy divisions at the enemy (organized in three corps —one of them commanded by Bullard) and breeching the enemy lines to an unheard of depth of 10 miles in a single operation. One of the divisions slated to lead the attack was the Thirty-Fifth.

The first and greatest challenge of such a bold maneuver would be getting the doughboys there in the first place. An attack in the Meuse-Argonne required moving 800,000 men with their accoutrement of vehicles, horses, and supplies. Two hundred thousand French had to be withdrawn and replaced by 600,000 doughboys. And it all had to be done in secret, getting six American divisions into the line for the attack and three in reserve before the Germans suspected that a major offensive was afoot.

The Americans accomplished this logistical feat in a manner that would have earned the admiration of Colonel Thorpe, the author of *Pure Logistics*. "War has become a business," Thorpe wrote, "like commercial activities. It is susceptible to analysis in order to determine upon a proper division of labor, to estimate necessities required to meet the situation, and to avoid inefficiencies."[39] For the Meuse-Argonne repositioning the doughboys had done their homework. Historian Robert H. Ferrell, who does not offer praise easily, concluded "that they managed it as well as they did was nothing less than a miracle."[40] He is right. It was an impressive achievement.

Much of the credit for the success of the maneuver went to the management skill of a brilliant and tireless assistant chief of operations. He was responsible for planning the routes, coordinating the timetables, writing orders, solving problems, resolving conflicts, and ensuring the whole thing was done at night and with limited radio and telephone traffic to escape the attention of the Germans. The colonel in charge of the miracle was George C. Marshall—the future Army Chief of Staff during World War II.

Marshall understood that miracles were an important part of combat. He even had a chapter on "miracles" included in the lessons of combat written under his direction at the U.S. Infantry School after the war. "Resolute action by a few determined men," the chapter proclaimed, "is often decisive."[41] The examples given in the chapter referred to individual acts of bravery on the battlefield, much like Huebner's efforts to reorganize his troops for the assault on the Paris-Soissons road. That was old-fashioned courage. The singular effort by Colonel Marshall was equally important to the war effort. But, there was a difference. Marshall's miracle was the product of doughboy genius.

## THE HARD-LUCK DIVISION

Marshall's best efforts, however, could get the doughboys only to the fight. Once they got there they were on their own. Among the units in place for the attack on September 26, 1918, was the Thirty-Fifth Division. The GIs who heckled General Lear on the Memphis golf course in 1941 were Missouri National Guardsmen from the 35th Infantry Division. The men of the hard-luck division in the Meuse-Argonne campaign were their fathers, Missouri men from the Thirty-Fifth Division.

The story of the Thirty-Fifth is another cautionary tale in the illusive search for genius. Parallels between the Thirty-Fifth Division in the Meuse-Argonne in 1918 and the 90th Division at the Battle of the Séves River in 1944 were striking. Normandy was the 90th's first campaign. The Meuse-Argonne was the first test of battle for the Thirty-Fifth. In both cases, senior theater commanders feared that the divisions had been inadequately trained and lacked a solid cadre of field-grade officers. Landrum led the 90th from a basement emerging only to fire any officer who crossed him. Major General Peter E. Traub commanded the Thirty-Fifth in a similar style. He was both remote and mercurial, removed from running the division and then firing several key commanders right before the battle.

The mission of the Thirty-Fifth Division was also similar to the 90th's at the White Witch—a simple task against a difficult objective. The division's assault was part of the effort to clear the flank for the main attack, clearing a corridor in the Aire River valley between the river and Montfaucon.

There were two serious obstacles in the division's path—the land and the Germans. The Argonne forest was a dense, almost trackless expanse of land that would be difficult for men and machines to navigate even in the absence of an enemy. And there was an enemy. The doughboys faced the *Kriemhilde Stellung,* one of the most entrenched segments on the vaunted Hindenburg Line.

The German defenses in the Meuse-Argonne did not look anything like the efforts thrown up to guard the flanks of the salients at Marne and St. Mihiel. The Meuse-Argonne front was guarded with multiecheloned lines of trenches and fortified positions miles thick. First, the doughboys would have to fight through an outpost line of observation posts, machine guns, and light artillery—certainly not an impenetrable obstacle, but enough fighting power to slow down even skilled and well-disciplined troops and certainly sufficient resistance to allow time to warn the enemy of an impending advance, its strength, and its direction. The second line would contain more troops and some counterattack forces. Successfully fighting through these would only lead to the third line, the main defense belt, laced with machine guns and covered by artillery support. Even if the main line was breeched, the battle was not over. The Germans had prepared subsequent defensive lines to which they could withdraw and continue the fight.

## INTO THE WOODS

Historians still dispute what happened to the Thirty-Fifth Division when it plunged into the dark woods of the Argonne forest on September 26, 1918. The Army's Inspector General conducted an investigation and authored a series of scathing findings. Congress held hearings. Recriminations flew. One fact, however, seems indisputable. The three great war engines of modern technology—artillery, armor, and airpower, largely failed the doughboys in battle.

The artillery plan for the offensive was quite extensive. It called for diversionary preparation fires in other areas days before the attack to confuse the enemy as to where the main effort would occur. The plan also called for the massive employment of chemical gas shells. Then on the night of September 25, there would also be a massive preparation with conventional artillery fires that would attempt to smash the Germans' main lines, followed by a rolling barrage that would precede the infantry advancing 400 feet per minute. None of the components of the artillery plan worked terribly well in practice.

Nothing illustrated the emergence of industrial-age warfare better than the opportunities to employ poison gas in the Meuse-Argonne. The rise of a global chemical industry and the associated research and development was integral to the rapid commercial expansion at the end of the nineteenth century. In turn, the chemical industry proved to be one of the great engines of war. The U.S. chemical giant DuPont, for example, saw its annual revenues increase to 26 times what they were at the start of the war.[42] One instrument it provided for war was chemical weapons in staggering amounts. Both sides used chemical shells during the war. When employed with surprise, these gas attacks had panicked and confused the defenders. In their 1918 summer offensive, one German innovation was how well they integrated the use of poison gas shells into their trench-storming tactics.

The decision to add a massed gas attack to the preparation was ambitious. Americans had studied the successes of the German offensive of 1918 and hoped to achieve similar results. While in theory the plan for a massive gas attack on the enemy lines involving tons upon tons of chemical munitions sounded terrifying, in practice it proved anything but. Division commanders were told to prepare their own plans for using gas. They lacked experience, expertise, and confidence in employing the weapon. As a result, the actual use of gas projectiles proved rather modest. By the end of the Meuse-Argonne campaign, some of the divisions had gained sufficient confidence and experience in employing the gas shells that they began to effectively integrate them into their operations, but it was too little, too late, an illustration of how slow the doughboys proved in adapting to new technologies on the battlefield.[43]

Likewise, the effects of the preparation with conventional powder explosives proved far less than commanders had hoped. The amount of artillery fire was incredible. "During the three hours preceding H Hour," military historian Carlo D'Este calculated, "the Allies expended more ammunition than both sides managed to fire throughout the four years of the Civil War."[44] The volume of artillery fire, while impressive, was largely irrelevant. Results proved disappointing because of the type of artillery available for the attack and how it was employed.

Almost 4,000 artillery pieces were assembled to support the Meuse-Argonne offensive. The Allies categorized artillery as light, medium, or heavy. The designations related not just to the size of the artillery piece, but also to the size and weight of the shell it threw at the enemy. The predominant light artillery piece used by the Americans was the French manufactured 75 mm (a gun that gave its name to a popular cocktail, the "French 75," a mix of champagne and brandy). The "75" referred to the diameter of the shell. The most common medium gun was the 155 mm, also French made. A heavy gun could refer to anything up to the size of the massive rail guns that could fire shells with the girth of a small wagon, 14 inches.

The diameter of the shell was an important designation because it gave an indication of the size of the projectile. The size of the projectile was important because the bigger the shell, the heavier the shell, and weight in artillery killing power meant everything. Most of the destruction by artillery was not done by the force of the explosion, but by the metal fragments thrown out from the exploding casing of the projectile, often called "shrapnel" (British Lieutenant Henry Shrapnel invented a fragmenting shell in 1803). The bigger the shell, the more and the heavier were the flying pieces of white-hot metal thrown out with the crack of an artillery round. Also, the larger the shell, the more powder could be packed into the shell. More powder meant a bigger explosion imparting a higher velocity to the flying fragments. The bigger the shell, the greater the combination of shrapnel mass and velocity, and mass and velocity equaled the killing force of the artillery.

Larger shells also had a larger killing radius. And since it was difficult to predict exactly where artillery shells might land, commanders were reluctant to use medium and heavy artillery in proximity to their troops out of fear of inflicting friendly fire. In addition, they preferred the light artillery because it was more maneuverable on the battlefield and could accompany the infantry as it advanced.

The problem with the fire plan for the Meuse-Argonne was that light artillery was used for all the close-in targets. The 75 mm was simply not a powerful enough projectile to take out a well-prepared defensive position. (In World War II, the Americans would adopt 105 mm as their standard light artillery piece, a weapon that proved to have far superior killing power.) While the massive preparation fires had an effect on the German observation post line, it did not eliminate all the enemy positions. In addition, stretching the fire over several hours diminished the shock and fear that a sudden intense bombardment might have achieved. The 75 mm could actually fire 30 shells a minute, though only for short periods; otherwise the tubes would overheat and malfunction or explode. Instead, the guns pooped rounds at a rate of one to two per minute spaced to cover the entire time allotted for the preparation.

The massive preparatory fires did not prevent the Germans from adequately readying for the Allied attack as the doughboys discovered when they went over the top and encountered heavy resistance. That is when the third component of the artillery plan failed. The infantrymen could not keep up with the rolling barrage that was intended to shield their advance. Exploding walls of artillery fire walked away as doughboys struggled through wire, shell holes, mud, and machine-gun fire. With poor means to communicate between the infantry and the guns and no way to accurately place fire on the battlefield, there was little that could be done.

One observer, appalled, watched the inept artillery effort. He wrote a highly critical account of the entire affair. He was one of the Army's most promising young artillery experts. His name was Lesley J. McNair. The future commander of the Army Ground Forces during World War II was disappointed by the inability of the Americans to innovate in battle. The Germans had already figured out how to adapt artillery in the attack. And they used the techniques to good effect in the summer offensive of 1918. They massed all their guns and employed gas and conventional shells together in massive bombardments that would last only about 15 minutes. These fires would impart maximum shock and disruption, creating a brief window of opportunity to advance before the enemy could recover and prepare an organized defense.[45]

The failure to master the employment of artillery was not the doughboys only problem. Tank support also proved disappointing. One of the most significant obstacles in the Thirty-Fifth Division's path was found to be a German stronghold at Cheppy, just about a mile from the start line for the attack. The defense of the village held up the division for hours. The infantry needed help. The tanks, however, were nowhere to be found.

Tank support for the Thirty-Fifth Division came from the command of Lieutenant Colonel George Patton. Integrating the maneuver of tanks with the infantry, as Patton had learned in his brief tenure as an armored commander, was nearly impossible. There was simply no way to communicate effectively. The small noisy compartment of the tank left only enough room for the driver and the gunner. Even if wireless sets could be built that proved durable to withstand the bumps, jolts, and dust of the battlefield (an unlikely prospect), there was no place to put them, no way to power them, and nobody to operate them. When tankers wanted to talk to anyone, they would have to stop and stick their heads out the turrets.

Patton decided the only way to effectively facilitate tank/infantry cooperation was to do it himself. So at 6:30 A.M. on the morning of battle he struck out for the front. What he found appalled him. When the fog and smoke that shrouded the battlefield lifted around 10 A.M., the scene proved to be one of utter chaos. Patton discovered he was over 100 yards ahead of his tanks, which had become mired in the barbed-wire lines strung in front of the forward enemy positions. The fact that Patton could see what was going on plainly enough meant that the German defenses on the high ground above him could see everything as well. They drenched the attackers with artillery fire directed by observers. In addition, the advancing doughboys found themselves in the midst of the first German defense line (which had not been obliterated by the weak bombardment of the 75-mm guns). They were attacked by machine-gun fire from virtually every direction. German machine-gun nests to their front, flank, and rear all peppered the tanks and infantry in equal measure.

The machine-gun and artillery fire were not only a danger to men and tanks, it made the prospect for running back and forth between them very hazardous duty. Most field-grade leaders, like Huebner in the First Division at the Battle of Soissons, were killed or wounded exposing themselves to enemy fire as they tried to pick their way from place to place simply to give directions and confer with other commanders. Such was the fate of Lieutenant Colonel Patton. At the height of the advance on Cheppy, a German machine-gun bullet struck him down and he was evacuated to an aid station of the Thirty-Fifth Division.

Only a chance encounter of two platoons of Patton's tankers and troops from the division's 138th Infantry Regiment saved the moment. Both had managed to reach the flank of the German position at the town, where the infantry and armor officers in charge in a hasty conference arranged a joint assault. It "may well have been the first-ever situation of tank-infantry cooperation in an offensive situation," concluded Carlo D'Este in a fine biography of Patton. "Nothing recorded about the earlier Saint-Mihiel campaign even approached the capture of Cheppy by tanks and infantry working together as team. If there was evidence that the tank had a future, it was this small but important tank infantry-action. Unfortunately, whatever useful lessons might have been learned were to be lost… ."[46] Cheppy proved a fleeting bright spot in a disastrous day.

The taking of Cheppy proved disappointing in two respects. First, only an accident, a chance encounter between forces and commanders on the battlefield took the town. One veteran of the battle summed up the situation well, "The 138th got a lot further that day by accident," he mused, "than they could have gone in a well-organized attack… ."[47] It was a triumph not repeated elsewhere. Second, it came too late, well after noontime, to sustain the momentum of the division's attack.

Airpower's role on the battlefield proved even more ambivalent than the contributions of armor and artillery. Some 800 aircraft had been assigned to support the attack. Among the planes in the sky on that September morning, one was piloted by Eddie Rickenbacker, the famed American air ace. Rickenbacker recalled the opening artillery barrage on the German lines. The scene, he recalled, looked "like a giant switchboard which emanated thousands of electric flashes as invisible hands manipulated the plugs."[48] Rickenbacker was, however, like most airmen, an observer of the ground war whose efforts had little impact on the land battle.

It was difficult to identify targets on the ground and coordinate air-land operations, and it was far too dangerous to have planes operate in the forward area. Instead, air-ground attacks were more often than not, as another air ace, Major Charles J. Biddle, described, "a strafing party on some roads well in the German lines. Strafing … is aviation slang for bombing and shooting up troops, etc., on roads, from very low attitudes, two or three hundred meters.

It is most unpleasant and dangerous work, for one gets shot up from the ground, against which there is no protection, and then any Huns [Germans] who may come along in the air have you at a great disadvantage."[49] Ground support was not a simple task.

Biddle had no enthusiasm for the mission and no wonder. Airplanes were fragile structures made of soft wood, usually spruce, and fabric, hardly designed and equipped for this kind of work. One sergeant in the Thirty-Fifth Division described a typical ground-support mission in the Meuse-Argonne. "Or planes were buzzing all about, the high ones observing and the low ones strafing the hill ahead of our skirmish lines," he recalled, "One fighter sailed in close over the crest, made a tight turn and exploded. His wings and tail jumped out of a cloud of black smoke and the front end arched down like a flaming comet. Look like he'd run into a direct hit by a 77-mm."[50] The task was not only difficult and deadly, it was largely disconnected from efforts on the ground and irrelevant to turning the tide of the land battle.

## COLLAPSE AND REDEMPTION

By the end of the day, part of the attack had gone well: the divisions in Bullard's corps had pushed forward miles, clearing both the first and second lines of the German defenses. The divisions of the other corps fared far less successfully, the Thirty-Fifth least of all. The division had advanced little more than a mile. On September 30, 1918, the Thirty-Fifth was relieved from the front by the First Division. Estimates vary; the command had lost somewhere between 6,000 and 8,000 men.[51] And for all that loss, the soldiers of the Thirty-Fifth had gained precious little ground. They had been inadequately prepared for battle and poorly led. The results spoke for themselves.

Despite the first day's tough fighting, Allied operations continued—and the Americans played the predominant role. Over 1,250,000 doughboys participated in the offensive. All of them were needed. The days stretched into weeks, the weeks into months. On November 1, 1918, the American offensive forced the German front to withdraw across the Meuse River; on November 5, the first U.S. troops forged a crossing and three days later held the high ground overlooking the city of Sedan from which they could direct artillery on the Germans' main rail supply line. On November 8, the Germans dispatched a delegation to a railroad siding at Compiègne west of Soissons. November 11, 1918, the war ended. The doughboys' work was over. Their achievement was impressive.

## LEARNING LESSONS

Americans contributed more to winning the war than just numbers.

Over the course of the campaign, the doughboys mastered the ways of modern fighting. And victories were the result of something more than just the raw courage of men like Huebner and Patton, risking their lives at the sharp end of war. The American Army learned lessons in combat and adapted as it gained battle experience. "A perusal of the volumes of Military Operations in the Official History of the American Expeditionary Force," observes historian Kenneth E. Hamburger, "impresses the reader with just how far the organization progressed in its capabilities and efficiency in relatively a short time."[52] American soldiers attended Allied schools where they absorbed the experience of the first three years of the war. Commands published tactical instruction memorandums filled with their own lessons from combat. After the war, the Army organized the Superior Board on Organization and Tactics to study the American combat experience. The board's findings were published in June 1920, crammed with recommendations on improving organization, training, and equipment.

How the Americans tried to make sense of their wartime experience says a great deal about how they approached the problem of being better at battle. The doughboys proved more concerned with improving the practices they had been taught than improvising new methods of war fighting. If all this effort seemed a bit much like Taylor's *Principles of Scientific Management,* that is perhaps not far off the mark. The Americans focused on making the processes of war more efficient. That after all was the essence of doughboy genius.

Lesson learning, with the exception of the lessons burned into the memory of men such as Lear, Marshall, Patton, Huebner, and McNair, proved largely fruitless in advancing the cause of genius in the postwar era. Anemic budgets and shrunken numbers precluded institutionalizing many of the organizational practices the American Army had honed in its efforts to raise, equip, train, ship, and then manage masses of men in battle. Doughboy genius would continue to be practiced in Army schools and War Department offices, but much of it would have to be relearned for the next war, as would the attributes of GI ingenuity.

## CHAPTER 3

# The Innovation Revolution

## HEROES AND HOLLYWOOD

TOMMIES AND DOUGHBOYS RETURNED from World War I very different people. "Tommy" was the popular nickname for the British soldier in the Great War. It was actually a nickname of a nickname, a shortened version of "Tommy Atkins," the British version of "John Doe" in uniform used as far back as the eighteenth century. Interestingly, Tommy remained the public nickname for soldiers in World War II. The continuity of nicknames reflects the nature of British society in the interwar years—stagnation. Tommies came home after World War I happy with victory, but weighted down with the years of sacrifice and physical and economic burdens of paying the price. The war also marked the high-water mark and the beginning of the precipitous decline of Britain's reign as an imperial and industrial global power.

In *The Great War and Modern Memory,* Paul Fussell illustrates the listless spirit of the era in an analysis of British war literature, noting the emergence of the "victim-hero," men, like the British nation, victimized and exploited by war, casualties, just like the million crosses for the boys left in the French earth. The literature had a powerful pull on the generation of Britons who saw their lives bifurcated by the Great War and disillusioned with the results of their sacrifice. They became the "lost generation."

In contrast, the war was both a remote and an inspiring image in American culture. While Tommy poets lamented that they wallowed in mud, stench, and death within sight of the coast and their bucolic homeland, doughboy popular culture portrayed the war as a great adventure akin to exploring and conquering the Old West. "To Americans, the Great War in France," Fussell writes, "was as remote as, say, the Second War in the Solomon

Islands: 'Over There' (meaning *way* Over There) is characteristically an American, not a British, song of the war."[1] Many Americans romanticized the war in a manner the British did not.

There were exceptions. A few American writers such as John Dos Passos, who served as an ambulance driver during the war, shared the dissolution of British intellectuals. His novel *Three Soldiers* (1921) was a critical and financial success, but its reception illustrated what mainstream America thought about its achievements in the Great War. "Critics, while generally praising it," Townsend Ludington noted in the *Virginia Quarterly Review,* "recognized that an attack on the military was controversial. Conservatives attacked it: the reviewer for the *New York Times* condemned it for its 'unmanly intemperance both in language and plot.' It lacked any 'voice of righteousness' and had only the 'voice of complaint and petty recrimination.' In March 1922 the *Chicago Tribune* published a diatribe against *Three Soldiers* under the headline: THREE SOLDIERS BRANDED AS TEXTBOOK AND BIBLE FOR SLACKERS AND COWARDS."[2] Unlike Dos Passos, most Americans had loved their war ... or at least their warriors.

When the doughboys returned from France, the hometown image of World War I reflected the nature of stateside society: a society that was confident, hopeful, with an expanding economy, thriving industry, new scientific discoveries, a nation never physically molested by the horror of the trenches. The Great War was an American adventure. It remained only for the window of American culture, a small group of thriving entrepreneurs and artists in Southern California, to tell Americans what they already believed about war. The place was called Hollywood and the people there made movies.

Hollywood more often than not has been a mirror, rather than a leader, of American culture. This era was no different. America was blossoming in the postwar world and so was Hollywood. "They were a new race these men and women of the movies, said a writer of the 1920s," according to film historian Robert Sklar; "They were a people dedicated completely to the body, to beauty, and health, than any the world had seen before. They marked the dawning of the Aquarian Age ... ."[3] And film captured that spirit—even in war.

In 1927 one of the most spectacular adventure films of its time hit the screen—*Wings*. In *Wings* the war is an escapade for the brave and beautiful. When the United States declares war on Germany, Buddy Rogers and Richard Arlen join the fledgling Air Corps to learn how to fly and fight. Of course, both are strikingly handsome and courageous, and the story of their adventures is just an excuse for showcasing good-looking heroes and the daring of aerial flight. John Monk Saunders, the writer who sold the idea to Hollywood and Washington, declared, "the very magnitude of the subject demanded heroic treatment."[4] And grand it was; Saunders talked the Army into providing a half dozen planes and pilots for the movie. The climactic battle scene, the assault on the St. Mihiel Salient (actually filmed in Texas, not Hollywood) included everything to create the most realistic combat scene ever filmed: 3,500 men, 60 planes, and 45 cameras.[5] Audiences swooned.

The larger ironies of the film escaped most Americans. The film glorified the kind of fighting that had the least impact on winning the war. The role of aircraft at St. Mihiel was almost insignificant. Likewise, the film hyped the emergence of airpower at a time when the U.S. postwar investments in aviation were next to pathetic. Equally incongruous was that Hollywood inadvertently trumpeted one of America's greatest failings in the war. Despite the fact that the United States was the greatest industrial power in the world, virtually none of the planes flown in France had been made in America. And the film, like all the first generation of Hollywood postwar movies, virtually ignored the soldier's greatest contribution to winning the war—doughboy genius.

Americans showed little interest recalling the genius that doughboys had shown harnessing the industrial age in the service of modern conflict. America's notables were not technocrats, such as industrialists and staff officers who helped field the mass army that won the war. Nor were they victims (like those in the British lost-generation literature). Rather, Americans loved heroes. They chose to clothe the doughboy's mastery of business, science, and technology in the imagery of the heroic adventurer.

Efforts to romanticize the relationship between Americans and technology were not new. It had been an enduring feature of nineteenth century life. Americans tended to describe their great inventors, from Eli Whitney to Thomas Edison, in romantic language. One contemporary writer suggested all inventors had in them "something grand and heroic."[6] Americans envisioned their warriors, even those enabled by the mundane technologies and practices of the industrial world, in the same way. That was a tradition they carried into the Great War. *Wings* was a case in point. The film merely perpetuated a popular wartime fiction of air combat as a duel between elite, masculine heroes, something more akin to sports or hunting than combat.[7]

The deification of heroism was not just reserved for the air war. In film, books, and the American imagination the battle of the trenches was won by blood and guts and grit of doughboys (both Army and Marine), not doughboy genius. The first big box-office war movie, *The Big Parade,* released in 1925, brought in over $15 million. In the film (also made in Texas with Army cooperation), three men, a millionaire's son, a riveter, and a bartender, become friends and bravely go off to fight together. The next hit movie, *What Price Glory?,* was actually made from a pacifist Broadway play (coauthored by

Lawrence T. Stallings, a combat veteran who lost a leg from war wounds), though the film version softened the message and focused on the individual heroism of men at the front.

What all the success of Hollywood's efforts had in common, notes film historian Lawrence Suid, was that they "demonstrated that moviegoers wanted to see them not because of the antiwar sentiment they might contain, but simply to watch great battle scenes, scenes of men fighting and dying, of planes flying, and of men loving on their time away from combat."[8] In the popular memory, strong, masculine individuals—doughboys—had made the difference. "The tough, wise-cracking, hard-as-nails, heart-of-gold" sergeant played by popular screen figures such as Edmund Lowe, Victor McLaglen, and Wallace Berry became a stock character of the Hollywood war movie.[9]

The war's real life heroes paralleled their fictional counterparts. In the air, men such as Eddie Rickenbacker, America's ace of aces, were among perhaps the most notable. The story of Rickenbacker's wartime experiences, *Fighting the Flying Circus,* became an instant best-seller when it was published in 1919.

On the ground, the war's two most popular heroes were individual enlisted soldiers, both awarded the Congressional Medal of Honor, America's highest decoration for valor. Samuel Woodfill grew up in the wilds of Kentucky, joined the army in 1901, and won the Medal of Honor during the Meuse-Argonne offensive when he single-handedly charged a machine-gun nest. The title of his biography penned by adventurer and famed broadcaster Lowell Thomas says it all—*Woodfill of the Regulars: A True Story of Adventure from the Arctic to the Argonne* (1930). In the introduction, Thomas wrote Woodfill was an "American frontiersman, a real survivor of an earlier day, thrown into the infernal mechanism and modernistic terror of the greatest of all wars. It was pretty much as if Daniel Boone or Kit Carson by some miracle were brought back and thrown into the middle of the bloody fire-swept ground of the Argonne, with his primeval riflemanship and game-stalking, cover-taking cunning … ."[10] Woodfill filled the image of the archtype American hero better than Hollywood could ever imagine.

Sergeant Alvin York's fame proved even greater, his story being even more compelling to an American public hungry for heroes. York grew up in the backwoods of Tennessee. Like Woodfill, he was renowned as a hunter and a crack shot. York requested an exemption from military service for religious reasons, but he was drafted anyway. The reluctant warrior proved an incredible soldier. During the Meuse-Argonne campaign he led a squad of men that captured 132 enemy soldiers. York personally killed nine Germans. General John Pershing, the Commander of the American Allied Expeditionary Force in France, called him "the greatest civilian soldier of the war." York received the Medal of Honor and a hero's welcome when his ship docked in New York; he was whisked off to the Waldorf-Astoria Hotel for a grand reception. For years, Sergeant York remained a household name. When George Marshall ordered the lessons of World War I recorded in the Infantry School study *Infantry in Battle,* in the chapter on "miracles," the accomplishment of a small group of soldiers is given the ultimate compliment: "one of these examples," the lesson exclaims, "rivals the case of Sergeant York."[11] Next to Rickenbacker, York may have been the most famous American in uniform.

While General Pershing and other senior leaders in the Great War garnered their share of acclaim and admiration, they were austere, remote figures, like the cooperate giants ensconced in their offices far above the factory floor. As far as the American public was concerned, the war was won by their brave boys in the trenches. If war came again, the pioneer spirit, an All-American attitude, and old-fashioned teamwork would pave the way to victory once more.

## THE AGE OF UNPREPAREDNESS

While Americans nurtured their romanticized version of the terrible conflict in the trenches, the doughboy genius that had helped win the war quickly atrophied. Pershing's Superior Board on Organization and Tactics made sweeping recommendations for refining military organizations and training and operational processes. The War Department proposed retaining an active-duty military of 600,000 and three months of mandatory military training for all young men in the country, so that the nation could quickly mobilize if war came again. Americans wanted none of it.

Planning for demobilization began a month before the war ended. Within nine months over 3 million doughboys were mustered out of service. Resources for the Army's ground and air forces continued to decline through the mid-1930s. Most of the Army divisions existed only on paper. Skeletonized regiments were spread among small garrison posts throughout the United States, Panama, and the Philippines. In 1932, not counting the National Guard, there were only about 130,000 men in uniform. The United States ranked seventeenth in military strength behind such global powers as Yugoslavia.[12]

The American Army was not only small, it was poorly equipped. The Army Chief of Staff, General Douglas MacArthur, complained that outside of a dozen experimental tanks, the entire American armor corps was unfit for modern battle. Likewise, the U.S. Navy and the Army Air Corps experimented with various kinds of aircraft, but bought few of anything. Of the 1,400 planes owned by the Army, only 400 were considered of "modern type."

In a similar manner, research and development on field artillery continued, but the United States lacked an up-to-date artillery force. "A well developed arsenal [government manufacturing] system for field artillery existed," wrote American field artillery historian Boyd L. Dastrup, "but they could furnish only a small fraction of the Army's demand during wartime. This meant the War Department would have to rely on private industry that had neither expertise nor experience."[13] In the meanwhile, almost the entire extant artillery force was of World War I vintage. All this guaranteed that when the next great war occurred America might well again have to scramble to get ready.

While the Army evaporated, the spark of doughboy genius continued to sputter in a few places where the winds of indifference and unpreparedness did not blow them out altogether. Marshall's tenure at the infantry school was one place. Marshall not only schooled soldiers and thought about future war, he measured the quality of students and faculty that passed through. One of the instructors that caught his eye was a young officer named Omar Bradley. And professional development went on in quiet studies and offices where papers (the interwar army's principal weapons) were shuttled back and forth at a languid pace. This is where Dwight Eisenhower learned much of his trade, serving on the staffs of Great War veterans such as Fox Conner, Pershing, and MacArthur.

And the spirit of doughboy genius walked the halls of the ornate building at the confluence of the Potomac and Anacostia rivers. Elihu Root had first proposed creating a military war college to address the utter failure of the Army to mobilize efficiently for the Spanish-American War. The college suspended operations during the Great War and then resumed them again in 1919. In 1921, the school standing majestically on the banks of "Buzzard Point" was renamed from the General Staff College to the Army War College. Until 1940, the college served to keep doughboy genius alive in a number of ways. The War College, and the Command and General Staff College at the old cavalry post at Fort Leavenworth, taught up-and-coming officers the processes for managing militaries in battle. The War College also trained officers for the War Department staff and taught subjects related to the strategy and logistics required to mount large-scale wars.[14]

During this same period, the War Department established an Industrial College to train military staff officers in procurement and mobilization. While a student at the Industrial College, Dwight Eisenhower wrote his course paper on the role of the War Department in industrial mobilization.[15] (Eisenhower would later put the skills he learned in the classroom to work when he drafted the first detailed industrial mobilization plan for the War Department.)[16] The Army tried to do in the classroom what it lacked the men and material to do in real life, exercise the practice of doughboy genius.

The Infantry School Staff. George Marshall is seated center. Bradley stands to his right. (Courtesy, Army Signal Corps)

Perhaps most important, while formal war plans were drafted by the War and Navy Department staffs, the students at the Army (and the Navy War and Industrial Colleges as well) conducted studies and war games to help inform these efforts. During this period the staffs first developed a series of "Color" plans; each plan envisioned a U.S. war against a major adversary. In the mid-1930s the color plans were replaced by the "Rainbow" plans, which considered the United States fighting on multiple fronts against multiple enemies with different combinations of allied support. At least a few soldiers, somewhere, were thinking about the unthinkable, even if the rest of America slept.

## FREEDOM AND FEAR

While a few American military thinkers mused of war, American industry continued to mass-produce what made modern war so terrible: the marriage of science, technology, industry, and business, a marriage that, when needed, could birth mass armies of unrivaled sophistication and power. And no one understood how to adapt technology to everyday life (whether for conspicuous consumption or combat) better than Americans. People around the world began to speak of an "American System of Manufactures."[17] This system included not just the use of standardized parts and assembly lines made famous by the factories of the Ford Motor Company. The American system comprised an intricate network of organized industrial activities from the delivery of raw materials through manufacturing and on to the distribution and delivery of products on a mass scale, with all these activities done under the umbrella of a vast democratic, free-market enterprise.

Only the intervention of the Great Depression in 1930 cast any doubt on the supremacy of the American economic ideal. By the end of 1931, almost 2,300 banks had failed. Gross National Product (the measure of all the goods and services produced by the country) dropped 20 percent. Unemployment was almost 16 percent. And the depression had gone global, crushing the economies of Western Europe and affecting most nations around the world. The nosedive in the global business cycle proved not only to be a setback to the economy, it also kept the recovery of military preparedness at a snail's pace, despite the rise of worldwide tensions suggesting that another major conflict might not be far off.

Depression, however, was not war. Factories had not been bombed. The workers were still alive. Thinkers kept thinking and inventors inventing. In large part, President Franklin Roosevelt was right when he told Americans they had "nothing to fear but fear itself." When the business cycle began to turn up, America was on the cutting edge of the upswing. Economic recovery began in a serious way in 1938, though unemployment remained high until 1940, as the United States began to gear up to feed the dogs of war again. As a result, in 1942 when the American military needed to exercise its dough-boy genius again, America was primed and ready. The only problem was that the rest of the world had gotten ready first.

## DREAMS OF WAR BETWEEN THE WARS

By the mid-1940s the American genius for industrial innovation had become common knowledge around the world. Every modern power knew how to exploit the advantages of the assembly line. And many had invested far more effort in preparing for the next industrial-strength war. They made the period between the wars one of the most remarkable ages in military history.

Historians have given periods in history resulting in dramatic changes in warfare different names and argue incessantly over which names fits best, a preoccupation of the craft. Whatever these eras are called, the results are the same—the next war is fought very differently from the last one. That characterization certainly fits the difference between World War I and World War II.

The reason for the dramatic shift in the ways of war between the two global conflicts has much to do with the innovations made by militaries during the interwar years. The efforts of no country contributed to this period of change more than the country that lost the last war—Germany.

Understanding what the German military accomplished requires reading a book. There are a handful of books every student of the military art should read. Clausewitz's *On War* is one. *Truppenführung* is another. Published in 1933–1934, *Heeresdienstvorschrift 300, Truppenführung* (unit command), as James Corum writes in his foreword to the English translation, is "one of the most important expressions of doctrine in military history."[18] *Truppenführung* is perhaps the first and most influential coherent expression of modern combined-arms warfare in much the same way as Carl von Clausewitz's *On War* is recognized as a founding document of contemporary strategic thought.

The origins of *Truppenführung* can be found in the waning days of World War I. No army could effectively "combine arms," in other words, use artillery, armor, aircraft, and infantry in an integrated manner. Artillery upset everything. Attackers crossing no-man's-land had scant means to counter the withering rain of shells and shrapnel that saturated their path. In contrast, artillery proved a clumsy instrument for the offense. Massing fires, coordinating infantry and artillery, and conducting effective counterbattery (shooting at the enemy's artillery with artillery) fire were all in their infancy. In its summer offensive of 1918, Germany experimented with innovative tactical concepts to break the stalemate of trench warfare, but collapsed from strategic exhaustion (in large part because of the efforts of the American Army) before it could employ its tactical initiatives with decisive effect.

During the interwar period, General Hans von Seeckt, the head of the *Reichswehr* (the German Army of the Weimar Republic, the country's postwar democratic government), undertook a comprehensive review of the war's lessons and initiated a series of exhaustive experiments, war games, and exercises to develop new war-fighting concepts. Von Seeckt codified the insights gained in a series of doctrinal manuals. The general never allowed a lack of resources to constrain innovative thinking. Germany developed tank doctrine even before it had any tanks and air-ground operational concepts before it established the *Luftwaffe*. Automobiles and bicycles covered in canvas stood in for tanks. Simulated air reconnaissance and attacks were accomplished by giving a former aviator a motorcycle and letting him ride unmolested through the enemy lines. When he returned he issued a report to the umpire who ruled on the effects of the "aerial" sortie. It was all more than just fun and games. It was a deadly serious effort to map the processes of modern war and determine how to make them as efficient as possible.[19]

Intellectual change preceded technological capacity. As German factories in the 1930s began to turn out the instruments of modern war, the German Army updated its doctrine. *Truppenführung* was a revision of von Von Seeckt's work, rewritten to account for emerging developments in motorized warfare, aviation, and electronic communications. And when Adolf Hitler and the Nazi Party turned the German military toward global conquest, the army was ready for the job.

Frederick W. Taylor would have been proud, not of the Nazis, but of the methods used to restructure the military. War, the manual proclaimed in its opening sentence, is "founded on scientific principles."[20] The German efforts to implement effective combined-arms warfare were nothing less than the principles of scientific management on steroids.

There was, however, a subtle but important difference between Taylor's vision of merging man and machine into one flawless perfect process and von Seeckt's efforts to reinvent the conduct of ground combat. Von Seeckt had read his Clausewitz. The general appreciated the importance of unpredictable factors, chance events, and unintended consequences in battle and recognized that scientific study could never eliminate their effect. While the opening sentence of *Truppenführung* emphasized war's scientific roots, it also stated that "war is an art, a free and creative activity."[21] Genius in battle was still important.

The solution adopted in German doctrine was to establish a style of command that encouraged junior officers and even enlisted soldiers to take initiative, improvise, and adjust to conditions on the ground as long as they operated within the intent of orders issued by higher headquarters. The concept was called *auftragstaktik* (mission-type orders). The object was to institutionalize the concept of flexible, adaptive command, particularly for fast-moving offensive situations.

Germany was not the only great power experimenting with the ways of modern war during the interwar period, but its efforts certainly garnered the most attention, particularly after its dramatic conquests of Poland and France, the opening campaigns of the Second World War. An American journalist called it *blitzkrieg* (lightning war).[22]

The handsome, smiling face of Walther von Brauchitsch, commander-in-chief of the *Wehrmacht* (the new name for the German Army after the fall of the Weimer Republic and the onset of the Nazi regime) beamed on the front cover of the September 25, 1939, issue of *Time* magazine. Inside the newsmagazine, a journalist reported on the remarkably swift victory over Poland. "For this was no war of occupation," he wrote, "but a war of quick penetration and obliteration—Blitzkrieg, lightning war. Swift columns of tanks and armored trucks had plunged through Poland while bombs raining from the sky heralded their coming."[23] The victory marked the return of combined-arms warfare, not with infantry muskets, smooth-bore artillery, and sword-wielding cavalry (as in the days of Clausewitz), but with armor, quick-firing artillery, and airpower.

## PLAYING CATCH-UP

By the time the United States joined the war, after the Japanese sneak attack on the U.S. military bases in Pearl Harbor and Schofield Barracks, Hawaii, on December 7, 1941, every major nation had adopted some version of modern combined-arms warfare. As in World War I, the United States had a lot of ground to cover before it was ready to compete in another modern global war.

The American boys sent off to fight the war were, however, a very different breed than the doughboys. At first, they worried over whether they were even up to the challenge of doing what their fathers had done. The novelist James A. Michener recalled, "Many observers considered us a lost generation and feared we might collapse if summoned to some crucial battlefield."[24] There was also a measure of guilt. World War II veteran Army Chaplain Russell Cartwright Stroup wrote he felt that "as part of a generation that failed to prevent this war, I should suffer with those who are victims of our failure."[25] The fresh-faced kids, the Yankee fans from New York, the meat packer from Kansas City, and the orange grower from California came from a different America.

Americans that could claim kinship to the Sergeant Yorks and Woodfills of the Regulars were fewer in number. The American frontier was largely gone and, with it, a generation that had reached mythic proportions in the eyes of men and women preparing to fight World War II. "Life on the frontier," taught General Lear's *School of the Citizen Soldier,* "emphasized individual strength, ingenuity, and resourcefulness. The frontier was not a place for weaklings; it bred hard and tough individuals, it emphasized the fact that if a man would survive, he must learn to stand on his own feet."[26] This was the ideal stock for soldiers. It was a story the GI generation read about many times in juvenile literature, heard on the radio, and saw in films. It was not the world in which most GIs grew up. It was a world (whether it actually existed or not in the way they had imagined) that they thought they had lost.

GIs' childhoods unfolded in a new technological age. "Modern technology was made in America," concludes Thomas Hughes, a professor in history and sociology at the University of Chicago, "Even the Germans who developed it so well acknowledged the United States as the prime source. During the inter-war years, the industrial world recognized the United States as the pre-eminent technological nation, and the era of technological enthusiasm reached its apogee."[27] Its children were the GI generation.

GIs were the first generation of Americans raised in an age where industry permeated every aspect of their lives. They grew up in an electrified, gasoline-powered world. Even on the farm, kids lived with machines every day—fixing tractors, driving harvesters, and greasing well pumps. In 1900, there were 45,000 engineers in the United States. In 1930, there were 230,000.[28] And engineers and inventors increasingly worked in corporate America. They were employees of large industrial and engineering concerns. And they frequently became managers. By the 1920s, during their careers after leaving university two-thirds of college-trained engineers had moved into management.[29] And they were not lonely; "middle management," Frederick Taylor's solution to complex managerial challenges, became an endemic feature of modern com-panies. And the ranks of middle management were filled with college-edu-cated men, schooled in science, mathematics, history, English, and a host of other useful fields of knowledge.

They were a smart generation, but not necessarily a "soft" generation. An abundance of technological know-how had not meant an age of luxury and leisure. The Great Depression had seen to that. Even before war, the GI gen-eration knew hardship and hard times. Douglas Kinnard, who graduated from West Point in the D-Day class of 1944 remembered that in 1930 "the shadow of the Depression was beginning to be visible even to nine-year-olds. Grown men, who a year before had commuted daily to New York, were selling apples on the corner."[30] The Depression put many college-educated and col-lege-bound men out on the street, where they learned in the school of "hard knocks." They were a generation that went off to war knowing the challenge of adversity.

When Americans finally girded for battle, they found they did not lack gutsy individual heroism and leadership qualities with the likes of men such as York, Woodfill, Rickenbacker, George S. Patton, and Clarence R. Huebner. But they discovered they were indeed different from the doughboy genera-tion. The changing character of the U.S. workforce had two significant impli-cations for the nature of the American fighting forces.

(1) GIs were a generation comfortable with modern technology. Every GI shared some of the engineer and inventor spirit. "Contrary to popular myth," writes Hughes, "technology does not result from a series of searches for the 'one best' solution to problems. Instead it presents practitioners of technology confronting insolvable issues, making mistakes, and causing controversies and failures. ... creating new problems as they solve old ones."[31] That

description fit the American GI well. They were head-scratchers, problem solvers, and innovators. They were a generation that moved beyond simply creating formulaic industrial and business processes; they began to toy innovatively and creatively with machines, adapting existing technologies to do different things or do things in a manner different from the way they had been designed to be used.

(2) The GI generation was led by a cadre of men educated and practiced to exploit creative adaptation with technology. One argument for creating fewer, larger divisions during World War I was that the Americans lacked a sufficient cadre of skilled and educated men to fill out all the staff and field-grade command positions that would have been needed if they organized their 2-million-man army along the lines of the smaller divisions of the French and the British.[32] In contrast, the corps of men qualified to fill the ranks of middle management during World War II, the field-grade officers who would occupy the command and staff positions in battalions, regiments, combat commands, and brigades, would be vast.

Indeed, one of the successes of the Army during the interwar years was that it began to groom its middle management for the next war, and not just at its traditional training ground for officers, the academy at West Point. The National Defense Act of 1920 expanded and regulated the Reserve Officer Training Corps program. While the military had had a haphazard relationship with some colleges where military courses were taught in the past, after World War I the program was completely reorganized. By 1928, 85,000 students in colleges and universities around the country received some military education before many of them went off to serve in corporate America, ready to be recalled when war came.

A few college graduates joined the Army and became regular officers, rather than taking commissions in the Reserve or National Guard. While there was little prospect for getting rich or receiving quick promotions in the Army, there was the promise of steady pay, job security, and guaranteed housing—not a bad life during the Depression. And the Army valued its middle-grade officers. "The Army, like other great corporations, has among its executives all types of men," wrote the author of the 1940 book, *How to Be An Army Officer* (a book in a series that included titles such as *How to Be a Bandleader* and *How to Be a G-Man*), "Just as the corporation picks promising graduates, so too does the Army pick its second lieutenants ... . All Army officers are executives ... ."[33] And they became the nucleus of the next army.

Within the military ranks, despite its paucity in many areas, the Army did invest in educating its field-grade officers during the interwar years. In fact, military historian Charles E. Kilpatrick contends, "officer education, and most particular junior officer education, was the key factor," in success during

World War II.[34] Complaints about the lack of qualified field-grade officers (colonels, lieutenant colonels, and majors) would prove constant throughout the war. That was because commanders recognized their incalculable value to improving the fighting quality of the force—they could never get enough.

And their ranks were bolstered during the course of the war with an infusion of junior leaders, many of whom would become field-grade officers over the course of the European campaign. "The job the Army did," writes historian Stephen Ambrose, "in creating and shaping the leadership qualities in its junior officers—just college-age boys, most of them—was also one of the great accomplishments in the history of the Republic."[35] In Normandy, their contribution would be immeasurable.

Having the raw material for GI genius, however, was not sufficient. First, the Americans would have to get their boys ready for war. And in that regard, they had a long way to go to catch up with the rest of the world. Before Pearl Harbor most Americans had lived their lives untouched by military service; a 20-year-old private fighting in the Normandy hedgerows was born six years after the armistice of 1918. By 1943, these citizens had swelled the Army to its peak combat strength of 90 divisions, almost nine times the number that existed before the war. The veterans of the interwar army found themselves outnumbered 40 to 1. A typical division fighting in Normandy would have regular army regimental commanders, an even mix of regular, Reserve, and National Guard battalion commanders. Two-thirds of the company-grade officers (captains and lieutenants) would come from Officer Candidate School (a 90-day military course of instruction for enlisted soldiers). The other third came from the National Guard, the Reserve, or West Point. The division's noncommissioned officers and soldiers were a mix of volunteers and draftees.[36]

## DOUGHBOY REPRISE

Repeating Pershing's triumph, massing an army of unprecedented power in an unbelievably short period of time, was no simple matter. But mobilization for World War II showed that, despite the privations of the interwar years, doughboy genius, the skill at fighting industrial-age warfare, was alive and well in the American Army. Albert C. Wedemeyer proved that.

On April 26, 1941, Major Wedemeyer reported for duty to the Army General Staff. Until this point in his career he was renowned for—nothing. His service had been wholly unremarkable. Commissioned from West Point in 1918, the closest he got to war was a class tour of the front after the armistice and the chance to meet General Pershing and an impressive young colonel named George Marshall in Paris. In 1936, Wedemeyer (already a

graduate of the U.S. Command and General Staff College at Fort Leavenworth) was posted to the German *Kriegsakademie,* the school that trained
the German Army's general staff officers. There he discovered two things:
(1) the value of German military thought in books such as *On War* and
*Truppenführung* and (2) how far ahead the Germans were in seriously preparing for the next war and how determined they were to avoid a repetition of
the failures in the last one.

By the spring of 1941, there were still a few in Washington who doubted
that America would be drawn into World War II. Wedemeyer was not one
of them. Neither was his boss, Army Chief of Staff George C. Marshall.
Marshall ordered the General Staff to draft a new mobilization plan, a realistic
plan that accounted for the massive needs of providing support for the Allies
under the Lend-Lease program and creating a massive army, navy, and air
corps to fight a two-front war. The task was given to Major Wedemeyer.

In 90 days, Major Wedemeyer produced a 14-page report. Popularly
known as the Victory Plan of 1941, it became the blueprint for the mobilization of the Army. The plan was not only remarkable for its scope, but for the
incredible assumptions Wedemeyer had to make. He had to presume the
maximum capacity that the American manufacturing base could produce,
how much manpower could be mobilized without undercutting domestic
production, how the United States would fight a two-front war with the
forces available, what kinds of units would be needed, what kinds of technology they would be equipped with, and how long it would take to get them
ready for battle. It was a daunting achievement even to attempt to address
such weighty strategic issues.

What was even more incredible was how close the plan came to predicting
the capacity of the United States to wage modern war. "In 1941," Kilpatrick
writes, "Wedemeyer estimated that the Army Ground Forces and Army Air
Forces would need a grand total of 8,795,658 men to fight the war. As the
Army was attaining its peak strength in March 1945, it had a total of
8,157,386 men in uniform—very near the figure that Wedemeyer had estimated almost four years earlier."[37] Wedemeyer's assessments were not perfect,
but they were none the less a miraculous achievement of doughboy genius.

## DESIGNING A DIVISION

Raising and arming the Army was one thing; figuring out how to fight
with it was another. That effort began before Wedemeyer had entered the
*Kriegsakademie.* And it began with figuring out a new structure for the Army
division.[38] On November 5, 1935, the Army ordered a study undertaken of
the problem. Select committees met in January and in July 1936. Instead of

the square division used to fight World War I, it recommended a "triangular" division design (eliminating the two brigade headquarters and building the division around three infantry regiments).[39]

In World War I, the most critical element for determining the division design was staying power—the capacity to stay and fight in the trenches. For World War II, the principle design feature was ensuring the capability to conduct fire and maneuver using all the assets available to the modern combined-arms team. The answer was the "rule of three." At each echelon, commanders would have three forces: one for fire, one for maneuver, and one to exploit success. This organization was thought the most suitable for a highly fluid fast war of movement.[40]

The Army also believed the division should be smaller. Proposed troop strengths for the new division were as few as 10,000, though the Army eventually settled on a structure with a little over 15,000, about half the size of the World War I division. To make the division smaller, the Army achieved personnel savings by assuming the divisions would be part of a larger force that could provide combat and logistical support. Additional units, such as tank, artillery, and engineer support organized in separate battalions and brigades were to be pooled at echelons above corps. The corps would be a small command headquarters responsible for controlling the divisions and, as the tactical situation required, augmenting them with the additional assets allocated from the field army. In this manner, Army commanders would have greater flexibility in allocating assets to reinforce divisions to suit specific tactical situations.

In addition to enhancing flexibility, strategic factors heavily influenced the size of the division. The Army would need a tremendous number of divisions for global war. At the same time, as Wedemeyer reaffirmed in his analysis, there were definite limits on manpower and equipment procurement. In particular, shipping assets proved a significant constraint. Throughout the war, cargo space would be at a premium. Planners constantly puzzled how to squeeze the most combat power into the fewest number of ships. Smaller divisions simplified their problem.

With plans for the new division design drafted, in 1937 the Army set out to test the triangular design. The mission was given to the Indian Head—the 2nd Infantry Division. The man in charge of the tests was Lesley J. McNair. After the field exercise, changes were made and a second test was conducted in 1939. McNair described them as "the most searching and thorough tests ever made" and as "realistic as was permitted by the conditions of peace and lack of funds and of modern equipment in quantity."[41] The field tests were systematic with step-by-step evaluations of each design element and detailed findings and recommendations on everything from the frontages and firepower per unit to the turnaround time for ration trucks. In many ways the tests were a homage to the methods pioneered by von Seeckt a decade earlier.

The results of the test came none too soon. As German forces began their *blitzkrieg* across Europe, the new Army Chief of Staff, General George C. Marshall, ordered that the triangular design be adopted for all infantry divisions. The first was reconfigured by January 1940, less than a year later.

In addition, the Army developed a variety of specialized forces, including armored, motorized, light infantry, mountain, and airborne divisions. In particular, the design of the armored force earned special attention. The armor design had to be carefully thought through. It came with a hefty price tag. Though an armored unit had fewer men than an infantry unit, the support requirements to put an entire force on wheels and tracks were enormous. Just the logistical effort needed to deploy armor forces was breathtaking. Every tank sent to Europe contained 500 items that had to be unpacked, cleaned, mounted, and checked. It took a minimum of 50 hours to get one tank ready for combat. Armor was a big investment. The Americans tried hard to get it right.[42]

Requirements for the armored force differed significantly from the infantry division. Armored commands were to be exploitation forces, operating independently for extended periods. They needed to be more flexible and self-sufficient.

The armor design eventually evolved into an armored division including two tank regiments and an armored infantry regiment. Two combat commands (CCA, CCB) were also included in the division. The addition of these headquarters allowed the division commander to task forces to a combat command for a specific tactical mission. In other words, if the combat command had a mission that called for heavy, close-quarters combat, it might be composed of an equal mix of infantry and tank battalions. On the other hand, if the task was rapid exploitation, the command would be predominantly tank heavy with only minimal supporting arms.[43]

Within a year, the Army had approved plans for all the types of divisions it thought it would need for global war—and none too soon. Men swelled the "boot camps," where they would receive individual training and be sent off to units. Factories began to churn out everything from boot laces to bombers. America was readying for battle.

## ORGANIZING FOR COMBAT

The man in charge of fielding, training, and deploying the divisions was Lesley J. McNair. In regard to his task, McNair and Marshall, the Army Chief of Staff, were of one mind. Both planned for the Army's immediate future on the remembrance of things past. Both had witnessed the Americans' greatest offensive in the Meuse-Argonne, and while they were proud of the effort to get the doughboys to the fight, they were less than satisfied with how many of the American divisions performed in battle. McNair had railed about the poor artillery support plans. Marshall characterized the opening of the campaign as "stumbling, blunderings, failures, appeals for help, and hopeless confusion."[44] This time they would better. They would train the Army before it got to the fight.

The centerpiece of McNair's preparations was large-scale maneuvers, the first of which took place in Louisiana in the summer and the fall of 1941 (at the same time Wedemeyer was working on his victory plan). McNair intended the Louisiana field exercises to be "combat college for troop leading" and to use the maneuvers to test combined-arms concepts.

There was no question that McNair used the large-scale exercises, which involved tens of thousands of troops spread over hundreds of square miles, to grade leadership. Six of the eight National Guard Division Commanders were gone within a year of the field exercises. Lower officers were not spared either. In one division 119 officers were removed.[45] Men such as Eisenhower and Bradley saw their reputations rise. Others, such as Lear, saw their stock sink. Mistakes were made. Some of the reliefs proved highly controversial.[46] Some of the men who passed the McNair test went on to fail miserably in battle. No doubt, in the rough and tumble race to get ready for war, all the personnel decisions were not perfect. But, it was not a bad effort either, much better than waiting till casualties piled up on the battlefield to gain a glimmer of which leaders had the smarts and stamina for war.

The utility of the exercises as a test of combined-arms warfare was more problematic. Units still lacked much of the modern equipment they would take to war, and it was difficult to simulate their effects. There was only so much that could be learned, one participant remembered, from "flour-sack bombs, broomstick guns, and beer can mortar shells."[47] Like von Seeckt's field exercises for the *Reichswehr,* where the Americans lacked the equipment they needed, they improvised. Short of "blank" ammunition (cartridges with only powder and no bullets) to emulate the sound of war, the Army spent $15,000 for seven sound trucks with giant loudspeakers that would blast out recorded battlefield noises to make the mock engagements seem more realistic.

Perhaps the greatest difficulty in the exercises was determining how to assess the lethality of weapons, some of which had not yet even rolled off the factory floor. Determining the effectiveness of various forms of firepower was particularly important. Americans built their doctrine on the concept of fire and maneuver ... with fire coming first. If commanders could not bring accurate fire on the enemy and have a decisive effect, then (as the GIs discovered in Normandy) there would not be much maneuver.

McNair came up with a simple answer. For the field exercises, he would have three armies: two to fight each other and an army of umpires to adjudicate engagements. The umpires were issued a manual of complex rules explaining how to assess the value of firepower that units employed in battle and allocate casualties to the other side. Each division in the exercise was accompanied by 50 officers armed with their thick rule books and red, white, and blue flags, who functioned much the same way as an umpire in a baseball game. Given the resources available, it was the best system that could be devised. Still, without many of the real weapons of war, learning real lessons for the application of armor, artillery, and airpower would not be easy.

Learning how to employ armored forces may have been the most disappointing lesson of all. McNair was a zealous proponent of mobile antitank forces, perhaps, too much so. The umpire's manual underestimated the losses that could be incurred in tank-on-tank engagements and woefully overestimated the power of the U.S. Army's antitank weapons. The rules allowed antitank guns to take out one to two tanks per minute. Tanks, on the other hand, could not silence antitank weapons with their main guns; they had to overrun the enemy position to register a kill.[48] Even more limiting was the lack of imagination senior commanders had shown, especially Lear, in employing armored forces. Only some high-spirited advances by Patton's 2nd Armored Division showcased any of armor's promise to restore fast movement to the American way of war. Perhaps most disappointing of all, however, was how little attention was played to the most significant problem GIs would face in Normandy, coordinating infantry-tank action at the small-unit level.

The employment of artillery was a little more satisfying. The gunners did have some of their newest equipment for the exercise, including the first motorized versions of the 105-mm howitzer being built especially for the armored divisions. The guns were standard howitzers mounted on the chaise of a Sherman tank. But the impact of speed, mobility, and the effects of massed artillery proved difficult to replicate. Since commanders could not see the effects of waves of shells bursting over the enemy and smothering the battlefield in smoke and fire, they tended to underappreciate the value of fire support. Some commanders simply left their artillery behind when they moved their infantry forward. Others made scant efforts to mass fires, leaving artillery tubes idle in the most heated moments of battle. After the first maneuvers, McNair, an artilleryman himself, castigated commanders for their inability to effectively bring fire upon the enemy.[49]

Air-ground combat also left much to be desired. General Delos Emmons, who headed the Army Air Forces Combatant Command, did not want to

Patton Posing for a Publicity Shot during the Louisiana Maneuvers. (Courtesy, George S. Patton Collection, Military History Institute)

participate in the maneuvers at all, arguing it was a waste of good aircraft, fair summer flying weather, and valuable training time.[50] He was overruled. Nonetheless, the Army even had to borrow planes from the Navy to muster enough modern fighters and dive bombers to support the ground troops. In the end, perhaps Emmons was right. Perhaps it was all a waste of time. Doctrine for air-ground support proved to be so primitive and perfunctory, it was virtually useless. Means for communicating between aircraft and ground troops were laughably inadequate.

When all was said and done, the exercises failed to address the two major problems the GIs would face in battle when trying to obtain effective air support: (1) how to allocate air assets to the ground forces for different missions, whether air assets should be assigned to the ground commands or held under Army Air Forces' control and parsed out for each mission as needed, and (2) how to accurately identify friendly troops on the ground so that they would not be inadvertently attacked by American planes. No concrete solutions for addressing either problem emerged from the maneuvers or the reviews of the exercises that followed.[51]

Flawed though they were, the Louisiana Maneuvers and the Army Ground Forces' other efforts to raise and ready a mass army for battle turned Wedemeyer's Victory Plan into reality.[52] The Americans had not completely lost their doughboy genius. There was no question about that. But that would not be enough.

The Germans, building on the systematic efforts of von Seeckt, had gotten there first. The British, the Japanese, and the Russians had years of actual combat experience in combined-arms fighting. And in some respects, they all practiced industrial-strength warfare as well or better than the Americans. And the Louisiana Maneuvers demonstrated that with all the doughboy genius in the world, they still had not figured out how to effectively integrate infantry, artillery, armor, and airpower in battle. It would take more than doughboy smarts to give the U.S. Army the edge this time around. That was where GI ingenuity came in—though at the time few Americans appreciated the unique skills they were to bring to battle.

## WAR COMES AGAIN

When war finally came, Hollywood was ready. Once again, however, popular culture did not reflect the reality of war in practice. Hollywood started World War II where ended World War I, glorifying the hero: the bravery, determination, skill, and resourcefulness of the soldier. One of the first great World War II films the studios produced focused on the achievements of a single individual in battle. It was a movie about World War I.

On August 22, 1940, more than 20 years after he left the battlefield and put his uniform aside, Alvin York found himself in a first-class seat on the *Santa Fe Chief* bound for Hollywood. He was going there to meet the screenwriters who would make his life into a movie and be introduced to the actor who would play him—Gary Cooper. A little less than a year later, on July 2,

1941, *Sergeant York* premiered on Broadway to rave reviews, huge audiences, and not some controversy.[53]

Isolationist senators, who opposed U.S. entry into World War II, accused Hollywood of using the film to whip up "war hysteria."[54] In August 1941, a Senate resolution called for investigation of the film industry. The fact that York had been an outspoken advocate for increasing military preparedness and had been highly critical of Charles Lindbergh, who had stridently argued for American neutrality, only fanned the criticism. Lindbergh (the former famed aviator who had made the first solo flight across the Atlantic) was the principal spokesman for the America's First Committee, a group with over 800,000 members that lobbied in opposition of supporting the war effort against Hitler. York called Lindbergh an isolationist and an appeaser, earning the ire of Lindbergh's supporters and the enmity of the antiwar faction in Congress.

The release of *Sergeant York* did much to help turn the debate. After the premier of the film, York became as popular as he had been when first driven down New York City streets in a ticker-tape parade. Following Pearl Harbor, both York and Woodfill were recalled to active duty, given commissions as officers, and served as spokesmen for the Army giving speeches to the troops and the public to boost morale. The American hero was back.

When GIs finally got in battle, Hollywood started making movies about their exploits. The hero motif returned. One of the first big war movies was based on some of the first combat Americans saw overseas, captured in war correspondent Richard Tregaskis's best-selling book *Guadalcanal Diary* about the war in the Pacific. Rushed into production, *Guadalcanal Diary* (1943) had no real stars. It was mostly filled with stock players whose faces and characters were familiar to most moviegoers, even if few could recall their names. This was, perhaps, one of the great strengths of the film, enhancing the image of the "everyman" as hero.

Playing to packed theaters across the country, *Guadalcanal Diary* bore all the elements of great war movies and bad history. The film followed the story of Marines who landed on the island on August 7, 1942. A narration by actor Reed Hadley, who plays a war correspondent accompanying the troops, gives the film a documentarylike quality. The action focuses on what was to become the ultimate movie war cliché, the typical squad of all-American boys. Actor William Bendix is the working-class Joe, "Taxi Potts." Anthony Quinn plays the ethnic member of the squad, Jesus Alverz. Richard Jackel (discovered in the Twentieth Century Fox mailroom) is the squeaky-clean farm boy.

*Guadalcanal Diary* features the obligatory moments of heroism and sacrifice, but it was nothing like real war. The actors look sweaty and unshaved, but amazing well rested, healthy, and well fed, especially the portly William Bendix. They talk about home, moon about the girl they left behind, share pictures of newborn babies, reminisce about the old neighborhood and mom's cooking, and obsess about baseball. It was all, except for the brief moments of battle, a bit too idyllic, like a hot, sweaty summer camp.

What *Guadalcanal Diary* was not was anything like real war. Charles McDonald, a World War II veteran, recalled what he had told a reporter when asked what the captain had wanted most from home—a question that seemed to come right out of a Hollywood movie war script. "I've got something to say," McDonald growled, "Tell them its too damned serious over here to be talking about hot dogs and baked beans and the thing's we're missing. Tell them its hell … they're men getting killed and wounded every minute, and they're miserable, and they're suffering." Optimism, teamwork, fair play, hope, heroism, sacrifice, the stock and trade of World War II movies, had nothing to do with what it took to reach the next hedgerow.

The GIs headed to France would not learn what was demanded of them in war watching movies in the camp theater or mess hall anymore than they learned how to soldier in the swamplands of Louisiana. They would discover real war on the beaches of Normandy.

# CHAPTER 4

# D-Day Disasters

## CAMELOT

DAWN, JUNE 6, 1944 was a bad day. On Omaha Beach technology failed the GIs in virtually every respect. And there was very little they could do about it. Omaha was a horror show—a bloodbath of showering sand, ear-splitting noise, chaos, and death. Neither doughboy genius nor GI ingenuity was much help. The unpredictability of amphibious operations was difficult for industrial-age armies to deal with—too many variables and unknowns. If anything, trying to treat assaulting a hostile beach bristling with wire, mines, machine guns, concrete bunkers, mortars, and artillery like the task of running an assembly line virtually guaranteed that the graves registration teams would be collecting fistfuls of bloody dog tags.[1] On the other hand, there was not sufficient time in the space of a few hours on the beach to practice real technological innovation. U.S. forces triumphed because of the determination of individual soldiers. It was a real-life heroic achievement.

The accomplishments of GIs on Omaha (the code name for one of the two Normandy landing sights assigned to the Americans) were doubly spectacular given the odds they faced. The beach defenses, despite a vicious preinvasion bombardment by air and naval forces, were intact and fully manned by disciplined troops who fought well. The terrain was impossible, a shallow rocky beach covered with obstacles, wire, and mines and scant cover overlooked by a high bluff infested with machine guns and mortar pits. And the generals sent their boys onto the shore with less usable combat support than the Thirty-Fifth Division had going over the top in the Meuse-Argonne. It should all have been a terrible disaster.

The only problem was, you could not tell that by the movies. To most Americans the battle for Normandy began and ended on a dreary June morning. And it was a triumph of the "big" Army. A methodically planned and well-organized invasion armada breeched Hitler's Atlantic Wall and, after a few harrowing moments on the beaches of Normandy, marched under the *Arc de Triomphe* in Paris. It was a myth Hollywood helped solidify with a single motion picture.

When *The Longest Day* premiered in 1962, it was the most expensive war film ever made. Up to that time, for World War II movies, studios had used official combat footage and newsreels to save the expense of trying to recreate scenes with masses of men and equipment. For *The Longest Day,* producer Darryl Zanuck intended to make an epic film with real tanks, planes, and ships recreating the landings in historical detail. He spent almost $10 million on the project, more than any other black-and-white motion picture in history. The question most Hollywood insiders asked at the time was, Why make the film at all? Most of the movie-going public had not even been born when the GIs hit the beaches in Normandy.[2]

The year of 1962, however, was the perfect time to release a cinematic version of the D-Day landings. It had been almost a decade since the Korean War ended. American memories were no longer raw with the nightmares of real combat. The Cold War was well under way. But it was, with the exception of the Korean War, largely—cold. In fact, in the autumn of 1962, it looked like America might well survive the threat of the Soviet menace. The fears fanned by confrontations in Berlin, the launch of the Russian sputnik satellite, and the science fiction films of the 1950s had calmed (*The Longest Day* opened before the outbreak of the Cuban Missile Crisis in October 1962, which briefly rekindled the apprehension that a nuclear confrontation with the Soviet Union was imminent). America was in good shape.

Dwight D. Eisenhower, the greatest of the greatest generation, had just left the White House and turned the country over to John F. Kennedy, a veteran of the war who had served as a very junior naval officer. The musical *Camelot,* the story of the magical reign of an idealistic King Arthur, played to packed houses on Broadway, and many used the term to describe the Kennedy presidency. And it was a time before the nation became embroiled in the Vietnam War. General William Westmoreland, a lieutenant colonel during World War II and the future commander of forces in Vietnam, was serving as the superintendent at the academy at West Point (hosting Kennedy's visit to give a graduation speech to the cadets). West Point, the Army, the presidency, and indeed most of America were run by World War II veterans, and they seemed to be nurturing the nation fairly well through the turbulence of the postwar

Real War. Troops in the First Wave Head for Shore at Omaha Beach. (Courtesy, Army Signal Corps)

years. It was the right time to take the American public on a victory lap of the war's greatest battle.

Based on the 1959 best-seller by Cornelius Ryan, both the film and the book drew on a conventional and largely uncritical view of the assault on the beaches of Normandy, a view that had emerged in the years following the war. Although Ryan, a journalist and former war correspondent, humanized the drama of D-Day by lacing his narrative with vignettes garnered from a number of personal interviews, the book was still set in the framework of an already well-established story line.

The D-Day story had two principal sources, official military history and the general's tale. The official histories came from a generation of historians and journalists who went off to war wearing a uniform, but armed with a pen and typewriter—the men of the Army's historical detachments. It was their job to collect the documents and record events that would be used to write the official history of the war. And they got to their task with dispatch. Prepared "in the field" by the 2nd Information and Historical Service, attached to the First Army, and the Historical Section, European Theater of

Operations, the Army had its first official publication on the assault on Omaha in print before the end of September 1945. *Omaha Beachhead* was part of the *American Forces in Action* (the same series that produced the narrative of the attack on Hill 192 in *St. Lo*).

The Army's definitive history of the invasion, *Cross-Channel Attack* by Gordon A. Harrison, who had served as the historical officer for George Patton's Third Army during the war, came out in 1950. *Cross-Channel Attack* was the second volume published in what would become known as the Army's "green book" series (named for their hardback green covers). Published by the Historical Division, War Department Special Staff (later renamed the U.S. Army Center of Military History), the books were meant to provide an authoritative account of U.S. operations. Kent Roberts Greenfield, the Army's chief historian, was the project's architect. Greenfield insisted on three things: (1) high standards of excellence, (2) open access to all records (even records marked top secret), and (3) academic freedom for his authors. Unlike most Army publications, Greenfield insisted that writers get authorship credit and take individual responsibility for their work.[3]

The Army's official historians had enormous advantages over their civilian counterparts. By way of contrast, compare the green books to the first public histories such as Francis Trevelyan Miller's *The Complete History of World War II* (1945). Written largely from press accounts, *The Complete History of World War II*'s historical accuracy was almost laughable. On the other hand, researchers such as Harrison could draw on all the Army's official records, as well as records the Army had captured from the *Wehrmacht*. They also had ready access to senior military leaders (Eisenhower allowed Harrison to use his personal papers) and many had real-world experience as war historians, some in the commands they later wrote about. Not surprisingly, when the Army published the green books, they were taken not only as authoritative, but definitive, leaving the impression that there was little more to the "big story" to be told.

The green books, however, were not the final word. While they included battle narratives, they were intended to be operational histories, providing an overview of the Army's campaigns. As a result, they tended to focus more on what generals did. In addition, while author's had academic freedom, they were required to vet their work with an editorial board chosen by the Army Historical Division and circulate the manuscripts with senior commanders and staff officers who had fought in the campaigns, many of whom were still in the service, some in very, very senior positions. This correspondence, like the Army's war records themselves, is retained at the National Archives in College Park, Maryland. The flurry of letters that preceded the publication of a green book makes for interesting reading, as participants argued over how events should be interpreted. What it suggests is that while the author's work may have been independent, it was not totally free from pressure to shape events one way or another.

As it turned out later, the Army historians did not have access to all the classified material available. They could not, for example, consult or even acknowledge the existence of ULTRA, the supersecret classified intelligence intercepts of German communications that provided Allied commanders detailed information on enemy operations.[4] Such shortfalls in green-book scholarship, however, were not widely known at the time. It was assumed Harrison had said it all, or at least an awful lot, and civilian historians and the general public drew on *Cross-Channel Attack* for an authoritative understanding of World War II.

The general's tale reinforced the big story in the official histories. After World War I, John Pershing waited until 1931 (seven years after he retired) to publish his memoirs, *My Experiences in the World War*. In contrast, Eisenhower's *Crusade in Europe* was published in 1948; Omar Bradley's *A Soldier's Story*, in 1951, and *Eisenhower's Six Great Decisions* by Walter Bedell Smith, Eisenhower's Chief of Staff, in 1956. Patton died right after the war, but in his papers are manuscripts suggesting he, too, was going to write about his wartime command. There was, in fact, a kind of arms race by senior Allied war leaders rushing to get their stories into print. It would be disingenuous to call them all self-serving, but with few exceptions they were hardly self-critical, and they were without question self-important. Generals won wars.

As the first draft of war scholarship, the green books and the general's tale did something to American popular culture that did not happen after World War I. The focus of attention shifted from GI Joe to GI generals and heaped credit on something, which was, after all, very important to success in battle and sadly neglected after the Great War, the organizational genius of the American military. In World War II doughboy genius got its due.

That generals became the iconic figures of the times was perhaps not surprising. Some 8 million men had worn Army uniforms during the war, experiencing the discipline of working for a large-scale bureaucracy and the value of teamwork on a heroic scale. They saw the genius of fighting industrial-strength warfare firsthand. After the war, many of the greatest generation now found themselves running factories and boardrooms. They could relate to the challenges of generalship and came to respect and admire the organizational skill and leadership of the senior commanders who had ordered them about during the war.

Generals were heroes for the corporate age. Following World War II, economic growth in the United States continued a pace. Big business got much bigger. In December 1954, the stock market closed at a level higher than the levels reached before the crash of 1929. "The Great Depression," wrote economic historian, John Steele Gordon, "was finally over, psychologically as well as economically."[5] Corporate profits soared. It was the era that William H. Whyte described in the title of his best-selling book, the age of *The Organizational Man* (1956), an age when men would spend their entire adult lives having worked for only two big organizations—the U.S. Army and companies such as RCA, General Motors, IBM, Boeing, or General Electric. It was an age when football, an exercise in violent organized teamwork that deified leaders like Vince Lombardi (a former West Point coach who led the Green Bay Packers to a national title in 1961), a game that veterans of World War II combat squads could relate to, began to rival baseball as the national game. (It was no coincidence that many of World War II's most notable generals, including Eisenhower, played football in college.) It was an age when football coaches and GI's generals represented the epitome of the American spirit.

*The Longest Day* did much to embellish this image. Though there were many individual stories in the star-studded film, including the portrayal of personal acts of courage and sacrifice, the movie was really the story of the triumph of industrial-age warfare and the capacity of generals to organize masses of men and drive them toward a common goal.

While *The Longest Day* offers a collage of the various activities occurring on the longest day, the pivotal dramatic moments in the film are reserved for generals, such as Eisenhower's momentous decision to launch the attack on June 6, 1944, despite the promise of only marginal weather. Even Bradley makes an appearance in the film, though he had almost nothing to do with affecting the course of events on the beaches. At least Bradley could be thankful that the producers did not strive for perfect realism in their combat scenes. Bradley watched the landings on Omaha from the deck of the USS *Augusta* with ill-fitting dentures, cotton stuffed in his ears to muffle the sounds of the ship's big guns, and a plaster to cover an infected carbuncle. He hardly struck a very heroic-looking figure. The actor playing Bradley in the film stood stoically on the deck of the ship—clean shaven and without cotton in his ears.

It is also noteworthy that in a film laced with movie stars, the biggest stars of all, Eisenhower and Bradley, were played by unknown actors chosen more for modestly resembling the real-life generals than their acting talents. Five-star generals could not be played by movie stars.

The other climatic moments in the movie also include generals. Henry Fonda, playing Brigadier General Theodore Roosevelt, Jr., makes the decision to lead the troops inward off Utah Beach, even though the first assault wave of the division had landed in the wrong place. On Omaha, Brigadier General

Norman Cota (actor Robert Mitchum) organizes the shattered and disorganized troops in an attack that breaks through the fortified exits (draws in the line of the bluffs that lead to the high ground above the sands). While both these events did happen on D-Day as they are portrayed in the film, portraying them as decisive moments is misleading and contributed to the myth over how the battle of the beaches was actually won.

While Cota did lead troops through one of the beach exits, the advance was possible only because small groups of GIs, often leaderless, worked their way through wire and fire onto the bluffs over the beaches and often in bitter hand-to-hand combat overcame the German defenders, taking out the machine-gun nests covering the beach exits with enfilading fire and the observation posts directing mortar fire down on soldiers huddled below.

## SAVING D-DAY

Camelot was not real. Neither was *The Longest Day.*

Camelot ran for only 873 performances; the myth of who won the day on bloody Omaha persisted almost to the 50th anniversary of the battle. In the end, the myth was shattered by a book and a movie.

The book was *D-Day, June 6, 1944: The Climactic Battle of World War II* by historian Stephen Ambrose (1994). Ambrose added the largely unknown story garnered not from official records and the remembrance of generals, but compiled in over 1,400 oral histories, many from participants in D-Day who had never publicly told their tales before. From these stories, Ambrose revealed that "[b]ut for all that American industrial brawn and organizational ability could do, for all the British and Canadian allies could contribute, for all the plans and preparations, for all the inspired leadership, in the end success or failure in Operation Overlord [the D-Day invasion] came down to a relatively small number of junior officers, noncoms, and privates or seamen in the American, British, and Canadian armies, navies, air forces, and coast guards."[6] D-Day was a GI victory in much the same way men such as Huebner and York had made the difference the last time an American Army came to battle in France.

The film that told this story best was *Saving Private Ryan* (1998). The plot of director Steven Spielberg's homage to the American GI could have come straight out of an old-fashioned Hollywood studio. It was a movie of heroic adventure. Captain Miller (actor Tom Hanks) leads a small all-American squad on a search for Private Ryan, whose three brothers had already been killed in the war and who has been ordered by the War Department to be returned to his family. The plot is implausible, as is the journey of Miller's squad, which manages to move fairly freely across the Normandy countryside while the rest of the American Army is bogged down in deadly fighting in the hedgerows. While most of the film is more Hollywood than hedgerows, the first combat scene of the movie, which recreates the assault on bloody Omaha, is something entirely different.

*Saving Private Ryan's* opening sequence, heavily influenced by Ambrose's research, replicated the absolute chaos of the landings on Omaha. "I wasn't really looking to make a World War II film," Spielberg recalled, "I didn't want to shoot the picture as a Hollywood gung-ho Rambo kind of extravaganza. I wanted the audience to be fairly uneasy sitting through the invasion of Normandy."[7] For the assault on Omaha Beach they were.

In the film, after wading through surf frothy with blood, deafened by artillery explosions, and disoriented by the scream of casualties and disorganization on the beach, Captain Miller leads a small group of men up the bluffs. The action is about as close to real war as a film can possibly be. In fact, Miller's actions recall those of Captain Joseph Turner Dawson, a company commander in the 1st Infantry Division, who helped lead a small group that penetrated the bluff defenses on Omaha.

Spielberg's recreation of Omaha was a memory of indescribable slaughter and undaunted courage brought to life. In theaters across America, in the opening minutes of *Saving Private Ryan* for a few moments the children of the GI generation got about as close to the battles of World War II as film could take them. They glimpsed the real world of their fathers' nightmares. Hollywood, the world of make-believe, helped save D-Day's real history.

## AN ABSENCE OF GENIUS

Absent from *Saving Private Ryan,* save a cameo scene featuring veteran actor Harve Presnell playing George C. Marshall, generals are completely missing from the film. Spielberg's movie is about GI war. That's fitting—particularly for the scenes on Omaha where the genius of generals little affected the day's fighting.

Given that generals and their staffs had spent so much time getting ready for June 6, 1944, it is ironic that they played such a small role in the outcome of events. If there was any military operation that called for doughboy genius it was amphibious warfare, landing on army on a hostile shore in the presence of an enemy force. Yet, after spending over two years planning and training for the great invasion, somehow they managed to get so many things so terribly wrong.

A near disaster on Omaha might have been more forgivable if it had been the first amphibious operation ever undertaken by the Allies. It was not. They had the experience of almost a dozen major amphibious operations to draw on. And all of them suggested one thing: Clausewitz's caution on the unpredictable influences of the friction of battle applied to no operation more completely than an amphibious landing.

The difficulties of conducting an opposed landing on hostile shores was a lesson the Allies learned early and often during the course of the war. On August 19, 1942 (a little more than a week after the Marines landed on Guadalcanal in the Pacific, the first major American amphibious landing of the war), the Allies made their first significant attempt at cracking the Atlantic Wall (a network of defenses the Germans had erected along the French coast) with a large-scale commando raid on the port at Dieppe. It was to be a miniature D-Day with over 6,000 troops, mostly Canadians, air and naval support, including some 200 ships. Operation Jubilee (the code name for the raid) ended nine hours after it started—an absolute unmitigated catastrophe. Almost 1,000 died. The Germans captured over 2,000. Another 1,000 never got off their ships. Also 119 planes were lost.

A published account of the raid in *Combined Operations: The Official Story of the Commandos* (1943), written under a forward by Vice-Admiral Lord Louis Mountbatten (one of the first among the Allied commanders to race his version of history into print), described the attack as anything but a failure. The greatest value "was the first-hand experience we acquired of the conditions which may be met with a large-scale assault on a strongly-held channel port. The details of these experiences must not be revealed. The enemy will know in due course how we have profited … ."[8] Mostly what they learned was how pathetic their ability to plan amphibious operations really was.

Nevertheless, of the landings on D-Day, Miller wrote in *The Complete History of World War II* that "all the lessons learned so dearly almost two years before on the blood-soaked beaches of Dieppe were proving their worth."[9] That was hogwash.

In *Cross-Channel Attack,* Harrison offered only a slightly more qualified assessment of the Allies' efforts to apply lessons from the Dieppe raid to D-Day. He wrote, "the Dieppe raid provided some valuable experience for the tactics of amphibious operations and specifically for the planning of Overlord."[10] Harrison, however, had trouble pointing out successes in the D-Day plan that benefited from the lessons of Operation Jubilee.[11] Today, historians are not so confident that admirals and generals learned much of anything at all.

## FROM THE SEA

As might be expected, amphibious operations proved to be an integral component of a global war fought by Americans on three continents and two oceans. Among the many aspects of large-scale war planning the Army nurtured during the interwar years, attacking from the sea was not one of them. After the nearly comically inadequate amphibious maneuvers during the joint Naval-Army exercises in Hawaii in 1925, Major General John Hines, who commanded the Army troops, told students at the Army War College about the problems encountered in words echoing Clausewitz's dictum about the simplicity of war. He held, "no doubt, that highly-trained-well led infantry can establish a beachhead once the troops are ashore—but getting ashore, there's the rub."[12] The Army simply had no modern equipment designed to deliver men and machines to a hostile shore. Nor, he might have added, did they have doctrine to employ them even if they did.

In the interwar years, it was the U.S. Marine Corps, not the Army, that invested the most intellectual capital in the problem of amphibious warfare. After the 1925 maneuvers, amphibious warfare pioneer Marine General Dion Williams argued that the challenge was not trivial. In fact, the task could well be daunting in the face of uncertain weather, difficult surf and shore conditions, the presence of hostile shore defenses and enemy air planes, and the complications of coordinating the employment of air, land, and sea forces. In the face of all these obstacles a way had to be determined "to get men and materiel ... on the beach in the shortest possible time with the least confusion and in the best possible condition for immediate action."[13] And Williams believed figuring out how to solve this dilemma was a mission for the Marine Corps.

Williams was not alone in his commitment to amphibious operations. John A. Lejeune shared his view. He was an important ally. Lejeune was the Marine Corps Commandant, the service's senior officer.

When America entered the Great War, the Marine Corps, a separate military service reporting to the Department of the Navy, was mobilized alongside the Army for combat duty in Europe. Marine brigades fought as part of Army divisions. Among their number was a veteran infantryman, John A. Lejeune. In the final phase of the Meuse-Argonne offensive Lejeune commanded the Second Division. On the last night of the war he led his troops across the Meuse River. When the armistice was declared, he was one of the most respected officers in the Corps. In 1920 he became their commandant.

Lejeune was determined that the Marines would be ready for the next war. That required identifying a unique mission for the Corps to base future funding requests upon. The role Lejeune argued for was seizing and defending forward bases for the Navy. It was a mission that seemed to make sense given that the Marines were totally dependent on the Navy Department for their funding.

In part, the commandant's vision was inspired by a member of his staff, Lieutenant Colonel Earl H. Ellis. Another veteran of the Meuse-Argonne, Pete Ellis wrote Operation Plan 712, "Advanced Base Operations in Micronesia." Ellis predicted war with Japan, a war in which the Japanese would strike first, denying Navy bases in the Far East. The Navy, Ellis argued, would have to fight its way into the Pacific—and it would need the Marines to take and hold the bases. Ellis went on to recommend the tactics, equipment, and troops that would be required for these operations.

In 1927, the Marine Corps was given the principal responsibility for developing amphibious assault doctrine. Ellis was not there to see it. In 1923 he died mysteriously while conducting a personal reconnaissance of islands in the Pacific. It was rumored he had been poisoned by the Japanese. Others argued he died from chronic alcoholism. In fact, he died from a fever aggravated by liver disease.

While the prophet of amphibious warfare was gone, his mentor was not. Until his retirement in 1929, Lejeune continued to make the case for specialized equipment and training for amphibious operations and forces organized to conduct expeditionary warfare ashore. It was frustrating work. The Navy could not, for example, be convinced to build a motorized assault boat to carry the troops to shore.

It was not until 1933 that the Navy authorized the first unit dedicated to amphibious assault, the Fleet Marine Force. In the years following, Marines developed joint doctrine for beach-landing operations and tested their concepts, though they lacked suitable landing craft and rugged ship-to-shore communications up almost to the outbreak of the war.

The hard thinking paid off, but even hard thinking about warfare from the sea did not save the Marines from the friction of battle. Their first major landing against a fortified Japanese position on the island of Tarawa (November 21, 1943) was a disaster of the scale of the Dieppe raid. After the first day of the attack 1,500 of the 5,000 assault troops lay dead or wounded. Though the Marines took the small island, the three-day battle cost them over 3,300 dead and wounded.

The tragedy at Tarawa was due in large part to the fact that the Marines failed to get the three major weapons of modern war (airpower, artillery, and armor) into the fight. They lacked sufficient armor-piercing shells for the big naval guns (needed to reduce the fortified concrete bunkers on the beach), and there were not enough landing craft to bring in all the tanks and artillery required to support the infantry in the first wave.

America's Marines learned from their disasters as well as their success and applied the lessons acquired in battle to subsequent operations. The Marine Corps' effort to develop the skill to fight from the sea during the interwar years, despite a poverty of resources, and then to develop the tools and talents of amphibious warfare over the course of World War II serves as a remarkable example of doughboy genius. What was shocking was how few of these lessons transferred over to the Army and that even fewer of the lessons were applied to the war in Europe. The inability to replicate advances in joint operations was a real problem. It was a serious issue because during the war more Army forces made amphibious landings than Marine units. And all the major operations on the second front in the West were made under Army direction, including the landings in North Africa, Sicily, Southern Italy, Anzio, Normandy, and Southern France.

## A SERIOUS SECOND FRONT

The Army had fair warning that it would have to get its feet wet sooner or later. In 1935, students in the "Participation with Allies" portion of the War Plans course at the Army War College were presented a theoretical problem: America in concert with European allies faced a confederation of "Nazi" states. From the onset of the exercise, however, the students assumed that Japan would take advantage of the situation. "The United States is committed to the war in Europe," they concluded, "but sooner or later will have to deal with Japan."[14] It looked like a two-front war to them. Nor did the students find the problem overly academic. They had, according to one student officer, "experienced some difficulty in keeping separate the developments of the problem from the news in the daily press."[15] They were not the only ones.

The planners in the War Department had struggled with the challenges of mustering the resources for a two-front war and the daunting prospects of conducting amphibious operations in two oceans. And before 1938, one of the American Color-Coded War Plans, Red-Orange, envisioned a two-front confrontation. The only problem with the plan was that while Japan was one of the enemies, the other was Great Britain.[16] And the planners knew that made no sense. They had, however, little choice. By and large, during the interwar years the military could not plan against real foes because the State Department would not tell them who they were. "With a few exceptions," diplomatic historian Mark Stoler found that most State Department officials "maintained the traditional American beliefs that war was an aberration rather than a normal phase of international relations and that force constituted a separate category and last resort to be used only if diplomacy failed. Along with this went the corollary belief that military officers should have no role whatsoever in policy matters until war actually began."[17] As a result, war planners received scant real policy guidance to shape their war plans and had to determine the future capabilities required based on studying campaigns against hypothetical opponents.

All that changed in 1939 with the start of the war. The silliness of planning for war against Great Britain was dropped. A new set of directives, the Rainbow Plans, was developed that considered wars against various combinations of the Axis powers (Germany, Italy, and Japan).

American planners assumed they would be fighting a two-front war before the first bombs landed on Pearl Harbor. At a secret Washington conference in March 1941, the British and American Joint Chiefs of Staff (the senior military leaders from both countries) agreed that "[i]f and when America enters the war, she will exert 'the principal United States military effort' in the European theater. America will try by diplomacy to prevent war with Japan, but even if that proves impossible, operations in the Pacific will be conducted in such a manner as 'to facilitate' the effort against the European Axis."[18] When war came it would likely be fought on two fronts and Germany would have to be defeated first. Since all of Western Europe was occupied, that would mean the attack would have to come from the sea.

The Allies formerly assigned priority to the defeat of Germany at the Arcardia Conference in Washington, D.C. (December 22, 1941 to January 14, 1942), though through December 1943 more troops and supplies went to the Pacific theaters to block the onslaught of the Japanese advances in Asia than to the war in the West.[19] Even when significant forces were launched against the Nazis, they did not head to France. First, the GIs invaded North Africa. At the Casablanca Conference (January 14–24, 1943), the invasion of France was put off again. Instead amphibious operations put the GIs ashore in Sicily and then Salerno and Anzio as Allied forces pushed toward Rome. It was only at the Trident Conference in Washington, D.C. (May 15–25, 1943) that the fateful decision for the cross-channel invasion was made.

The series of pre-Normandy invasions had not grown out of any grand strategic vision, but as series of great power compromises. "North Africa led to Sicily," wrote Wedemeyer (now a general and temporarily attached to Eisenhower's staff), "and Sicily led to the Italian boot."[20] That the Americans had not tried to go directly from New York to Paris and Berlin via London was probably a good thing. In 1942, the American Army was not ready to tackle Hitler, anymore than the doughboys had been prepared for the Germans in 1917. As the Americans in the Great War progressed from Cantigny to Soissons, St. Mihiel, and the Meuse-Argonne, each operation in the Western theater during the Second World War gave the Americans an opportunity to prepare their leaders and their army for the eventual main effort.

There were lessons from every landing that were applicable to Normandy. The most important was that cooperation between air, ground, and navy forces was essential. And when things did not go right, disaster usually followed—especially in Sicily.

Sicily had its fair share of the unpredictable elements of war from the sea. A fierce 40-mile-an-hour gale buffeted the invasion, sickening the troops and endangering small craft. The winds scattered the gliders carrying British airborne troops to support the landings. A total of 144 gliders went up—12 landed on target, and 69 crashed in the sea; the rest landed all over the island, an area the size of Vermont. On July 10, 1943, an invasion force including a field army commanded by Patton and a corps under Bradley, as well as troops from the 1st Infantry Division (in their second major amphibious landing of the war), hit the beaches. But when Patton ordered up dive-bomber support for the troops, the planes were late and were then fired on by friendly antiaircraft guns that mistook them for German aircraft. There was worse to come. When Patton called for reinforcements to be parachuted in on the night of July 11, it happened again.

The paratrooper landings should have been, as military historian Carlo D'Este wrote, "a milk run."[21] They were not even jumping into enemy territory. As the planes carrying the 504th Regimental Combat Team of the 82nd Airborne Division (2,300 men) approached the island, they came under fire by naval and ground-based antiaircraft guns. It was one of the most deadly cases of "friendly fire" in the American war to date. Allied guns brought down 23 C-47 transport aircraft. There were 318 casualties with 83 dead.

Eisenhower was furious. And when he met with Patton on the morning of July 12, 1943, he told him so.[22] Appointed by the Joint Chiefs to command the Allied forces in North Africa and the Mediterranean, Eisenhower now had overseen his second major amphibious operation. Compared to what they would see in trying to crack the Atlantic Wall, these were cakewalks. And yet, as in the first landings in North Africa (November 8, 1942), so many things had gone so terribly wrong. On the beaches of Sicily, the enemy, it had turned out, had been the least of the problem. The Italian coastal defenses were poorly organized. Things should have gone better.

As Eisenhower railed, a small group of staff officers who had accompanied him respectfully stood off to the side. One of them was Major General Clarence Huebner, veteran of the Great War and hero of the Battle of Soissons.

When Eisenhower wrote Marshall on July 17, 1943, his frustration with the landings seems to have subsided. Patton was "doing well." Ike went on, however, to explain the 504th's disaster in some detail. In the end, he found the whole incident "odd."[23] They would have to do a much better job training and coordinating joint forces in the future.

Despite the miscues in Sicily, few reputations suffered. An official investigation into the firing on the 504th blamed—no one. Even after Patton was relieved for striking an enlisted soldier, Eisenhower still wanted him back as a field army commander for the invasion of France. As for Bradley, "There is very little I need to tell you about him," Ike wrote to Marshall, "because he is running absolutely true to form all the time. He has brains, a fine capacity for leadership and a thorough understanding of the requirements of modern battle. He has never caused one moment of worry."[24] By and large, Eisenhower was satisfied with the genius of his generals.

Not every reputation, however, survived the Sicily campaign. Eisenhower had Terry Allen and his deputy Teddy Roosevelt pulled out of the 1st Infantry Division.[25] Serious thought would have to be given as to who would replace them. The division, as in the First World War, was one of the first to go into battle and now had extensive combat experience, considered one of the most dependable units in the theater. Some of the troops in the division expected the command would be rotated back to the States to train others for war. Ike knew better. The division would go to England to prepare for the invasion of France—hence, giving rise to the popular saying, "the Army is made up of the 1st Infantry Division and eight million fucking replacements!" Content or not, they would spearhead the attack in Normandy. And they would get a man of reputation, approved by Eisenhower, to lead them.

## OVERLORD

The reputation that came out the best of all from the campaigns in North Africa and Sicily belonged to Eisenhower. He received the appointment to lead the invasion of France. And Ike knew it was an important job. "I clearly appreciate," he wrote Marshall, "that the coming venture is the decisive act of the War from the viewpoint of the British-American effort."[26] With that, he promised to make every effort to make the attack as powerful as possible, getting every plane, ship, and soldier he could muster into the fight. It was the kind of effort that called for the ultimate measure of doughboy genius. In the end, there would be over 2,200 ships off the coast of Normandy on the first day of the invasion, over 150,000 troops on the beaches and another 23,000 paratroopers inland, and over 170 squadrons of planes. And he had his pick of the best of the generals to lead the way. He selected Bradley to command the U.S. ground forces. Doughboy genius should never have been better. But it was not.

The generals made bad choices. "The lessons of Dieppe, Tarawa, Sicily, and other hard-fought amphibious campaigns," writes military historian and former Army officer and West Point professor Adrian Lewis, "appeared to have been forgotten by the planners of the Normandy invasion."[27] Lewis, Ambrose, and other historians who revisited the planning for D-Day in recent years have found a good deal wanting in what was done.

Chief among the problems was the old bugbear of modern war, putting the fire into fire and maneuver. This failure, Lewis contends, was because the Allies failed to follow their own doctrine for amphibious warfare developed painstakingly over the interwar years and refined with the experiences of wartime operations. In fact, he argues if the other beaches had been as well defended as Omaha, the success of the Allied landings might have been in doubt.

American doctrine with its reliance on fire and maneuver emphasized daylight assaults where airpower and support from naval guns could be employed to best effect because fires could be observed and directed more precisely on enemy targets. What was unique about amphibious operations, as a training memorandum from Bradley's headquarters made clear, was that "ground must be gained before field artillery can emplace and support infantry. Field artillery fire support, therefore, cannot be expected until at least H + 2 hours. During this critical time, only two means of support are available; air bombardment and naval gunfire … . Medium artillery in general support is necessary before the landing force will have sufficient fire power to be independent of naval gunfire."[28] That meant for at least the first day's battle the infantry would have to rely almost exclusively on fire support from the other services, particularly naval gunfire, which was the most suitable, accurate, powerful, and responsive weapon available to the invading army.

Advances in naval gunfire and their contributions to amphibious operations were another example of doughboy genius in action—a genius that derived from the last war. Jutland had been the greatest naval battle of the First World War; and its greatest lesson to many, wrote Samuel Eliot Morison, the great naval historian, was that naval officers believed future war would be "a succession of Jutlands, to be decided by big guns on battleships."[29] Navy men believed their future was in navy guns.

As a result, in the interwar years admirals aggressively sought to apply America's industrial genius to naval gunfire developments. Much of that genius came from Elmer Sperry and his Sperry Gyroscope Company. Sperry pioneered a compass that could take bearing far more accurately than a magnetic compass and paired it with a stabilizer system that compensated for the roll of ships at sea. Sperry used these inventions to create a naval fire-control system that turned ships into stable firing platforms. He also developed an electronic means to send and display the information from the gunnery officers to the firing crews and an analog computer that could be used to accurately locate the ship and its target and help compute firing data.[30]

The only problem with the Navy's vision was that other technologies were marching along as well, including the application of Sperry's gyroscopes to the evolution of airpower and torpedoes. Gyroscopes made these accurate and deadly long-range naval weapons, ensuring that most naval battles were fought at arm's length out of range of naval guns. On the other hand, the immense expense and energy invested in the development of guns, ammunition, and fire-control systems did not go to waste. "The accuracy and efficiency of our naval gunfire," Morison wrote in 1963, "was a great asset in the war. Gunfire support almost opened a new dimension to amphibious operations."[31] Naval guns were designed to rapidly throw heavy shells at high velocity at fast-moving steel-clad battleships on rolling seas. Tackling reinforced concrete beach defenses and armored counterattack forces that might threaten a bridgehead was a simple task in comparison.

There were three main challenges to employing gunfire support: (1) protecting the ships from land-based guns, air attack, mines, and submarines while they provided support; (2) dealing with the problem of a high "range-probable error"; naval shells flew flat and fast; thus a small error in trajectory, particularly over flat ground, could result in a significant error in where the round landed along its flight over land; in addition, hitting targets that were defiladed, in other words, behind a terrain feature, was difficult; and (3) communicating targeting information from ship to shore. All these problems, however, had been confronted and overcome before D-Day. At Sicily, the day after the Allies landed, naval gunfire had helped save the beachhead from an Italian counterattack. Patton, who had come ashore to check on the progress of the operation, witnessed firsthand the column of enemy tanks bearing down across an open plain. He spotted a young naval officer with the beach party and ordered, "Hey You with the radio! If you can connect with your Goddamn navy, tell them for God's sake to drop some shell fire on the road."[32] The USS *Boise* opened fire obliterating the tank column. "Kill everyone of the goddam bastards," Patton later growled.[33]

In Normandy, however, it was a different story. Lewis calculates that the assault beaches had only a fraction of the naval gunfire support demanded by doctrine and far less support than that available for comparable amphibious operations.[34] Nor did the Army allow much time (about 40 minutes) for the naval prebombardment to reduce the German defenses before the first wave of Allied troops went ashore.[35]

There were two more phases for naval fire support. The destroyers and the landing craft were supposed to be able to call in "drenching fire" on selected targets. In addition, the assault troops would be accompanied by nine naval fire-control teams that could radio requests for additional support. That meant, however, that success would rest heavily on the "chance" of battle—the fire-control parties not being shot, the ability to see targets in the smoke and chaos of battle, the capacity to accurately locate targets, and the ability to maintain reliable communications with the ships. In practice, none of these things happened.

The field artillery in the invasion force proved virtually useless on D-Day. By June 10, 1944, the Americans had almost 624 artillery pieces ashore (one gun for every 100 yards of front), but the first wave of GIs to hit the beach, as the First Army artillery assessment had predicted, could not count on the gunners for much support.[36] The landing crafts carrying the howitzers, scheduled to land between 6:00 and 8:00 A.M., had trouble negotiating the heavy seas; most foundered. Only five guns made it to the beach. They were M7s, the mobile 105-mm howitzers mounted on tank chassis. To provide some armor protection for the crew, the guns were wrapped in an armor skirt that sat on top of the tank chassis, but that created a problem. The gun could not be depressed for low-angle fire because the tube would bump up against the skirt. Nor could it fire effectively at a high angle. When the tube was elevated too high, the gun's breech would hit the top of the tank chassis. With less than 800 yards of beach to operate on, the gunners had a problem. They could not lower the tubes enough to strike at the beach fortifications above them, but less than 2,000 yards away. Nor could they lob shells onto their targets by firing at a high angle.

A failure of fire support might not have been so important if the main means the Allies were depending on to reduce the beach defenses had worked. The generals expected a preinvasion air bombardment to flatten the German positions. They were flat wrong.

The Allies flew 14,000 sorties on D-Day. (A sortie was the flight of one aircraft on an operational mission.) Many pilots flew three missions on the first day of the invasion. It was a lot of effort—but it did not have much impact on the fate of the first wave at Omaha.

An air-support plan called for 1,200 bombers to strike the beach defenses for half an hour at first light. At Omaha, however, there were problems. Dropping a bomb during World War II from 20,000 feet and having it hit within a quarter of a mile of its intended target was considered very good shooting. The bombardier, the member of the crew responsible for operating the bomb site on board the aircraft and releasing the bombs, had to find the target. That was difficult enough on a clear day in broad daylight. D-Day on Omaha dawned with thin morning light, overcast with thick cloud cover, shrouds of smoke from the naval gunfire, and a smoke screen laid down to mask the fleet. In addition, the bombers' targets were close to friendly troops. There was a real risk of bombing GIs as well as Germans. With the target zone of German beach fortifications only a few hundred yards wide, only a few thousand yards away from the incoming waves of landing craft carrying the assault troops, a small error could result in big casualties for the wrong side.

The preinvasion bombing overshot its targets and obliterated empty fields behind the German beach defenses. The good news was not one bomb hit the beaches or friendly troops. The bad news was none hit the defenses on the bluff either. What the generals had hoped would provide the main firepower punch for D-Day proved a bust.

In addition to the bombers, there were over 5,400 tactical fighters in the sky above Normandy on D-Day as well. They carried machine guns and bombs and could provide both air cover for the fleet and support for the ground troops. They spent most of their day dodging friendly antiaircraft fire. And although pilots could see the devastation going on on Omaha Beach, there was little they could do about it. They lacked direct radio contact with friendly troops on the ground, and distinguishing friend from foe in the cramped space of the battlefield from the seat of a plane zipping over the coast at high speed, dodging explosions, and watching out for enemy fighters was no easy task.

Armor was the infantry's last hope for firepower on Omaha. It was a forlorn one. Tanks were an important weapon in amphibious warfare. At Tarawa, for example, on D + 2 (two days after the first landing), armor support, after some problematic fits and starts, helped reduce the Japanese main defenses, turning a disaster into a victory. Armor was a great asset once it got to the beaches. The biggest challenge, as the Marines found out all too well, was getting the armor from the sea to the battle.[37]

As with their approach to fire support on D-Day, the generals took risks with their armor for Omaha that did not pay off. Amphibious doctrine called for relying heavily on naval gunfire support to reduce prepared defenses. Instead, the generals placed their faith in an unproven technique—air bombardment. It failed. Their luck with the plan for armor proved little more successful. The generals assigned each assault division a battalion of 32 tanks. All of them were to go in with the first wave. To get them into the battle they placed their confidence in another unproven innovation. It failed, too.

The armor plan called for a small fleet of Landing Craft Tanks, each one carrying four armored vehicles. At 6,000 yards from the beach, the crafts would drop their ramps and the tanks would swim to shore wrapped in a 13-foot high inflatable, rubberized canvas screen. The screen would displace the weight of the tank keeping it buoyant, though disconcertedly bobbing below the waterline (with the screen extended up keeping the water from flooding into the tank's hatch). The tanker steered through the use of a periscope and two maneuverable 26-inch propellers attached to the tank's drivetrain and powered by the engine. They were called duplex-drive (DD) tanks.[38]

Once they touched ground, the armor would pull up to the waterline and, still obscured by the surf, provide support for the infantry, firing at the defenses on the bluff. By having the DD tanks launch at sea, they would leave room for more craft carrying infantry to hit the beach. The tanks would also be smaller and less inviting targets for the enemy artillery covering the approach to the shores. In this respect, the innovation would benefit both the armor and the infantry. At least, that was the plan.

One observer, a veteran of amphibious operations in the Pacific, was skeptical. "Without an invitation," he remembered, "I drove down to the Southern Coast of England to observe one of the Divisions in the VII Corps make a practice landing. I was distressed at what I saw. In my opinion these troops were six months or a year behind the Pacific in amphibious technique and apparently nobody knew it. ... the DD tanks ... worried me a lot. In the Pacific we put our tanks on LSMs [landing ships] and fired them from their water-borne bases at shore targets and hit targets. Apparently this had never been considered on the Atlantic side."[39] The DDs seemed like a very complicated and risky solution to a simple task.

The concern proved to be well-founded. DD tanks had been tested in moderate seas, where they not only worked surprisingly well, they made a respectable four knots as they motored confidently to shore. On D-Day, the waves were two to three feet higher than the lip of the canvas. The DD tanks sank like a stone. The battalion supporting Omaha lost 27 tanks.

Most of the armor that got to the beach did so only because the crafts carrying them ran aground and discharged the vehicles right onto the sands. These tanks were, however, too few in number to make a difference on D-Day. The ones that did arrive soon fell prey to mines, enemy artillery, and obstacles.[40]

An official summary of events prepared by the British Naval Historical Office shortly after the landings summed up the problem with the English flair for understatement. "It has to be admitted," the report stipulated, "that conditions could not have been less ideal for this novel weapon, but even so the consensus of naval opinion is that ordinary water-proofed tanks, landed on the beach in the normal manner, would have served the purpose equally well."[41] It was a polite way of saying the generals had taken an unreasonable risk for little profit.

One of the great controversies surrounding the landings was the refusal by the Americans to employ the British "funny" tanks for their landings on Utah and Omaha. These tanks were a variety of improvised designs, including a

Testing the DD-Tank off the Coast of England. (Courtesy, Army Signal Corps)

"flail tank" with a rolling drum and chains that could be used to clear mine-fields.[42] Historians still debate the question—even though the issue is silly and irrelevant. The problem on Omaha was far more basic—not enough tanks got ashore, and the antitank defenses emplaced to stop them were intact when they got there.

## GENERAL COMPLAINTS

If there was one fundamental overriding flaw with the scheme for storming Omaha Beach, it was that the plan was a product of doughboy genius. None of the decisions made by the senior commanders and their staffs were heartless, thoughtless, or hastily made, but they were all made in the comfort that they were doing what doughboy genius knew how to do best: get the maximum number of forces to the right place at the right time. What their decisions lacked was an equal appreciation for ensuring that the infantryman standing alone at the furthermost spit of sand could use all the combat power brought across the channel to help him climb up a sand bluff.

In the end, the Americans did what they had always done well during World War I: get masses of men and equipment to the fight. And they deserve credit for that. It was no mean achievement. "The Overlord plan for Omaha was elaborate and precise," wrote Stephen Ambrose in *D-Day*.[43] But, that was the problem. Waves of troops, vehicles, and supplies were programmed to go ashore as if they were to be carted down a conveyor belt on a factory floor, with precise tasks to be accomplished on a precise timetable. The plan, however, required that everyone and everything had a place to go, and it assumed that fire support, air power, and armor would pave the way. When none of that happened, Omaha became bloody Omaha.

Not all the generals were happy with the genius of generals. The plans developed by the staffs after two years of study, debate, and modifications proved wondrous in their capacity to orchestrate the movement of hundreds of thousands of men and thousands of vehicles, planes, and ships. There was no question about that. The question was what would happen when a handful of men supported by little more than the rifles in their hands and protected by little more than the helmets on their heads hit the beach at Omaha.

One commander was very uneasy with the answer. His name was Clarence Huebner.

After the relief of Allen, Huebner seemed like the obvious choice to take over the Big Red One. Not only was he a veteran of the division from the Great War, he was a close friend of Patton. The two had known each other since before the days of chasing Mexican bandits on the border in 1916 under Pershing. Additionally, Huebner had been on the staff of British General Harold Alexander, who thought him "anti-English" and was glad to be rid of him.

Ike, Patton, and Bradley all agreed that Huebner was also exactly the kind of commander the division needed. During the interwar years, Huebner had picked up a reputation as a "flinty disciplinarian." Since many of the complaints of Allen's tenure with the division stemmed from concerns about the lax attitude of the Big Red One soldiers, rather than their fighting qualities, Huebner was the man to straighten things out.

On August 7, 1943, Huebner assumed the call sign "Danger 6." "Danger" was the telephone code word for the 1st Infantry Division, and "6" was the designation for a commander. After the war, Danger 6 wrote with nostalgia of his return to the division. "To me, it was a return home: a return to the Division I had served with in peacetime, which included the regiment where I had learned the first lessons of soldiering and with which I had served as a young officer through the great battles of the First World War. It was a homecoming ... ."[44] That was not how the troops felt.

At first, the marriage between the Big Red One and the flinty disciplinarian was troubled. Even before the end of the Sicilian campaign, Huebner ordered additional training for the division, including rifle marksmanship, close-order (marching) drill, and mandatory classes in military courtesy for the troops not at the front. These proved to be none too popular for combat veterans who thought they were above lessons in basic soldiering. In England, there was more training—endless hours of training. The troops found it all demeaning.

Over time, however, the division's attitude toward its commander changed. Once in battle the soldiers would come to respect him even more. "Later," one veteran recalled, "General Huebner showed himself to be a gentlemanly, kind man who appreciated his troops and who was, in reality, a fine commander. I can never be convinced that he was such a mean, despicable, and self-serving person as to try degrade those whom he expected to follow his orders to their possible deaths."[45] He was their general now.

And the general of the Big Red One was not happy with the scheme for fire and maneuver on Omaha. Huebner disapproved of the assemblylike approach to the landings. In particular, he objected to loading plans for the landing craft that were designed more to maximize the use of space than to preserve unit integrity. "Craft must be tactically loaded despite the fact that some of the space is not used," argued the division's critique of the Overlord plan, "the assault team based on craft capacity is impractical. All planning should be built around normal infantry units, squad, platoon, company, battalion, and combat team."[46] Huebner stressed organization over efficiency because he believed that, despite the preponderance of air power and fire support, the infantry might well have to fight its way off the beach and to do that the men would be better off fighting and dying with the organizations and leaders they knew and trusted.

## BOOTS ON THE GROUND

The months in England turned over one by one. The staff of the Big Red One complained about the plan, failed to obtain adequate changes, and waited, waited as they looked "to the day," as Huebner reminisced, "when the French coast would be over the bows of our landing craft."[47] When the day came the first troops from the 1st Infantry Division did not like what they found on the beach.

What they found was that a battalion of minimally trained German coastal defense forces had been, by coincidence, withdrawn shortly before D-Day and replaced by three battalions of solid infantry from the 352nd Division who were conducting training exercises. And these men, alerted by the early morning bombardment, were in their trenches and bunkers waiting for the GIs. And they were fully armed and ready.[48]

And their positions were virtually untouched by American firepower. "I took a look toward the shore and my heart took a dive," one veteran recalled, "I couldn't believe how peaceful, how untouched, and how tranquil this scene was. The terrain was green ... . 'Where,' I yelled to no one in particular, 'is damned Air Corps?'"[49] The scene did not stay bucolic very long. As soon as the American landing craft came in range, the battle for Europe was under way.

In the boats coming ashore on the cheerless morning of June 6, 1944, rode the GIs of the 16th Infantry Regiment, 1st Infantry Division. They had been here before. They had landed in North Africa and Sicily. And they had the same dead feeling, churning in choppy seas waiting for the order to go in, seasick, backs aching under 60 to 90 pounds of combat gear, wet, and cold. And then there was the strain of the engines marking the run to shore and the grunt of men spilling into the frothy surf, hoping not to drown on the way to dry land. They cast furtive glances at the beach obstacles, scanning for mines, looking for the flashes of fire that marked the enemy positions through eyes squinting with salty sweat, sea spray, and sandy grit.

One of the first off the boats was Captain Joe Dawson, the commander of G Company.[50] His craft was in the vanguard of the second wave hitting the beach at 7 A.M., exactly at the time and spot called for in the landing schedule.

Bad luck plagued Dawson from the start. Company G's landing craft took a direct hit from an artillery shell before it had even finished unloading. Over a score were dead, including the naval gunfire support officer.

The next terrible moments involved getting from the water to the beach. With a ramjet of adrenaline shot from the heart, the urge was to sprint up the sands, but running under the heavy weight of the pacts, the contents and the weight of which had been carefully calculated by higher headquarters, was impossible. "It was the feeling of the men," Dawson later reported, "that their losses would have been cut in half had their loads been cut likewise."[51] Instead, the men walked into battle. And the slow-moving GIs made big, easy targets.

Even without the shooting it was a miserable maneuver. The hours on the landing craft had left the GIs cold and shivering. Many suffered painful cramps as they came off the ramp. They smelled none too good either. The uniforms had been impregnated with a chemical in case the Germans were planning to use poison gas against the assault troops.[52] The coating made the uniforms stiff and uncomfortable, making moving simply an exercise in misery.

And there was no way off the beach. A company in the first wave was supposed to have cleared a path, but there was no path. The beach was just covered with bodies.

Dawson's company was hemmed in by barbed wire, a minefield, and patches of impossible swampy ground at the base of a small estuary. And the Germans were firing at them. Dawson's men blew a hole in the wire using bangalore torpedoes (long metal pipes filled with explosives).

As they moved inland they followed a path of dead bodies, making grim progress, walking carefully near the dead assuming that the mines near them had already been detonated.

Having cleared the wire and negotiated a stretch of sand loaded with mines, they moved to the base of the bluff. Dawson started the morning with 189 men. The artillery fire at the landing and the move from the water's edge to the bluff cost 50 casualties.

Dawson sized up the situation as follows: They were several hundred yards from the nearest German strong points covering the beach exits on either side of where G Company landed. There was a small bit of cover from three dilapidated stone buildings with stone walls on two sides and a small defilade straight ahead. He had a good bit of his company, some of his supporting weapons teams (machine guns and mortars). They could organize and maneuver as a unit. The question was, where?

It was time to forget the plan. Moving to the beach exits, the company's original task was suicide. That would take them right into the teeth of the enemy defenses, defenses that had obviously not been reduced by the bombing and naval gunfire. With his own fire-control officer dead, there was no way to bring more naval guns on the German position. The better option would be to follow the defilade up the bluff. The downside with that decision was that Dawson had no idea what they would encounter or how deviating from the well-rehearsed plan might interfere with other units.

Dawson decided for the bluff. He established his machine gun and mortar sections on the beach to cover the advance. And then the men of G Company started off into the unknown.

The next challenge was getting up the bluff, a climb of 130 feet over the course of 200 yards. Dawson's company began working its way up the shallow draw, in tandem with another group from E Company. A German machine gun opened up on the column, but the draw provided a slight amount of cover. When they reached the top, they found the lip of the bluff overhung the bluff face. The Germans above could not see or shoot directly at the climbing infantry.

Captain Dawson tossed grenades over the top into a chattering German machine-gun nest. The grenades went off with a crack, pelting Dawson with pebbles, dirt, and sand. They waited.

The firing stopped.

Dawson waived his GIs over the top. On the crest of the ridge they immediately fell into a pile of German dead in the trench line. They had reached the high ground.

The other enemy manning the cliffs had fled and worked their way down the trench to the positions at the beach exit. The company fired after them, but Dawson did not pursue. He needed to press inland and secure the beachhead. Once the Germans knew they were there in force, there would be a counterattack. They had to get ready. G Company needed to press on and make room for others to follow.

On the beach below, the follow-on forces saw the silhouettes of American soldiers standing on the crest of the bluffs with the sky above the Normandy countryside behind them. There was a way off the beach.

Dawson's men crossed the trenches and started moving to the woods and the town beyond. They may well have been the first Americans off the beach. But, they were only the first. Others followed. And that was how bloody Omaha was won.

There was little more to the success on Omaha than raw courage and resolute leadership. "When you talk about combat leadership under fire, on the beach at Normandy," one veteran remembered, "I don't see how the credit can go to anyone other than the company grade officers and senior NCO's [noncommissioned officers, i.e., sergeants] who led the way … . We sometimes forget, I think, that you can't buy valor, and you can't pull heroes off an assembly line."[53] In modern war, genius, any kind of genius is never enough without boots on the ground—men with the skill and courage to do the job. That was the lesson of Omaha.

# CHAPTER 5

# Trial and Error

## THE GENERAL'S LOT

GENERALS MAKE MISTAKES. AFTER mistake-plagued Omaha, there were 335 days between D-Day and the surrender of Germany, plenty of opportunity for more mistakes. Mistakes were part of the cost of combat.

Genius does not mean perfection. It would be an error to equate genius with error-free decision making in battle. Mistakes in war, even really bad decisions that in retrospect seem so maddeningly obvious, do not necessarily reflect a lack of a measure of genius or good generalship. Mistakes in war are inevitable. And the more responsibility, the longer the campaign, the greater the stakes, the more far-reaching the objectives, and the increasingly complex the myriad of forces and factors weighing on battle, the odds are the more misjudgments will occur. Napoleon made so many bad choices that one historian claimed that he was really just lucky and not that much of a commander at all.[1] That, of course, is rubbish. He was a fine commander—so were men such as Dwight Eisenhower, Omar Bradley, and George Patton. They just were not perfect. That frustrating fact makes for the tumult of history.

The chancy nature of combat ensures that its study will eternally be a lively subject. The lot that generals and armies must bear is that they cannot outlive all the historians who will write about them. And historians, for all their sanctimonious claims of objectivity and zealous obligation to truth telling, are storytellers. They write stories because we all need them. Narratives are a vital part of our culture. It is how we learn. And stories have a beginning, a middle, and an end; and heroes and villains; and lessons to be learned. Making a story also means some details get intentionally left out, while others are underscored. All of this has to be done to craft the sense of people, place, time, and plot that drive the narrative form. War stories are no different. And so, military history tends to conflate the practice of the art of war by one side or the other into good or bad, better or worse, black or white. It takes the confusing, obscure, ambiguous, and contradictory and makes it straight, logical, organized, sequenced, chronological, and unconfusing. All this makes for compelling stories. And sometimes that is how myths are born.

The great historical myth of the postwar years was that America's generals were flawless. They were not by a long shot. Omaha showed that.

The figure of the iconic American commander, however, crumbled long before the recent critical reassessments of bloody Omaha by historians such as Ambrose and Lewis. The Vietnam War killed the myth of the invincible general. After 50,000 lives and great national treasure were expended and failure was experienced, generals became the historians' targets, not their heroes. Even Hollywood deserted them. The most popular war movie of the era was *Patton* (1970), and the film's attitude toward generalship and battle was ambivalent. When Darryl Zanuck bought the rights to Ladislas Fargo's *Patton: Ordeal and Triumph* (1965), he hoped to match the success of his box-office hit *The Longest Day*. When the film finally came to the screen, however, America was a different place. Wearied by war and humbled by an economy that had seen both stagnant growth and runaway inflation (coining a new term "stagflation"), Americans were in no mood to be triumphal. This was an introspective generation. *Patton* was a film for their time.

*Patton* told the story of "old blood and guts" from the American defeat at the Kasserine Pass in North Africa to the occupation of Germany. It was an evocative motion picture. The director, Franklin J. Schaffner, thought he had made an antiwar film. The producer, Frank McCarthy (a former Army general and secretary to George Marshall), was not so sure. He believed people took from the film what they wanted. "Some people came out saying 'What an antiwar picture,' meaning wasn't it grueling, wasn't he rough. Other people came out saying. 'If we just had somebody like that in Vietnam."[2] Such contrasting views were not surprising. The movie focused more on Patton's complex and flamboyant character than his generalship.

Confirmation of the death of the Hollywood general came in 1977 with the release of *MacArthur*. General MacArthur was played by an aloof, austere Gregory Peck, aptly capturing the character of another controversial war leader. In contrast to *Patton,* the film revolved around the critical command decisions made by MacArthur in the Pacific during World War II and the Korean War. The motion picture flopped. The big box-office war movie that year was *Star Wars*. Heroism was now the stuff only of fantasy films.

Historians turned on the generals in kind. *Eisenhower's Lieutenants: The Campaign of France and Germany: 1944–1945* (1981) by the distinguished and influential military historian Russell F. Weigley offered the senior American military commanders decidedly mixed reviews. Others were equally critical and not just of GI generalship. The fighting character of Americans came under fire. No book advanced this thesis more stridently than Martin van Creveld's *Fighting Power: German and U.S. Army Performance, 1939–1945* (1982), arguing that the combat effectiveness of units in the *Wehrmacht* was much higher than in the American Army. In a way, they had easy pickings. There was a great deal of uncritical scholarship to go after.

Post-Vietnam scholarship killed one myth, only to try and replace it with another. If America's military prowess had been wanting, something had to account for victory. John Ellis, in *Brute Force: Allied Strategy and Tactics in the Second World War* (1990), summed the answer up in his title. In what he called a "radical reappraisal," Ellis argued America and its Allies proved victorious principally due to the weight of their material superiority and little more. There was no room for genius of any kind in Ellis's narrative. But it was no more accurate an assessment than the stories it attempted to supplant.

History built exclusively on finding or ignoring faults is just bad history. Real war is much messier. The tale of the Normandy campaign after landing on Omaha offers ample evidence. The story of how the Americans broke through the German defenses may offer the best example of all.

## THE BREAKOUT

Bradley's plan for breaking out of Normandy earned a scene in *Patton*, which is no surprise because Bradley's book *A Soldier's Story* was used to help shape the script, and the general served as an advisor on the film. In the scene, Bradley (Karl Malden) briefs Patton (George C. Scott) on the plan for the breakout of Normandy, Operation Cobra, and offers Patton the command of the field army that would be established after the operation succeeded. It was, in some ways, an odd choice of events to be included in the film. Patton played no role in shaping the plan for Cobra. In fact, he was rather critical of Cobra, recording in his journal that it was "really a very timid operation."[3] It was not a moment that Patton would have thought particularly significant. But, perhaps it was not so strange for Bradley. For the senior commander of U.S. ground forces in Europe, it was perhaps his finest hour in command, though not one without flaws.

Cobra was an achievement to which neither the myths before nor after Vietnam do it adequate justice. In fact, it debunks both of them. And it was a battle that has much to say both about the practice of doughboy genius and GI ingenuity. And it all started in the place pictured in the film, Bradley's trailer.

Seven weeks passed between Omaha and the advent of Operation Cobra on July 25, 1944, weeks that saw some of the most difficult fighting the Americans had seen since Guadalcanal and weeks that included battles such as the assault on the White Witch and the taking of Hill 192. In that time the Americans managed to link up the forces that landed on Omaha and Utah beaches, tie their flank into the British-Canadian Army attacking toward Caen, relieve the airborne forces that had dropped behind the enemy lines on D-Day, secure the port of Cherbourg on the tip of the Cotentin Peninsula, and press south toward St.-Lô. And it was all done over a stretch of difficult ground: 25 miles of lowland swamp, flooded fields, and hilly hedgerow country.

Like the assault on Omaha, the genius of generals did little to prepare the Americans for hedgerow fighting. In retrospect, it is a failure that seems unforgivable. The nature of the Norman terrain in the U.S. zone was no great secret. Bradley's First Army staff should have known better.

The veterans of Sicily, several of whom served on the First Army staff, could recall the impact that difficult terrain had on the conduct of operations. The First Army staff terrain estimate described the bocage country. The Chief of the British General Staff warned the planners. He had been over the ground in 1940. It would be tough terrain for modern armies to fight on. They should, he suggested, give the problem some thought. There were hedgerows in the English countryside. Nothing was done to test their impact on combined-arms warfare. Nothing was done to help the troops training in England prepare for hedgerow fighting. "I do not remember ever hearing about hedgerows and their effects on tactics," recalled William DePuy, a veteran of the campaign and future general officer.[4]

Bradley's staff should have had a plan to deal with the bocage country. And in a perfect world they might have. Getting ready for Normandy was anything but.

The First U.S. Army had its first taste of battle managing the attack on the St. Mihiel Salient in 1918. After that, the command, in a move organized by the operations officer Colonel George Marshall, supervised the massive redeployment for the Meuse-Argonne offensive. These were no mean achievements. Any legacy of their genius, the skills, knowledge, doctrinal insights, experience, and traditions that were passed down to the First Army headquarters that commanded GIs in Normandy, was—exactly zero. When the war ended, the field army became a paper headquarters, not a headquarters focused on paperwork, but a headquarters that existed only on paper. The Army reactivated field army staff-level headquarters in 1933. That did not make much of a difference. There were skeleton staffs and there were no realistic large-scale maneuvers to organize and conduct. The First Army staff, then stationed in New York, had a complement of two officers.[5] Then war came.

After participating in the stateside General Headquarters maneuvers of 1941, soldiers with the patch of the First Army (a black trapezoid capital letter "A") set up shop at Clifton College in Bristol, England, on October 20, 1943. That left about seven months to get ready for D-Day. And that seven months included not just writing the First Army plan, but allowing time for the plan to be coordinated and implemented, for training to be conducted and equipment to be issued. The Army rule of thumb held that a staff should reserve one-third of the time available to draft its plan and allow subordinate commanders two-thirds of the remaining time to prepare for battle. By that standard (since the invasion was originally scheduled for May), the First Army plan needed to be finished by Christmas.

And there was a great deal of planning to be done. In the Army scheme of organization, field armies commanded corps; corps commanded divisions; and divisions commanded regiments and battalions. Corps were meant to be small tactical headquarters, primarily responsible for managing the divisions, which did all the fighting. In contrast, the field armies planned and managed major campaigns, performed a myriad of logistical and administrative tasks, and commanded all the supporting combat support and service support units, allocating them to the corps as needed.

First Army had a particularly daunting challenge for Overlord. It not only had to plan for the crossing and the landing, but for all operational, supply, and administrative activities of all U.S. forces in Normandy for at least the first two weeks of the campaign. That meant it was responsible for everything from combat operations to air defense to medical treatment and graves registration, as well as taking control of the civilians in the French towns that would be liberated.

There were about 750 men on the First Army staff, little more than a battalion's worth of men for planning an operation in scale and scope unprecedented for the Army in modern times. And it was a team that came together only after the course of a few months. Bradley brought some of his staff with him from the Sicily campaign. Others came over directly from the United States. Courtney Hodges, who would serve as Bradley's deputy and later take command, did not show up until February.

The problem that preoccupied the First Army planners more than any other was figuring out how to get all the stuff they needed to the continent to fight the war. The Navy's job was to tell the Army how many ships and landing craft were available. The Army had to decide what went on what ship and what got unloaded in what order. It was like an enormous puzzle. And it was a zero-sum game, a never-ending series of Hobson's choice. If something got added, something had to be left behind. And everything depended on everything else. Infantry needed tank and artillery support. But tanks and artillery needed ammunition and fuel. But adding these meant less infantry. And not enough infantry meant there might not be enough troops to secure the beachhead. It was a maddening exercise and it consumed months of planning, debate, trial and error, late-night meetings with chain-smoking staff officers and strong coffee, writing, rewriting, estimates, plans, orders, memorandums, endorsements to memorandums, and it all had to be done in secret. In February, the First Army plan was approved by the army group headquarters that would command all the American, British, and Canadian ground forces in the opening phase of the invasion.

And the clock was ticking.

Parts of the Overlord Plan were not finished until May. And there was no detailed plan for what would happen after the Allies landed. There was, however, a general outline of a campaign mapped out by British Field Marshal Bernard Law Montgomery who would command all the ground forces for the invasion. Controversy over Montgomery's intent for the Normandy campaign continues to be the subject of some debate. It is a wearisome debate that has brought more heat than light to understanding the campaign and will no doubt never be resolved to historians' satisfaction (guaranteeing a fruitful source for doctrinal dissertations and books contracts for generations to come).

What is clear is that the Allied campaign did not progress in the manner Montgomery had hoped, despite claims in postwar years. On the other hand, as historian David Hogan points out, "Monty" had produced a "flexible plan that stressed keeping the initiative and taking advantage of whatever opportunities the Germans presented."[6] In general, the U.S. forces were expected to move through the hedgerows and then push north, opening the way for the establishment of another U.S. field army that would have the mission of securing the ports in Brittany that would serve as the base of the U.S. supply lines in northern France and support the drive on Paris and toward Berlin.

What perhaps the First Army did not anticipate was that the push of British and Canadian forces would be so slow that it allowed the Germans more time and troops to throw up against the Americans, troops that proved to be highly skilled at getting the most out of the hedgerow defenses. If the British and Canadians had taken Caen (the major city in Normandy and the hub of the area's road network) and reached the ground more favorable for tanks more quickly, then the Germans would have had to commit the entire weight of their defenses, particularly their armor, up against them. That would have left the GIs facing far fewer enemy in the bocage. But that did not happen.

In a perfect world the Americans would have had a more detailed plan for dealing with the hedgerows, what the military called contingency plans. But they did not. There was no denying that they could have used one. In a speech before the invasion, Bradley declared, "our training doctrines are sound. The old principle of fire and movement, whether it's two individuals or a battalion, is absolutely as it is in the book."[7] "Our tactics as taught at home are sound as a dollar," Bradley stated after the first battles of the hedgerows, "We only need to apply the things we learned in training."[8] His statement could not have been more wrong. It seemed an odd comment for a commander that journalist Ernie Pyle had nicknamed the "the GI general." It was a comment as divorced from the reality of the war that the GIs were fighting in the hedgerows as could have possibly been made.

By the beginning of July, it was obvious that the Allies were stuck. Eisenhower publicly tried to dampen expectations for a rapid advance. "Fighting will be most strenuous and there will be heavy losses," he told reporters, "The Allies will have to fight hard for every foot they gain."[9] Ike conducted a personal overflight of the countryside in a modified fighter so he could look at the ground himself. He wrote to Marshall describing the difficult nature of the bocage country, the troublesome weather, and the tenacity of the German defenders.[10]

Bradley ordered a general offensive in early July, 12 divisions assaulting the Germans head-on with a goal of expanding the size of the Allied lodgment area. It cost 40,000 casualties and made only modest gains.[11] The whole affair seemed like a bad day in the Meuse-Argonne. There had to be a better way. There was, but it required the genius of generals.

It was at this time that Bradley ordered a mess tent erected with a nice, dry, planked floor. He needed a place to lay out his maps, study the ground, and do what should have been done by the First Army in Bristol—come up with a solid plan for getting out of the hedgerows. The tent was later replaced by a custom-built trailer. Bradley's aid, Chet Hansen, had gone over to Monty's headquarters to see what his map trailer looked like. He then supervised the construction of something like it for the First Army commander. That was where the scene in the film *Patton* took place. And it was where Bradley laid out his plan for Operation Cobra.

Bradley had to make a simple choice—pick a plan for breaking through the bocage defenses. There are three options to defeating an enemy defensive belt: (1) go through it; (2) go around it; (3) go over it. The only problem was, none of those would work in Normandy.

Going over the top was not an option. The British and Americans had a limited number of airborne units and planes to deliver them. All the airborne forces had been committed to D-Day and were now back in England reconstituting. None of them were combat ready. And even if they had been, the terrain suitable to employ them was not the best terrain to support a breakout. In addition, airborne operations were feasible only if there was a degree of confidence that ground troops could link up with the paratroopers in a few days. Airborne troops had to travel light. They carried little food, ammunition, supplies, and no heavy equipment.

Going around the German defenses ("turning a flank") was not an option. On the east flank were the British and Canadian forces facing the preponderance of the German armor. The west flank was lightly defended by the Germans, but only because there were virtually no roads and lots of swamp. The area could not support an advance by a large number of American armored units.

Going through the German defenses was not an option. The Americans discovered that in the first July offensive. Unlike World War I, GI divisions were built for maneuver, not staying power. They could not absorb massive casualties and conduct sustained fighting for days, while retaining any degree of combat effectiveness for offensive operations. The Americans knew they would suffer high casualties in the opening weeks of the campaign. They had a pool of 20,000 replacement infantrymen ready to go. That was less than half the number they lost in the July offensive alone. The alternative to blast through the German defenses with firepower rather than forces was not an option either. There was not enough artillery ammunition for massive barrages. It had required 25,000 rounds just to support the advance up Hill 192. To support breaking through the hedgerows would have required on the order of 1.5 million artillery shells (an amount equal to what was fire in the 10-day preparation of the Battle of the Somme during World War I). And while the Americans had enough artillery pieces, they lacked enough ammunition for something like that.

It was a long way to Paris. The Americans did not have the combat power to exhaust themselves just trying to break out of the bocage. And even if they chose to do so, there was still a problem. There was not much room to bring a lot more men and supplies ashore or facilities to handle them. Normandy had become the end of a massive conveyor belt dumping into a warehouse that was filling up. Bradley already had the equivalent of another field army ready to go, but he needed room enough to get them into the fight.

The general was not out of options. There was a fourth alternative, and it was the one he picked. He would create a new flank in the German defenses, in the middle of the German lines, just east of St.-Lô. Rather than conduct a

Bradley's Map Trailer. (Courtesy, Omar N. Bradley Collection, Military History Institute)

broad frontal assault, he would mass three divisions and break through on a narrow front. He would then send three additional divisions through the breach. One division would turn west and block any major German counter-attack that might be launched to seal the breach. The other two divisions would turn east and encircle the German defenders on the Americans' right flank, driving almost all the way to the coast. Surrounded, these enemy troops could then be annihilated. This was called a "hammer and anvil" maneuver. The encircling division would act like the anvil, blocking the enemy troops and keeping them from retreating, and then the U.S troops to the north (the hammer) would attack crushing the enemy. (The 90th's attack on the Séves River was meant to prepare for the hammer strike after Cobra kicked off.) The result of the hammer and anvil maneuver would be a wide open flank, leaving plenty of room to send a second American field army (under Patton) to become operational to push into Brittany.

That was the plan.

And it was Bradley's plan. After the First Army commander settled on his course, he invited others into his map trailer to comment on Cobra, including Patton and Monty. Bradley took up some of their suggestions and modified the plan, but the basic concept and all the responsibility was his.

In *Eisenhower's Lieutenants*, Russell Weigley diminishes Bradley's contributions by arguing that it was really the generalship of "Lightning Joe" Collins that made the operation a major success. Collins commanded VII Corps during Cobra. He oversaw the six divisions that undertook the breakthrough.

Lightning Joe was a fine general. He had commanded Army troops in the fighting on Guadalcanal (where he had picked up his nickname as the commander of the 25th "Tropic Lightning" Division). After the D-Day landings, Collins led the successful assault on Cherbourg. He was without argument one of the best corps commanders in Europe.

In his war diary, Chester Hansen, Bradley's aide, perhaps a bit put out by Collins's emerging star status, described the general during a visit to the VII Corps command post as "hot mustard Collins and whom the hometown papers are calling 'Lightning Joe'. Smooth operator with a powerful gift for persuasion and people are already predicting great things for him in this operation. Walks with his hair slicked in a cow lick, shirt button to the collar but no tie. We found him living in an old French house that looked like a suite of a well to do French whore."[12] Still, Hansen had to admit everyone had great confidence in him and Collins and Bradley worked well together and respected one another.

Collins's contributions to Cobra, as suggested by Weigley, however, are either just flat wrong or grossly overrated. He performed well during the operation, but in neither the planning nor the execution of Cobra did he significantly affect the outcome of events.[13] Weigley simply got it wrong. There is no arguing—Bradley simply came up with a damn good idea and saw it through.

It was not only Bradley's plan, it was the right plan. The Germans definitely thought so. Germans excelled at maintaining a flexible defense belt and using local counterattacks to seal penetrations, maintaining the integrity of the defense. When enemy advances were made, they would fall back to the next defensible terrain feature and reestablish the defensive line. On the other hand, breakthroughs meant problems because they could be sealed only by large armored counterattack forces, and masses of armor meant only one thing to the Allied airplanes that dominated the skies over Normandy— excellent targets. The German commander responsible for the American sector knew it was the one kind of operation that their method of defense could not withstand, the same kind of maneuver that the Russians had used on the Eastern Front to take back large swaths of the motherland.[14]

It was the kind of plan that Americans excelled at, large-scale operations that required a lot of planning and coordination in short order. It was a task equivalent of Marshall's effort to move the First Army during the Meuse-Argonne, and this time Bradley's staff was up to the task. They were no longer the bunch of men thrown together meeting in drafty rooms at Bristol College. They were officers and men who had worked together for long months and who had plenty of practice at their craft. And they were now over 1,000 strong. They did not always get along. The stories of some of the rows between the senior members of the staff became legion. But, they worked well together and they were united in their support and loyalty to Bradley.[15]

## CULIN'S CUTTER

For all the excellence of Bradley's conception for the bocage breakout and the staff's work on the Cobra plan, there was still one very big problem. It relied on infantrymen fighting through hedgerow defenses in depth, a task not easily done.

Despite the GI general's fatuous comment that the tactics of fire and maneuver were "solid as a dollar," he knew better. He also knew that the success the divisions had made so far was due principally to the innovations of commanders who had figured out how to conquer hedgerows on their own. In fact, the techniques pioneered by the 2nd and 29th Infantry Divisions, and others as well, were perhaps the best expression of GI ingenuity made during the European campaign. The innovations are described well in Michael D. Doubler's excellent book *Closing with the Enemy: How GIs Fought the War in Europe, 1944–1945* (1998). Doubler, a former Army officer and history professor at West Point, provides a first-class study of tactical innovation by the Americans from Normandy to the drive to Berlin. *Closing with the Enemy* is a landmark work in understanding the impact of GI ingenuity on the course of the war on the Western Front.

Laudable though they were, hedgerow-busting tactics would not get the First Army out of the hedgerows. The example of the 2nd Infantry Division's remarkable success in taking the crest of Hill 192 offered a case in point. It had a taken a week of planning and rehearsal and a corps' worth of combat power and a full day of fighting to get a few battalions a few hundred yards up the hill. To break out of Normandy, VII Corps would have to cover a couple of miles and they would have to do it in a few short days before the Germans counterattacked in force. There was neither the time nor the resources to bust out of Normandy a hedgerow at a time.

Bradley had two ideas. Both became the stuff of myth. The most famous involves Curtis G. Culin's hedgerow cutter. The story by former war correspondent William L. White, published in the February 1950 edition of America's *Reader's Digest,* said it all, "Sgt. Culin Licks the Hedgerows." It all began during an inspection tour of a quiet sector of the line near St. Germain d'Elle, corps commander General Leonard Gerow turned to the commander of F troop, 102nd Cavalry Squadron, Captain James Depew, and asked what had been done to address the hedgerow problem. Depew admitted that they had not come up with any good answers. Gerow told them to find one.

That night Depew called a meeting of his officers and sergeants. Culin said he had an idea. The problem, Culin argued, was that the tanks and hedgerows acted like the bumpers of two cars ramming each other. What they needed was something like a snowplow that could get the momentum of the tank through the hedgerow rather than striking it head-on. Depew presented the idea to the squadron maintenance officer, Lieutenant Steve Litton. Litton suggested something like a "fork," something strong enough and long enough that it could dig under the roots of the bushes and trees on the hedgerows and something that could be bolted onto the front of the tanks. Litton thought of the iron beach obstacles that the Germans had littered about Omaha Beach. They were strong and had sharp cutting edges designed to rip the bottom out of landing craft trying to come ashore at high tide. They might work well if they were cut and welded to the front of the tank.

Two days later Depew reported they had a prototype ready for testing. The tank was taken out for a test-drive. It pulled up to a hedgerow and pushed forward. As it did, the tank started to lift its nose into the air, like a skinny kid trying to lift a load that was too heavy to bear. The tank went nowhere. The harder the tank pushed, the more it lifted. Culin's cutter was a big flop.

The tank then pulled back and instead of pushing through hedgerow, it tried running through the hedgerow. Heading toward the hedgerow head-on at a high speed produced an entirely different effect. The tanks sliced right through and broke into the field beyond flat and level. The damn thing worked.

Word went up the chain of command. Bradley excitedly mentioned it to Eisenhower. The First Army commander was going to see a demonstration of a new device that could beat the hedgerows. He got his preview on July 14, 1944. He needed some good news that day. That evening he was going to attend the funeral of Brigadier General Teddy Roosevelt. Roosevelt had landed with the first wave on Utah Beach (for which he received the Medal of Honor). Bradley planned to offer him the 90th Division if Landrum had not worked out. Roosevelt died in his sleep of heart failure. He was buried at the temporary cemetery at St. Mére Église (and was later moved to the U.S. cemetery above Omaha Beach where he rests beneath a cross emblazoned with gold letters signifying his status as a Medal of Honor recipient). It was a sad end to a good day.

For the cutter test, Gerow was there, as was General Robertson from the 2nd Infantry Division whose troops had cracked Hill 192 and who knew a thing or two about hedgerow busting. They were all impressed. Bradley featured the incident in his memoirs.

> Less than a week before the planned jump-off [weather postponed the attack until July 25], Gerow telephoned early one morning to ask if I could meet him at the 2d Division. "Bring your ordnance officer along [Colonel John Medaris]," he said, "we've got something that will knock your eyes out."
>
> I found Gerow with several of his staff clustered about a light tank to which a crossbar had been welded. Four tusklike prongs protruded from it. The tank backed off and ran head-on toward a hedgerow at ten miles an hour. Its tusk bored into the wall, pinned down the belly, and the tank broke through under a canopy of dirt. A Sherman similarly equipped duplicated the performance. It too, crashed into the wall, but instead of bellying skyward, it pushed on through. So absurdly simple that it had baffled an army for more than five weeks, the tusklike device had been fashioned by Curtis G. Culin, Jr., a 29-year-old sergeant from New York City.
>
> Medaris sped back to the CP [command post] where he ordered every ordnance unit in the army on round-the-clock production of the hedgerow devices. Scrap metal for the tank tusks came from Rommel's underwater obstacles on beaches … . Within a week three out of every five tanks in the breakout had been equipped with the device. For his invention Culin was awarded the Legion of Merit by the corps. Four months later he went home to New York having lost a leg in Huertgen Forest.[16]

Bradley ordered what came to be called "rhino tanks" held out of action until they could be sprung as a surprise during the breakout.

It seemed like the perfect marriage of GI ingenuity and general genius. After the war, Culin had an opportunity to meet Eisenhower at his office at Columbia University where Ike had gone to serve as president after he retired

Culin's Cutter. (Courtesy, Army Signal Corps)

from the Army. White wrote in his *Reader's Digest* article that Culin proved modest about his contribution. "No wait a minute," was Ike's rejoinder, "Of course we had the kind of army in which a really good idea could rise quickly. But remember someone has to have the idea. And that man was you!" And it was an idea that seemed poised to change the course of the war. Historians such as Richard Overy in *Why the Allies Won* (1995) and Russell A. Hart in *Clash of Arms: How the Allies Won in Normandy* (2001) even credited the rhino tanks with winning the Battle of Normandy.

## BOMBING THE CARPET

Even before Bradley learned about Culin's invention, he had come up with another way to break out of the hedgerows—firepower. There would, of course, be artillery. There would be 45 battalions of field artillery directly supporting the VII Corps, 550 guns. The corps on the flank of the breakthrough would also provide some supporting fires as well. Together, they would fire hundreds of thousands of rounds, a fair amount of fire support, but the zone designated for the breakthrough was six miles long. That was certainly not enough artillery to saturate the German defenses the way the 2nd Infantry Division had marched up Hill 192.

To put the fire back into fire and maneuver Bradley planned to use massed bombing from airplanes. In his war diary, Hansen wrote, "Brad is insistent on breakthrough with good use of our great air power ... . Brad wants 4,000 tons dropped on a tightly designated area which can be shown afterward. Wants them dropped in 100 and 250 lb bombs so that there will be a density of craters every sixteen feet in every direction. Greatest area bombing show in the world. 'I've been wanting to [do] this now since we landed. When we pull it, I want to to [sic] be the biggest thing in the world. We want to smash right through."[17] Airpower would bust through the hedgerow defenses.

It was easy to understand why Bradley wanted to use airpower. A medium bomber (the B-25 Marauder or the B-26 Mitchell) could carry a maximum of 4,000 pounds of bombs. The B-17 Flying Fortress, a heavy bomber, could carry up to 12,800 pounds of bombs. In one planeload a B-17 could deliver more firepower than 100 light howitzers firing at a time.

Yet, Bradley's faith in airpower seemed unwarranted. The bombers had not done any good at all on Omaha. Monty tried twice to use massed bombers in operations around Caen (Charnwood and Goodwood). Both failed.

Bradley thought he had the answers to all the shortfalls that had plagued previous attempts. The problem at Omaha had been the difficulty of identifying targets and too much of a safety zone between the friendly and enemy forces. As a result, all of the bombs fell behind the German beach defenses. Likewise, in the British operations a wide safety zone had been used. Thus, by the time the attacking forces reached the enemy troops, they had recovered from the bombing and reestablished their defenses. For Cobra, the safety zone would be only 1,200 yards (1,500 for the heavy bombers). To limit the possibility of friendly fire, fighters flying only at a low altitude (2,000 feet compared to 15,000 feet for the bombers) would attack targets in the strip closest to the American lines. In addition, Bradley proposed that the bombers fly a course parallel to the target, reasoning that if the bombs fell short of the target at least they would still land on the German side. Finally, the attack was planned across the St.-Lô–Périers road which Bradley reasoned would be an identifiable terrain feature that the pilots could use to help identify the target area.

Bradley's expectations for a more accurate aerial attack were bolstered by the implementation of the employment of radar for directing the bombers. In 1935, the British Air Ministry commissioned Scottish physicist Robert Watson-Watt to determine whether radio waves could be turned into a practical weapon. What he discovered was that waves transmitted in a focused beam produced an echo when they hit a plane. Using the direction of the beam and the time it took to send the radio signal and receive the echo, he could determine the location, direction, and speed of the plane. He patented his discovery: radio detecting and ranging—radar. In 1940, the Royal Air Force used radar to warn of impending air attacks. By 1944, the Allies had figured out how to use radar to help guide bombers to their targets across the British Channel. Using radar to guide the bomber fleet would help make sure the bombers got to the right place, even on a cloudy day when pilots and bombardiers could not see the ground.

A second problem in the British operations was that the bombings had heavily cratered the roads, creating serious obstacles that impeded the advance of the Allied armor. To eliminate this problem Bradley wanted all the bombs used to be less than 500 pounds, which would leave shallower craters for the tanks to negotiate.

A third problem had been that even after the massive bombings the Germans still managed to put up a strong defense. The last attempt, Operation Goodwood, had involved 2,000 planes that dropped over 7,000 tons of bombs. And still the Germans held. Bradley planned to overcome that likelihood by increasing the density of the bombs. There would be 3,000 sorties, including 1,800 heavy bombers, supporting the attack. And all the bombs would be dropped in less than three hours. The GIs would attack across a carpet of bombs.

## THE BIG ATTACK

As the day approached, the troops knew that something was up. One GI wrote in his journal, "keep hearing rumors of an offensive very soon. Hope they're true. This slogging through hedgerows and swamps has been rugged on the infantry boys. I never seen a line of them going up to the front that I don't think, poor bastards."[18] They did not have to wait long.

After a spate of bad weather Cobra was scheduled to kick off on July 24, 1944. The weather, however, worsened after the bombing run started and the attack was canceled and rescheduled for the next day. Cobra got under way July 25. Once the attack started two things happened that were not supposed to happen. One of them was an unmitigated tragedy.

The soldiers who witnessed the bombing firsthand, including Bradley's Chet Hansen, could not believe what they saw. "It was horrible. Ground belched, shook, and spewed dirt … . Huebner an old front line campaigner, said it was the most terrifying thing he had ever seen."[19] Among the GIs staring skyward on July 25 stood General McNair. He had wanted to see what Bradley called his "big attack" firsthand.

McNair had left the Army Ground Forces. Lear replaced him. Now he was in England. He did not know it, but Eisenhower was considering him for a field army command.[20] This was McNair's second trip to the front to see how the training provided by the Army Ground Forces had paid off. During the North Africa campaign, McNair had been wounded by artillery while out on an inspection tour. Once again, he was up at the front, in a foxhole less than 2,000 yards from the target area. He had been there for the aborted attack on July 24 as well. "The troops sure like to see you up front," one staff officer told him.[21] It was a rare opportunity to see the man who had made them march through the swamps of Louisiana.

There was a kind of irony for the Army's chief trainer to be witnessing a risky bombing technique that had already failed three times to break the Germans, a technique that was being attempted, in part, because he had not produced divisions that could accomplish the job by themselves.

McNair's training program had failed to ready the American divisions to handle the hedgerow fighting. In 1992, Paul Gorman, who had served as DePuy's deputy at the U.S. Army Training and Doctrine Command during the 1970s, wrote a report for the Institute for Defense Analyses. *The Secret of Future Victories* described DePuy's contribution to the training revolution that helped revitalize the Army after Vietnam. Gorman's study, however, started and went on to consider at considerable length the strengths and faults of McNair's Army Training Program. In a cogent assessment of the effort made, Gorman highlighted what McNair got right and got wrong.

The Army Ground Forces ran a methodical training system that with doughboy efficiency had turned out divisions for the fight. And he stressed the value of solid leadership and realistic training that acknowledged combat would be confusing and chaotic. But, the Army Training Program was an industrial process focused more on time and task than standards (ensuring units were qualified to perform the missions assigned) and the ability to adapt and innovate. "Get it done!" was how the World War II veteran DePuy recalled the strict requirements of the program, "Never mind whether or not the troops learned anything."[22] McNair had tried the best he could in the time that was available, but it was not enough. The problem was not just training leaders "who could draw arrows on the map to discomfort any enemy," Gorman wrote, "but also units capable of advancing those arrows."[23] That was where McNair had come up short. And the general probably would have acknowledged it … if he had lived.

McNair was in a trench that took a direct hit from an American bomb. He was killed instantly. His body was thrown so high and so far it took the day to find it, and when the troops did, it was mangled beyond recognition. And he was not the only one.

In the aborted attack on July 24, 1944, short bombings from American planes killed 29 and wounded 145. On July 25, it was a lot worse—bombs killed over 100. Almost 400 more were wounded. "Scores of our troops were hit," Hansen recorded in his diary, "their bodies flying from slit trenches."[24] More were missing. Others were in shock. Equipment was destroyed. Attacks were disrupted and delayed. Some battalions could not attack and had to be replaced. And there was still worse to come.

When the first infantry battalions reached the enemy lines, they found the enemy defenses as tenacious as ever. Collins received a disturbing call from one of the infantry division commanders, "there is no indication of bombing in where we have gone so far."[25] None of the initial reports were encouraging. The Allies had dropped 4,100 tons of bombs, and the Germans were still fighting tough.

Neither the short bombing nor its impact on the Germans should have come as much of a surprise. Under any circumstances 1,200 yards was an inadequately safe distance. Under perfect conditions, which meant (1) ideal weather, (2) accurate target location, and (3) perfect functioning release and detonation of the bombs, on average 90 percent of the bombs were calculated to fall within 1,000 yards of the center of the target.[26] They might, however, fall anywhere within that 2,000-yard circle, meaning the effects

Digging Out Soldiers Buried by the Short Bombing on July 25, 1944. (Courtesy, Army Signal Corps)

might well spill over outside that area. In addition, 10 percent of the bombs might fall twice as far away. Thus, even if everything had gone perfectly, statistically bombs landing on the U.S. lines were highly probable. And the odds were that conditions in Normandy would not be perfect. They were not even close.

The weather was not perfect. The bombing altitude had been set for 15,000 to 16,000 feet, but the clouds were too thick at that altitude to observe the target area. Some bombers dropped as low as 12,000 feet. The lower bombing required the formation to space farther out to make the planes less susceptible to ground antiaircraft fire; bunched-up planes at lower altitudes made very attractive targets. In addition, the sudden change in altitude required bombardiers to recompute the data for determining when to release the bombs and reset their bomb sites, significantly increasingly the likelihood for human error.[27]

Target location was not perfect. Artillery shells with colored smoke were fired to help mark the enemy locations. That smoked mixed with the clouds of smoke and debris thrown up by the fighter-bombers whose attack run preceded the heavy bombers. The Germans also started firing artillery as well. As a result, the location of the St.-Lô highway was difficult to make out as a prominent south breeze turned the whole area into a blanket of haze. And there was no accurate means to mark the friendly positions. And that everyone knew. It had proven a problem during the Louisiana maneuvers. The Army had conducted a test only a year before Cobra and found the most accurate means it had to identify targets was effective only to 2,000 feet (13,000 feet below the planned release altitude for the heavy bombers). Direct communications with aircraft proved useful at preventing friendly fire. But the bombers did not have radios that could talk to the units on the ground. Even during the campaign, units reported problems with short bombings because of the difficulty of accurately identifying friendly and enemy locations. And they warned against trying to use artillery smoke to mark targets for air attack. The accuracy of air support was troubling. Only days before Cobra, at least one division commander gave Collins "a first hand appreciation of the problem." Even units 2,000 to 3,000 yards from enemy targets had been accidentally bombed, and they had been hit by fighter-bombers flying at much lower altitudes.[28]

Humans were not perfect. In one case, the bomb site on the lead plane of the flight group malfunctioned. The bombardier released visually; other planes dropped on his signal. The bombs landed in the wrong place. On July 24, 1944, a bomber attacked an Allied airstrip when the bombardier accidentally hit a toggle switch. In the official investigation, all the short bombings were attributed to human error.[29]

In his memoirs, Bradley railed that it was all the fault of the flyers. To limit the time over the target and to get the most bombs on the ground, in the shortest time, and as close together as possible, they had elected to have the bombers cross perpendicular rather than parallel to the American lines. Given the probable range of errors involved, it is not clear at all that a different course would have made any difference.

Indeed, it is almost certain that a parallel bombing would have been less accurate. And that was because of one of the most important Allied technological innovations of the war—radar. For Cobra, the bombers were guided by the British H2X radar system. The radar's deflection error (bombs that would fall right or left of the target) was much greater than its range error (bombs that would fall long or short of the target). As a result, a parallel course might well have actually resulted in even more bombs hitting the American lines.

The importance of all this might have escaped Bradley. He was not a technology enthusiast. In 1943, he had called one of his staff officers in to brief him on radar because "he had heard about this radar, but he didn't know anything about it." After receiving a simple explanation of the physics, Bradley concluded, "Thank you very much. That's all I need to know. Pat [Colonel Charles G. Patterson, the First Army Antiaircraft Officer] that's your problem from now on. I'm not going to get myself involved in the technology of radar."[30] Clearly, Bradley was no expert on radar or airpower and was not qualified to be dictating bombing tactics.

The air staff knew what it was saying when it insisted that a perpendicular course would result in both a faster and more accurate attack. In fact, air analysts who studied the strike photographs determined that "bombing errors were actually less than anticipated."[31] Amazingly, only about 3 percent of the bombs fell short of the target line.

Bradley also failed to note that the air staff had warned him that there might be significant casualties from short bombings, which was why they had wanted a 3,000-yard safe zone to begin with.[32] It appears Eisenhower understood the risks as well. Before the attack he wrote Bradley that "speaking as the responsible American rather than the Allied commander, I assure you that the eyes of our whole country will be following your progress and I take full personal responsibility for answering to them for the necessary price of victory."[33] It seems highly unlikely that Bradley did not realize he was undertaking a serious risk, even if he refused to admit it in public. The First Army commander had a human failing—the GI general was loathe to admit that he knew his plan might well kill some of his GIs.

Mistakes were made. An official investigation into the bombing blamed— no one.

The fact that the bombings had not appeared to disrupt the Germans forward defenses should not have been much of a surprise either. As at Omaha Beach, the German positions closest to the American lines were inside the bombing safety zone. The enemy's main defensive belt was missed by most of the bombs. Some German positions were hit by bombs, as were some forward American positions. But just as the short bombings did not keep the GIs from attacking, they did not keep the Germans from defending.

Bradley's carpet bombing, however, did not go to waste. Dropping far more bombs behind the enemy lines than any previous saturation bombing operations, the density of the attack had a dramatic impact on the Germans. As the GIs discovered after the battle, "the German front-line snuggled close to our forces during the saturation bombing from the air. While enemy and artillery and other support weapons, lines of supply and communications, dumps, and other installations had been destroyed by the bombs, the German forward positions remained largely intact."[34] Touring the area after the battle, Hansen wrote in his war diary, "viewed tremendous cratering effect of the bombardment with destroyed Panzer tanks littering the road, their guns nose-heavy with the muzzle-break careening at crazy angles toward the sky. Shattered trees and dead cows, their legs stiffened in the early morning sun, gave evidence of the terrific effort there."[35] The carpet bombing wiped out reserve forces, crippled headquarters, damaged supply depots, and thoroughly disorganized the German rear area. While the enemy's first line of defense could still fight, behind it was a smoking shell of chaos and casualties.

In a typical day of hedgerow fighting, even when the GIs managed to gain a bit of ground, divisions lacked the combat power to sustain the advance, and they would usually be blunted or turned back by a timely German counterstrike. (That had been the fate of the luckless GIs in the 90th Division when they crossed the Séves River.) July 25, 1944, in Normandy was different. Because of the effects of the air bombardment, German commanders had no idea what was going on at the front, where counterattacks needed to conducted, and no way to organize reinforcements. As a result, when the three infantry divisions attacked, they found a typical day of tough hedgerow fighting and slow going, not much different than any other day in Normandy. The difference was—no significant German counterattacks. When the GIs took ground they held it. And even though none of the divisions reached all their first-day objectives, by the evening it was clear that a path had been made through the enemy's main line of resistance. There was room for the armored-heavy divisions with their rhino tanks to go in and clear the rest of the way.

## THE DRIVE TO MARIGNY

Collins assigned what he believed the most critical task for the breakthrough to Clarence R. Huebner's 1st Infantry Division. There was reason for that. The division was thought to be one of the best fighting outfits in the Army. A few weeks before Cobra, Patton had visited the division headquarters to talk about hedgerow fighting. "When you want to know about fighting," he told Huebner, "you must contact a fighting outfit, that has a fighting general."[36] That description fit the Big Red One. After North Africa, Sicily, and Omaha, nobody questioned whether it could fight.

The plan had called for the division to follow the 9th Infantry Division into the line. The 9th was to have driven south and taken the town of Marigny. Marigny would open a path to dive farther south and also serve as the turning point for the drive to the southwest where the 1st Infantry Division would set up the main blocking positions behind the Germans (the anvil for the hammer that would follow). The division was held on two hours notice, ready to follow up the 9th's advance.[37]

From the outset it was clear the 9th Infantry Division was going to have a tough time clearing its zone. Some of the front-line units were hit by friendly bombs. And the initial German defenses encountered were well organized. Fighting through them was tough. Huebner met with the 9th Infantry Division commander. "Let's call General Collins," Huebner suggested, "and let me take over right here and try to break through and complete my mission where it is. Let's take advantage of the fact that out in front of us the Germans are badly upset right now. We don't want to give them any time to recover."[38] Collins agreed.

By twilight on July 25, 1944, it was clear that while the 9th Infantry Division had dented the enemy lines, it did not have the combat power to get all the way to Marigny. Collins considered Marigny vital to the success of Cobra. He ordered the 1st Infantry Division to pass through the 9th Infantry Division and secure the town.

The division was ready for the job. It had been pulled out of the lines and wound up having 10 days before Cobra to prepare for the attack. To weight the Big Red One's combat punch, Collins attached Combat Command B (CCB) from the 3rd Armored Division to the 1st Division. And there was Bradley' secret weapon. On July 14, 1944, Huebner also had an opportunity to witness the demonstration of Culin's cutter, and over the next few days most of his tanks had been outfitted with the rhino devices.

All the preparations and elaborate plans the division made in the run up to Cobra proved worthless when the order came down that the mission had changed. For Huebner and his staff it meant a sleepless night as they had to come up with a new scheme of maneuver. Originally the infantry was to have been trucked to the front and then follow behind their tanks racing through open country to their objectives. Now they would have to pass through the troops of the 9th Infantry Division that were engaged with the enemy and then fight through the German lines to get to their objective. And there was not a lot of room to do all of this. The division would have to move on a much narrower front than it had hoped. There were few roads and few options in how to advance. All of this had to be taken into account, new orders prepared, issued, and the troops taken off the trucks and put on the road to march to the front. Ten minutes before midnight the division issued a new plan.

Huebner's new scheme called for his 18th Infantry Regiment under Colonel George Smith, Jr. to advance in the eastern part of the zone and take Marigny. By its side would be CCB. The division's other two infantry regiments with their accompanying tanks would follow.

Remarkably, by 7 A.M. the division had gotten its troops to the front and was ready to attack. That was no mean feat. The American lines were jammed with troops and equipment all pushing to get into the fight.

Colonel Smith was ready to go, but he was worried. CCB with its rhino-tipped tanks planned to move fast and hard. While Smith had his own rhino tanks, he did not have as much armor as CCB. He could only hope his troops could keep up and not leave the CCB flank exposed to counterattack.

The reports into the command post proved promising. The infantry units had made contact with the 9th Infantry Division just north of the St.-Lô–Périers road. At 7:15 A.M., the first units had made contact with the enemy. That was not bad news. The enemy troops they encountered were fighting in isolated strong points, not in a belt of interlocking defenses. And there were no enemy counterattacks. Smith found this promising.

There was, however, tough fighting and rough going. "Companies were literally drenched all of the way with shell-fire; every other hedgerow contained a stubborn pocket of resistance" and the terrain "naturally rugged … had been completely torn up by the aerial bombardment of the previous day. Painful hours were spent in clearing paths through Nature's debris to allow the rolling tanks to follow the infantryman."[39]

Smith ordered that pockets of resistance be bypassed and mopped up by follow-on forces. In a normal hedgerow battle a commander might never take that chance. Advances always faced the prospect of determined counterattacks, and the last thing any combat leader wanted was to be fighting an attacking enemy at his front with a dug-in enemy behind. For the breakout, however, it was a risk worth taking when speed was essential and it looked as if the enemy resistance was uncoordinated. Above all Smith did not want to fall behind CCB.

The biggest problem so far proved to be the roads. The armor had trouble keeping up. Bradley had hoped to avoid cratering, but the planes had carried some 500 pound bombs and these virtually obliterated the routes to Marigny. Aerial photos revealed that the main route had been cut in at least 25 places by craters.[40] Engineers had to be brought up to patch the roads. And there was more bad news. There had been no contact with CCB. Smith felt he was being left behind.

Smith finally made contact with CCB at 10:30 A.M. and found that its armored columns had gotten almost nowhere and were, in fact, fighting to catch up with the 18th Infantry Regiment. General Huebner's war diary reported, "the tanks on the right (CCB) moved slowly in a one tank front and had road blocked for miles. ... Situation moving slowly because of bomb craters from yesterday's bombing."[41] Cratered terrain and enemy fire had kept the armor from dashing anywhere.

The two commands made slow and steady progress throughout the day. By late afternoon they had advanced about two and a half miles, considered remarkable progress for a day of hedgerow fighting.

Smith decided to carry his attack into the evening. His troops had yet to secure Marigny and there were still no signs of an organized defense. Continuing the attack seemed like a prudent and necessary risk.

At midnight there were more new orders. CCB was to begin the turning movement and head southwest while the 18th Regiment finished securing Marigny. The burden of seizing the key objective now all belonged to Smith. And it did not seem as if it would be an easy task. That night there had been reports that some of the forward-most divisional units were in Marigny. Those reports turned out to be wrong. And when the first troops were sent into the town on the morning of July 27, 1944, they were cut off and surrounded. There were Germans in Marigny, and it seemed they had no intention of leaving town.

By midmorning there were two battalions from Smith's regiment in Marigny and the fighting was fierce. And there was no air support. The weather was dreadful: rainy and overcast all day. The division's artillery was called up and began pounding the enemy positions commanding the high ground south of town. Observers were stunned when they witnessed the incredible veracity of the bombardment, only to find that after the smoke lifted there was still plenty of fight left in the Germans. The enemy in the town was just as tough. Buildings were infested with automatic weapons. Every house became an enemy bunker, and every one of the town's narrow streets and alleys a deadly killing field of automatic fire.

Huebner was concerned. He made three visits to the 18th Regiment's command post during the course of the day.

It took all afternoon for one battalion to fight through Marigny to the other side. By the end of the day, however, victory was not in doubt. Huebner's war diary recorded, "the breakthrough is a success."[42] He ordered Colonel Smith to get four hours of sleep. Smith had not rested since the battle started.

It was not a pretty advance and it had taken longer than Huebner had hoped, but the division had accomplished its mission. Mistakes were made, but by July 28, 1944, a breakout was well under way.

## MEASURE FOR MEASURE

What was most remarkable about the advance of the Big Red One and the other infantry divisions during Cobra was how, at the pointy end of the arrow, the nature of combat was so similar to every other hedgerow fight. The rhino tanks, despite the high expectations, actually contributed only marginally to success.

There was more myth than miracle to the story of Culin's cutter, beginning with the fact that initially it was not even Culin's idea. During the "bull session" that led to the invention, Max Hastings reports in *Overlord: D-Day and the Battle for Normandy 1944*, "a Tennessee hillbilly named Roberts asked slowly: 'Why don't we get some saw teeth and put them on the front of the tank and cut through these hedges?' The crowd of men roared with laughter. But Sergeant Culin … said, 'Hang on a minute, he's got an idea there.'… An honest man, he [Culin] tried hard to give some of the credit to Roberts. But the weight of the great propaganda and publicity machine was too much for him. He became a very American kind of national hero."[43] Though it was not entirely Culin's idea, there is no denying it was a good idea, but it also was not a particularly unique idea.

Others had invented hedgerow-busting techniques before Cobra, including the 1st Infantry Division. A division report described, "Well we finally figured out some way to do a little bit, not too much, but it helped some. That was to put some heavy forked spikes out in front of a few tanks and run up and ram them into a dirt bank and then pull the tank up into where it lifted the dirt. What it would do would be to lift and push at the same time so that on the far side of the bank it would tend to cover up a foxhole and there was no telling how many Germans we buried alive that were trying to hide from us on the other side of the bank."[44] The 1st Infantry Division used their version of bocage busting with good effect, but it did not win the war by a long shot. Any hedgerow-busting technique, the rhinos included, was not a magic bullet for breaking out of the bocage. If it were, the Americans would have achieved that goal weeks before.

In part, the rhinos were no help because of the nature of the terrain. It had been so chewed up by the bombing that the craters, not the hedgerows, were what slowed the division down. In addition, even when the rhinos were used to bust through hedgerows, that did not solve the problem of bocage fighting. Unsupported tanks still fell victim to German antitank traps. It still took coordinated armor-infantry-artillery action to advance in hedgerow country. In the case of the 1st Division, as a record of the 18th Infantry Regiment makes clear, the road to Marigny was primarily an infantry fight. "Observation to the front was limited, restricting use of mortars and artillery. It was strictly a dough boy's show, with bullet, bayonet, grenade, and bazooka paving the way."[45] Beyond Marigny, some of the armored columns made amazing progress, but that too had nothing to do with the rhinos; once the Americans had broken through the main defensive belt, the tanks got on the road and raced to the enemy's rear.

Measure for measure what got the Big Red One division through to Marigny was not rhinos, but the same thing that had gotten it through most of its battles—a mix of GI ingenuity and sound combat leadership. The carpet bombing and the hedgerow cutters were, without question, marks of GI ingenuity. Sure other armies innovated on the battlefield, but the Americans toyed with technology consistently and often produced good results. The carpet bombing was a case in point. Strategic bombers had not been designed to support tactical ground operations. There was no doctrine, no opportunity to train, no air-ground communications system, and no adequate command structure. After three notable failures in trying to use the bombers, Bradley tried again anyway and, despite the short bombings, did it successfully.

And although Eisenhower swore it would never be done again, the tactic was repeated later in the European campaign and with success as the air corps developed a better system. On November 16, 1944, 1,204 bombers dropped 4,120 tons on the Roer River defenses as part of Operation Queen. According to Ian Gooderson, "Most of the bombers were equipped to receive signals from a vertical SCS-51 localizer transmitter beacon placed a short distance in the rear of the U.S. front line, and from two marker beacons. The SCS-51 indicated to the bombers their exact position in relation to the front line and the bomb release point, while the marker beacons kept the bomber on course. A ground control station was set up in radio contact with the bomber stream ... ."[46] Americans made it work.

Like good engineers, a lot of the good that was done in the bocage country was accomplished by trial and error. The tragedy of Normandy was that, in battle, trial and error costs lives. Perhaps if the Americans had started their mobilization sooner, had invested more in their national defense during the interwar years, if they had just had more time to learn their lessons before the battle (the very training system that DePuy sought to institute after the Vietnam War), then the losses might have been less, the genius of generals and GIs more apparent, and the victory more cheaply won. But they had not and that was the cost of unpreparedness.

# CHAPTER 6

# The Air-Ground Miracle

## HELL ON WHEELS

AN EXHAUSTED, BLEARY-EYED Maurice Rose needed a shave. He had had almost no sleep. He smelled, gasoline, grime, and days of sweat mixed together. His ears rang with a constant buzz from the grind of tank engines and the crackle of radios. It was dawn on July 30, 1944. He had been fighting and moving nonstop for three days.

Rose had been struggling against two enemies, and they had both proved pretty tough. The Germans were disorganized and desperate. They were attacking from every direction. Rose had to fight the Americans as well. With the success of Cobra, other divisions were pushing forward too, and competing for maneuver space. Everything was happening fast, too fast for much coordination. He had already been fired from his job as commander of Combat Command A (CCA), 2nd Armored Division, for an insubordinate argument with another division's commander. And then he was rehired the same day. Coordinating artillery fires was impossible. Nobody was sure where the front lines were. Hell, there were not any front lines.

Rose was in a foul mood. Life really was hell on wheels.

George Patton had done much to popularize the 2nd Armored Division's motto "Hell on Wheels." When he led the command during stateside maneuvers in the United States in 1941, he trumpeted the gruff-sounding nickname and staged brilliant, if impractical, demonstrations of armored raids deep into the enemy territory. But impressing newspapermen in mock battles decided by red and blue flag-waving umpires was one thing. Fighting in real wars was another.

In Normandy, the 2nd Armored Division was like the 1st Infantry Division, a veteran combat outfit. It had fought in both North Africa and Sicily. And while it had never achieved any spectacular victories that quite measured up to its Hell on Wheels moniker, it had proved to be a dependable outfit. It seemed the right force for a mission that required a dependable outcome.

The Cobra plan called for three divisions in the exploitation force that were to charge through the breach created by the carpet bombing, following the path opened up by the three infantry divisions in front of them. The three follow-on divisions were divided into what was called the "inner" and "outer" rings. The rings were a maneuver technique used to encircle and destroy an enemy force. The purpose of the inner ring was to cut off the force to be destroyed. Collins had assigned that task to the 1st Infantry Division and an armored division. They had what was considered the main task in the operation, trapping and crushing the west flank of the enemy line (in concert with other troops attacking from the north) and opening the routes in Brittany. The mission of the outer ring was to prevent the enemy from sending in a relief force to break the siege. In other words, the outer ring's job was to guard the back of the inner ring against a counterattack. That was the 2nd Armored Division's job.

And it was a real job. There was a real risk of counterattacks during Cobra.

From the onset of the Normandy campaign, the Germans had held back a significant portion of their armored forces in Northern France to guard against a suspected second amphibious invasion. After it was obvious the Allied buildup in Normandy was the main effort, the theater armor reserve readied to counter any breakthroughs. The question was where these might occur. So far the Allies main armored thrusts had come out of the British/Canadian sector—and they had been blunted.

After the American breakthrough near St.-Lô, it was clear that something had to be done. The answer was to destroy the 2nd Armored Division. The German high command ordered attacks from two directions. The units that had retreated south in the face of the advance of the Americans' inner ring were commanded to turn and strike east into the Hell on Wheels. Among their number were Lieutenant Colonel Hedyte and Sergeant Uhlig, who had ably bested the 90th Division at the Séves River. This time they were not so lucky. Their attack and every other unit that tried to hit the flank of the 2nd Armored Division by attacking west to east were beaten back.[1] Both Uhlig and Heydte would finish the Normandy campaign in a prisoner of war camp.

Still, the Germans were not done yet. There were two *panzer* divisions heading straight at CCA, attacking east to west.

The Germans always knew that if the Americans pushed too hard, the panzers could strike back. The Vire River was only 28 miles from where the Germans had concentrated their armor against the British. The *panzers* could move through the wooded *Suisse normande* countryside, and if they moved at night they would probably never be seen by the Allied airplanes that dominated the skies. Within 24 hours they could be on the Americans before they knew it.

The Americans were not surprised that the Germans were desperate to choke off the advance of Hell on Wheels. The division had achieved much more than serving as an outer protective ring for the breakout. During the course of its advance, it had split the boundary between two German corps and broken all the way through the enemy's main defensive belt. As a result, Bradley not only had an opportunity to drive into Brittany, but turn the entire western flank of the German Army in Normandy. If the Germans could not blunt the 2nd Armored Division, they would have to undertake a major withdrawal.

On the morning of July 30, 1944, Rose had new orders: begin rolling up the German flank. Rose planned an east attack. The objective was the little town of Tessy-sur-Vire.

That same morning the Germans planned to attack west. Their first objective was the little town of Tessy-sur-Vire.

The Germans had every advantage. They had more powerful tanks. They were fresh. Rose's boys were exhausted. The GIs had lost a lot of tanks along the way. The Germans had massed for an attack. Rose's command was strung out over miles.

The Germans had every advantage, except one. They sorely lacked for air cover. Rose did not.

## DREAMS OF WAR

That there would be air support for the ground troops was not a sure thing … not until Cobra began. From the start of the war, the airmen had dreams of things greater than serving the infantry in battle.

From the days of the Great War there were dreams of winning wars from the air. It was inspired in part by America's heroes.

When Eddie Rickenbacker returned from the war, he, too, as Sergeant York, received a hero's welcome and a banquet at the Waldorf-Astoria. His affair was sponsored by a group of automobile associations. There was no surprise there. Automobile manufacturers had made millions off of government defense contractors (particularly for aviation contracts that did not build many planes). One of the featured speakers at the gala evening was

Broken Field Running—The 2nd Armored Division's Infantry and Armor Advancing behind the German Lines. (Courtesy, Army Signal Corps)

Secretary of War Newton Baker. He called Rickenbacker "one of the real crusaders of America—one of the truest knights our country has ever known."[2] Such accolades were common for one of America's most famous war heroes —and totally out of balance with the contribution of aviators to defeating Germany.

What the aviators did accomplish was to inspire a generation of soldiers who believed that one day wars would be won from the air. And they knew that would never happen while ground soldiers ran the war.

Military aviation began not as an independent branch, but under the supervision of the Aeronautical Division of the U.S. Signal Corps. After the war, the aviators believed the potential of air power earned them a separate service. Senior Army leaders were not so sure. John Pershing's review board concluded that, whatever was to be done, aviation must remain under the preview of ground commanders; the airplane's function was to serve as auxiliary to the infantry. That the Army followed its recommendations was not remarkable. Pershing served as the Army's postwar Chief of Staff.

Still, it was not the last word.

General "Billy" Mitchell, the Assistant Chief of the postwar Army Air Service, zealously made the case for a separate air arm. In 1925, it earned him a court-martial. He resigned his commission.

In 1926, Congress acted, creating the Army Air Corps under the War Department. It was not much of a victory. The authorized size of the corps was no different than the Air Service, 1,514 officers and 16,000 enlisted men. The law did create an assistant secretary for military aviation issues, but his duties were unspecified and the entire aviation budget was controlled by the service secretary.[3] By 1935, senior air leaders gave up on the battle for creating an independent air force and invested their efforts in trying to get control over budgets and promotion lists for their officers, as well as creating a separate air staff. In June 1941, as America prepared for battle, the War Department was reorganized; the Air Corps became the Army Air Forces with is own commanding general and staff.

While the air staff was not autonomous, it did play the dominant role in determining what kind of air force would be built and how it would fight. Much of what it decided as needing to be done was determined by the air maneuvers that had been conducted in the years leading up to the outbreak of the war. Not surprisingly the "experiments" led the staff to conclude what it fervently hoped to believe—strategic bombing would be the air forces' most important mission in the next war.

Ground support played no role in the air maneuvers. Rather the exercises were designed to determine whether the United States should invest in fighters for air defense or offensive bombers. By 1930, the character of the exercises turned decidedly in the favor of strategic bombings. In the 1933 maneuvers, pursuit planes failed utterly to stop mock bombing raids on Los Angeles. The results led Colonel Henry ("Hap") Arnold, the future Commander of the Army Air Forces, to conclude that "pursuit tactics must be revamped or the pursuit passes out of the picture."[4] Some suggested fighter aircraft should be dispensed with all together.

One airman who read Arnold's proposal was Captain Claire Lee Chennault, who would later lead "The Flying Tigers" in support of the Chinese Army fighting the Japanese. Chennault argued the maneuvers were rigged. "All sorts of fantastic and arbitrary restrictions," he fumed, "were placed on fighters in maneuvers that were supposed to simulate honestly the conditions of actual combat." Chennault made an impassioned case for the fighter.

When Arnold saw Chennault's critique, he wrote, "Who is this damn fellow Chennault?" Who Chennault was, was an old-fashioned flyer fighting a rear guard action to preserve the preeminence of the fighter pilot. And he was losing. In their younger days, "fighter boys" had been the "prima donna service," recalled General Ira Eaker, who would command a bomber force in Europe, "Nearly everybody put his preference when he went to flying school for pursuit. That grew up of course from the First World War, the ace sort of thing."[5] That age, however, was rapidly coming to a close, despite Chennault's best efforts.

Another exercise was organized to test Chennault's proposal for making tactical fighters more effective. They worked. Nevertheless, airmen had little enthusiasm for them. They were bomber boys.[6]

Likewise, the limitations of strategic bombing failed to faze the air enthusiasts. According to John Perry, "between 1930 and 1938 the Air Corps dropped 200,000 bombs, mostly from 4,000 to 11,000 feet, and very few from over 16,000 feet [considered the minimum safe bomb altitude to stay above enemy antiaircraft ground fire]. Drops generally took place under optimum conditions—clear weather, low speed, no enemy opposition, and against targets clearly marked on the desert floor."[7] There were no clouds, no enemy flak (fragments from bursting enemy air defense shells), enemy fighters, or friendly troops to worry about. Rather than focusing on these distractions, men such as Arnold trumpeted the fact that it was possible to drop bombs from thousands of feet up in the air and have one or more land within a few hundred feet of a specific point on the ground.

As a result, airmen came to believe that the great contribution that they would make in the next war was breaking the back of the enemy nation through a devastating strategic bombing campaign. They would win the war without slogging through mud to take the next hill. There would, of course, be some ground combat. Aviators would help win that battle, too, primarily by clearing the sky of enemy planes—maintaining "air supremacy." The last mission in priority was providing fire support for the ground troops.

The air commanders never contemplated that they would play a significant role in a battle such as Tessy-sur-Vire. If the armor and infantry needed fire support, that was the job for the field artillery. Air power should never be used for targets that were within range of the gunners.

Air Corps Tactical School textbooks declared that ground support would be done only "under the rarest of circumstances" in "cases of greatest emergency."[8] The official Army doctrine at the start of the war, Field Service Regulations, 1939, offered exactly two paragraphs of discussion on air support for ground troops, reflecting, as West Point professor Bill Odom argued, "the broken state of close air support operations in the U.S. Army."[9] The Army's airmen assumed they would play only a minor role in the ground war.

In their dreams and on the drawing board, Army airmen had big plans for air power, industrial-strength plans, and they had every hope America's industrial genius would answer them. It was not an unreasonable dream.

The interwar years saw a significant expansion in the civil aviation sector. Following World War I, the automobile industry quickly abandoned airplane production after the lucrative government contracts dried up. In their place, a fledgling aviation manufacturing industry gradually emerged. Charles Lindbergh (Sergeant York's future nemesis in the preparedness debates before the U.S. entry into the Second World War) made his solo crossing of the Atlantic in 1927, giving an adrenaline shot to America's interest in civil aviation. As new aircraft designs appeared, civilian and military aviators vied to set new speed and distance records. On September 13, 1935, film producer, aircraft designer, industrialist, and world-class playboy Howard Hughes set a world-speed record, 352.322 miles per hour.

No company epitomized the industrial possibilities of air warfare more than the airplane-building business started by William Boeing. In 1917, when the United States entered the Great War, Boeing had 28 people on his payroll. Boeing had to lend himself the money to secure a loan to cover their wages. By the end of the war, he had 337 employees. By 1928, there were 800 on the payroll, and the company was one of the nation's largest airplane manufacturers.

In 1933, Claire Egtvedt, the first engineer Boeing ever hired, became the president of the company. Egtvedt's business strategy was to leverage research and development for the Army with the production of large commercial airplanes.[10]

In 1934, Boeing produced the XB-15, a long-range experimental bomber. The company also financed the prototype for what became the B-17, the workhorse heavy bomber of the American Army Air Forces. The design of the B-17 "flying fortress" also served the development of the civilian Model 314 "Clipper," which conducted the first scheduled trans-Atlantic passenger flight, and the "Stratoliner," the commercial version of the B-17. When George Marshall toured Boeing's Seattle manufacturing plant in 1938, he was impressed. He left believing that if it came to war, American industry would be able to supply the bomber force that the airmen pined for so longingly. As America recovered from the Great Depression, the appetite for commercial air service grew. By 1940, more than 2 million passengers had flown in Boeing manufactured planes.

Still when compared to other industries, the aviation sector on the eve of war represented more potential than capacity. General Motors, the car manufacturer, had 112,000 employees and 112 manufacturing plants. All the airlines together had 39,000 employees and 259 planes. They would need a lot more capacity than that for an industrial-strength air war.

In the summer of 1941, a small group of officers on the air staff produced the Army Air Force equivalent of Albert C. Wedemeyer's Victory Plan. One of the officers was a young major named Laurence Kuter. Kuter and the others in his group had all been trained at the Air Corps Tactical School at Maxwell Field, Alabama. By the time they had attended courses there, the age of the air ace was long dead. They were taught "[a] well planned and well organized air attack once launched cannot be stopped." This motto became the "creed of the bomber."[11] And it was reflected in their planning. Air War Plans Division-Plan 1 set out the blueprint for the Army Air Forces in World War II. It called for over 2 million men (the peak size of the air forces in the war was 2.3 million), more troops than the entire American Expeditionary Forces in the First World War. And it called for 13,000 bombers. It laid out a strategic bombing campaign to win the war. It was as fine an expression of industrial-age genius as Wedemeyer's plan for the ground war.[12] All they needed was men and planes.

When war came, America's aviation industry responded, even before Pearl Harbor. Pan Am helped camouflage U.S. war preparations, ferrying material to build up U.S. bases in Latin America, West Africa, and the Pacific. And American industrial production went into high gear. By March 1944, Boeing's Seattle plant alone was turning out over 360 bombers a month. The Ford Motor Company even got back in the airplane-making business, cranking out B-24 Liberators at its Willow Creek plant.

## AIR TO GROUND

With the preeminence of the bomber, there might have been scant aircraft at all to support ground operations if one of the most cherished hopes of the "bomber boys" had not proved false. As an airpower innovator, Hap Arnold, like many others studying the problem of air combat, believed that technological innovation in bomber construction would outstrip fighter developments. Fighters could not keep up with heavily armored, high-altitude, high-powered heavy bombers. Bombers might not even need fighter escorts to safely get to their targets. That was what they had hoped and what their air maneuvers had suggested was in fact true. Their premise, however, turned out to be very wrong, as both the British and the Germans discovered during their strategic bombing campaigns in 1940. Bombers were vulnerable to fighters and would remain so throughout the war. America's air forces would need a cadre of fighter planes to compliment the bomber force.

The fighter planes developed for World War II were built with the primacy of supporting the bomber force. Speed and range essential for pursuit, in other words, chasing down the enemy's bombers and fighters, and fighter escort (protecting the friendly bomber force) were more important than armored protection and heavy firepower, essential for supporting ground troops.

In the end, the Army Air Forces developed "multirole" fighters that were to provide air defense, offensive air support, and close air support for ground troops. They were not perfect for any of these missions. They were, however, decent enough for all of them.

The principal fighter aircraft available to support U.S. ground troops in Normandy was the P-47 Thunderbolt. Designed by the Republic Aviation Corporation, the plane was originally conceived in the summer of 1940 as a lightweight interceptor. That vision did not last long. The plane was to be powered by a new 2,000-horsepower Pratt & Whitney Double Wasp engine, which required an enormous supercharging duct system that was so big the designers wound up designing the plane's fuselage around it. Then they had to create a huge 12-foot diameter four-blade propeller to efficiently use the power of the new engine. That required a larger undercarriage to ensure the propeller did not strike the runway. Finally, to up-gun the fighters, a battery of eight .50-caliber machine guns was added. With fuel and ammunition, the P-47 weighed in at over 12,000 pounds. The nimble, featherweight interceptor had become a rugged, heavyweight fighter, one that could perform air sweeps, escort duty, and ground support.

The first prototype of the plane took to the air on May 6, 1941. The production model was in the hands of the Army Air Forces less than a year later, March 1942. In April 1943, the Thunderbolt flew its first combat mission. From the onset the plane gained high marks for toughness and reliability. Its sturdy construction and design features made the plane well suited to close air support. The Thunderbolt had a radial air-cooled rather than a water-cooled engine. Water-cooled engines were vulnerable to ground fire; one hit might be enough to cause the loss of coolant, causing the engine to overheat and seize up. P-47s, in contrast, were known to return from battle with gaping holes in their fuselages and whole cylinders blown off their engines ... and still be flying.

The P-47 could also carry a fair amount of firepower. In Normandy, 80 percent of the ground support sorties carried two 500-pound bombs and 400 rounds for each of its machine guns, enough to knock out both infantry troops and armored vehicles—exactly the kind of targets CCA would face at Tessy-sur-Vire.

While the P-47s were adequate planes, there were three significant problems to employing them in the ground-support role. None of them were easy to solve.

Problem number one was the weather. Close support at night, for example, was chancy in the extreme. The Army first developed techniques for night flying during World War I, but they had no application to ground support.[13] And no progress had been made by the Second World War that allowed

The P-47 Thunderbolt, the Workhorse of the Western Front. (Courtesy, Army Signal Corps)

planes to identify targets in proximity of friendly forces at night. And the problem was the same the other way around. Ground air defense units could not visually distinguish between friendly and enemy planes. The density of Allied air defenses in Normandy was amazing, with some areas covered by as many as forty-eight 90-mm guns. At least 12 friendly aircraft were shot down by friendly ground fire. The risk of U.S. lines in the dark might have been more dangerous than flying over enemy territory.[14] Fortunately for the Americans, the Normandy campaign took place during the long days of summer when the GIs had the maximum amount of daylight available for close air support. That was if the weather cooperated—which it rarely did.

Low cloud cover and fog were endemic during the hot, wet summer of 1944, and often when Americans could use fighters to the best advantage to kick off a dawn attack before they moved on the objective, the weather was not good enough for the planes to find their targets. That is what happened to the 90th Infantry Division at the Séves River. Air support might not have saved the day, but it was sorely missed during that disastrous attack.

The problem of weather was made worse by the different weather patterns in England and in France. Planes might take off from England in sunny, clear weather and report that air support was on the way only to find their targets socked in. Or GIs could be sitting in their foxholes staring at open skies watching for their planes, not knowing that the fields in Britain were covered in fog. During the first weeks of the campaign, control of tactical air support for the First Army was split between bases at Middle Wallop, England, and Grandcamp near the beaches in Normandy.

As the Allied bridgehead expanded and more tactical air groups moved to the continent, that not only helped with the weather issue, but made for shorter flight times and more responsive air support. By the advent of Cobra, that was less of an issue. There were 18 fighter-bomber and reconnaissance groups, 15 air bases and temporary airfields, and a radar control system in free France.

Problem number two was more intractable. Air-ground communications were unreliable. It was not an easy obstacle to overcome. The radio sets were heavy and fragile and had limited power and that meant limited range. And they were less useful in close air support. At lower altitudes terrain interfered with the propagation of radio waves.

On the ground things did not work much better. The standard ground communication radio was the SCR-197. It took 10 minutes to set it up. It could not be operated on the move.[15] Like all radio equipment of the day, it was sensitive to moisture, shock, and dirt—things that were found on the battlefield in abundance. The SCR-197 was hardly the kind of equipment GIs wanted to take into a fast-moving, shooting battle.

And air-ground communications were vital for both finding targets and avoiding attacking friendly troops by mistake. The Allies had an air-ground system that could guide fighters using radar and microwave transmitters to the general area where they were needed. Once they got there, however, target recognition was done with eyeballs. None of the marker systems used in Normandy—colored smoke, reflective marker panels, or stencils painted on the tops of vehicles—proved particularly effective for fighter pilots swooping down at high speed looking for targets, friendly troops, civilians, enemy fighters, other Allied planes, U.S. artillery and antiaircraft guns (which might knock a plane out of the sky on purpose or by accident), and German air defenses all at the same time.

Most targets were identified using terrain features, no easy task for pilots who had to scan the ground and the map strapped on their knees to orient themselves. Ground-to-air communications were essential to make sure both pilot and ground pounder knew what direction the plane would be coming from, its time of arrival over the target, its altitude, the type of ordnance the plane would deliver, the nature and location of the target, and the location of friendly troops. It was a lot of information to be exchanged in the heat of combat with chancy communications and little room for error.

There was no question, the systems they had were not measuring up in Normandy. A July 5, 1944, report noted that in a recent 48-hour period of the 18 missions requested by the First Army on 15 occasions the pilots could not find the target.[16]

While failing to aid the infantry was a disappointment, the prospects of hitting the wrong target were even worse. The 2nd Infantry Division's successful attack on Hill 192 was almost derailed by short bombings. During the carpet bombing, the supposedly more accurate fighter-bombers made their fair share of attacks on the wrong side. Bradley's aide Hansen, who watched the bombings from the front, was attacked by fighter-bombers twice. And this was not uncommon. Amid not finding targets, missing targets, and hitting friendly forces, more close support air missions were failures than successes.

Problem number three was the most intractable of all. Airmen and ground soldiers disagreed on how close air support should be conducted to begin with.

It all started in North Africa. Close air-support coordination could not have been more of a disaster. The Germans were fighting back. While there was supposedly a centralized command, the air units were widely separated and poorly coordinated. Laurence Kuter was not happy. He had been called to North Africa by the nominal commander of the Allied Air Force. American aviators had always argued that airpower was most effective when it operated under the central control of an air commander. Air assets should be massed and employed where they would have the greatest effect on the enemy. In North Africa there was one air commander, and he had two subordinate commanders: one to support the American troops and one the British. Each of the Air Support Commands controlled all their own strategic, tactical, and reconnaissance assets. The Air Support Commander was supposed to collaborate with the Army Ground Commander who, in turn, was supposed to determine the level of air support required for each operation.

In practice it was not working so well. The Allies had been unable to maintain air superiority. Troops and port facilities were being constantly raided by German planes. Ground and air commanders lacked experience in working with one another. In late December 1942, Eisenhower, who had overall command of all the forces, agreed to create a single, integrated, centralized, combined air force, including control over tactical air support, but he insisted on putting off implementation for the new scheme for a while.

He should not have waited. In February 1943, the Germans routed the Americans at the Battle of the Kasserine Pass. Bad weather kept most of the air force grounded, but the air and ground commanders debated bitterly over priorities for air attack, frittering away the little support that was available.[17] It was the sorriest day, in a sorry effort to affect integrated air-ground operations.

The battle of flyboys versus GI generals is little remembered today. It did earn a scene in the movie *Patton*. When Patton replaces the corps commander relieved after the catastrophe at Kasserine, he meets with a complement of air generals to complain about the lack of air support. Moments after Patton was told that the Allies had complete "air supremacy" in North Africa, the head-quarters is strafed by German fighters. The scene in the movie was based on a real-life incident. One of the generals present was Laurence Kuter.[18] Despite the acrimony between ground and air commanders, the difficulties are now almost forgotten history. The most recent best-selling book on the campaign, Rick Atkinson's Pulitzer Prize-winning *An Army at Dawn: The War in North Africa, 1942–1943* (2002) hardly mentions the story. Yet, it was an experience that had a significant impact on the future of the ground war.

The disaster gave added impetus to restructure the air command in North Africa. Kuter helped with the implementation, but he did not stick around long. He was recalled to Washington, D.C. After he left, the organizational benefits of consolidating all Allied air assets under a single command proved ephemeral. For the Sicily invasion, the air forces did not coordinate their plans with the ground forces. Naval- and ground-based air defense units accidentally shot up the airplanes carrying U.S. paratroopers. And the best the air forces mustered during the whole campaign was 18 sorties a day to support Patton's entire field army.[19]

Back at the War Department, Kuter did his best to address the sorry state of air-ground coordination. And Kuter was no ordinary brigadier general. He had flown with Claire Chennault. He had served on both Marshall's and Arnold's staffs and both generals favored him.

Kuter's briefing on the problems he saw in North Africa was damming. "Airmen, operating against their sense of correct practice," writes Daniel R. Mortensen of Kuter's critique, "obeyed orders from subordinate army commanders who demanded air support missions over small fronts, other commanders who demanded expensive air caps, and yet others who ordered missions for obsolete bombers that were predictably shot down. The list went on, but the sentence was clear. To Kuter, certain air-ground practices explained why air support failed in the opening months of Tunisia [North Africa] and why they needed to be corrected in the future."[20] Kuter became a zealous advocate for consolidating theater air forces into a single command and making the air command independent and coequal with ground command.

Lesley J. McNair and Ben Lear fought a rear guard action against radically revising doctrine. Lear argued if the air forces got too much independence, they would ignore the needs of the ground troops.[21] While their voices carried great weight on the subject of land combat, they were at a disadvantage in arguing for how air assets should be employed. General Arnold and the air staff had great authority over all matters dealing with the air forces. When the Army's revised air doctrine came out in 1943, what Kuter had wanted was exactly what it said.

By the advent of Normandy the organization of air defense had matured somewhat. Army and air headquarters were collocated, so that commanders and staff could coordinate on a daily basis. Air sections were established in the G-3 (the part of the staff responsible for operations and planning) at the field army, corps, and division levels. Dedicated radio nets were established to direct air-ground communications. And ground liaison officer ("Rover Joes") teams were established. They would travel from the division headquarters to battalions at the front to coordinate air strikes. They would carry a very high frequency (VHF) radio with them in a jeep.

Two procedures were developed to allocate air support to the ground troops—preplanned and immediate. Preplanned requests were developed by the tactical commanders and their staffs and relayed up to higher headquarters by radio, telephone, or teletype to the division and corps G-3 air officers and representatives from the air commands at their headquarters. Based on a proposed allocation of sorties for the next day's fighting, the command would deny or approve the requests. Requests were then sent to the field army headquarters which was collocated with the tactical air command post where they were collected and reviewed between 6 and 9 P.M. jointly by the army and air operations and intelligence staffs. Approved requests were sent to the fighter-bomber groups. At the groups a ground liaison officer would brief the pilots for the next day's mission.

Immediate requests were reserved to respond to unforeseen tactical situations when an urgent need for air support occurred. For immediate requests, Rover Joes would radio directly to the joint operations center at the field army/air tactical command post. Intervening headquarters monitored the requests on the radio. Their silence was considered consent. Approved requests went directly to the tactical control center, which alerted forward command posts who contacted the planes and vectored them toward their targets using radar.

It all sounded great—in theory.

But little of this system had been realistically practiced before the invasion. Bradley had wanted to conduct joint training, but the air commanders had no planes available as all of their assets were being used to establish air supremacy over France. By the time they were ready to conduct mock air-ground operations, it was too late. The ground troops had already been sent to the marshalling areas to prepare for the invasion.

Even if training had been conducted, it was questionable how realistic or useful it would have been. Most of the tactical staff had little experience in joint operations. It turned out that most G-3 air officers responsible for coordinating ground-support operations were wanting for talent. By the end of the first two weeks of the campaign, all of the corps G-3 air officers had been replaced.[22]

In practice what happened was that air and ground commanders figured out the most expedient procedures in battle based on intuition, trial and error, and experience. It was GI ingenuity in action. For Cobra, it was GI ingenuity on overdrive.

And GI genius was not reserved for ground pounders alone.

## BUCK ROGERS PAYS OFF

In the two decades following World War II, when the great heroes of the second great war were the great generals, not the greatest generation, some of those generals wore wings. The heroes of the air war were not combat aces, they were generals like Hap Arnold, Jimmy Doolittle, and Carl Spaatz. And they were bomber generals.

The great postwar air combat movie was about a bomber general. *Twelve O'Clock High* (1950) featured Gregory Peck as the austere and aloof bomber commander General Savage. The character by temperament and style greatly resembled Peck's portrayal of MacArthur. But while 1970 audiences turned a cold shoulder to *MacArthur,* 1950 moviegoers relished the professional, decisive General Savage, whose leadership, organizational genius, and personal sacrifice helped win the war. Bomber generals were the epitome of the industrial-strength hero.

In contrast, the air generals who fought the ground war were the forgotten generals of World War II. The best of the least known was Elwood R. ("Pete") Quesada. In 1995, when Thomas Alexander Hughes penned Quesada's biography, *Over Lord: General Pete Quesada and the Triumph of Tactical Air Power in World War II,* he wrote his book was "an effort to recover the lost memory" of the general and his wartime innovations.[23]

In Normandy, Quesada commanded IX Tactical Air Command (TAC) responsible for providing close air support to the First Army. It was his job to provide air cover for the breakout. It was a job that, before the war, Quesada would have never envisioned. When he attended the Air Corps Tactical School in 1935, it had really looked like the day of the fighter was over. In

1930, "pursuit," the principal role of the fighter, accounted for 50 percent of the classes. In 1935, it accounted for less than 15 percent. Bomber operations were over 80 percent. The class on "Aviation in Support of Ground Forces" consisted of one day of instruction.[24]

After the air school, Quesada attended the Command and General Staff College at Fort Leavenworth. There he got a slightly different appreciation of the role of airpower. At Leavenworth, Quesada made friends with a young armor captain named Maurice Rose. One tactical problem they worked on together posited the problem of an armored column under attack away from the main body—an engagement not dissimilar to the Battle at Tessy-sur-Vire. Quesada took notes about his observations. "Future war," he scribbled, "will require all sorts of arrangements between the air and ground, and the two will have to work closer together than a lot of people think or want."[25] Quesada was not a vocal proponent for the fighter like Chennault. In fact, at the time he saw a great deal of merit in the arguments made by the bomber boys. Still, he knew there was more to war than dogfighting and bomber raids. He just never thought he would be the one responsible for it.

Quesada was not the smartest officer that ever attended the Army's schools, but he was a skilled flyer and an energetic and creative officer that produced results. His talents did not go unnoticed. Before the U.S. entry into the war he served on Arnold's staff and as Marshall's personal pilot. When war came he was promoted to general. After a combat command in North Africa, he reported to England to prepare for the Normandy invasion. He would be Bradley's airman for the first two months of the American war in France.

In *Soldier's Story*, Bradley had hardly a harsh word for any general officer, but he went out of his way to offer special praise for Quesada. Bradley wrote,

> He was a brilliant, hard, and daring air-support commander on the ground. He had come into the war as a young and imaginative man unencumbered by the prejudices and theories of so many of his seniors on tactical air. To Quesada the fighter was a little-known weapon with vast unexplored potentialities in support of ground troops. He conceived it his duty to learn what they were. In England, Quesada first experimented with heavier bombloads for fighters by hanging their wings and bellies with more and heavier bombs. He even converted a squadron of fast, sleek Spits [Sptifires—British tactical fighters] into fighter bombers. When the British protested this heretical misuse of the fighter in which they took such pride, the imperturbable Quesada retorted, "But they're not your planes anymore—they're mine. And I'll do anything I want to with them."[26]

The GI general loved the GI genius in his air general.

Nor was Bradley's praise in his memoirs anything less than sincere. There is nothing but accolades and warmth for Quesada in Hansen's war diary of

Bradley's daily activities. In Hansen's sketchy war notes Quesada cut a romantic and admirable figure in his leather jacket and rumpled pilot cap. He did not wear his stars. He did not wear any insignia at all. He drove his own jeep and flew his own plane. He told funny stories at Bradley's mess. But he was more than just colorful. "Quesada and General [Bradley] agree perfectly on the use of air power," recorded Hansen. They see, "eye to eye," he added.[27]

Quesada saw it pretty much the same way. "I liked him right off," he recalled, "Brad did not tell me how to run the air war, and I did not interfere with the alignment of divisions along his front. We spent an awfully [sic] lot of time together in Normandy and we never once had a substantial disagreement."[28] There was no lack of goodwill between them. They would need it to solve the problems of air support for the breakout.

Both knew that neither the deliberate or immediate air-support procedures would be adequate for Cobra. They were designed to serve on relatively static battlefronts. If the divisions in the inner and outer rings moved as far and as fast as Bradley hoped, the deliberate procedures would be too slow. And if the armor units cut through and bypassed the German defenses as called for in the plan, the immediate procedures would not work either. Friendly and enemy forces would be intermingled on the battlefield without clear front lines. The likelihood of attacking the wrong targets or not finding the targets at all would be greatly increased.

Cobra required responsive and accurate air support, and that could be achieved only by close and continuous coordination between the ground columns and the air sorties.

Effective air-to-ground communication was the key. And since there was not a way to do that, the GIs came up with their own system.

Quesada developed a "column cover" technique. Each armor column would be supported by four to eight fighters armed with 500-pound bombs and machine guns. They would remain continuously with the column flying ahead and to the flanks to provide reconnaissance and always be available to conduct ground-support attacks. By flying with the column, communications would be less of a problem because the distance between the ground and air radios would be kept short and there would be less intervening terrain features to interfere with transmissions. Also, pilots and ground observers could remain in constant contact exchanging critical information. To ensure contact was continuous, new planes would be rotated on station with fresh ammunition and full stocks of fuel.

If additional support was needed, the pilots could call back to the tactical control center, which could either divert more in-flight aircraft to the target or launch additional fighters that were on "strip alert" (fueled and loaded with pilots aboard waiting at the airfield for orders to take off).

Quesada's command also developed means to get the planes to their targets when visibility was poor. The radar systems, such as the H2X, used to guide the bombers were not accurate enough for the fighters. In Normandy, the fighters were to be controlled by a radar system called a microwave early warning radar (MEW). Once the system was set up, it proved decent enough as a flight control tool, but it was virtually useless for directing planes to targets. The IX TAC signal staff wired a SCR-584 Close Control Unit (a very accurate close-range radar used for ground antiaircraft positioning and gun laying) combining its accuracy with the range of the MEW.[29]

Effective column cover tactics, however, required not only dependable, accurate, and responsive support from the air, but reliable direction from the ground. Quesada had figured that out, too. He insisted that the Rover Joes be not only Army Air Force officers, but experienced combat pilots who would understand fighter capabilities and tactics and more expertly advise the ground commanders. In addition, he took them out of their jeeps and put them in tanks, so they could keep with the armor units and have a decent chance of surviving in the chaos of battle.

There was just one problem with Quesada's idea—the radios in the tanks were not built to talk to airplanes. First Army had to come up with a means to install the air-to-air VHF radios in the tanks and make them work reliably.

Weeks before Cobra, two tanks were ordered for the IX TAC command post; the First Army ordnance officer thought it was mistake and sent them to the 9th Infantry Division. But the 9th Infantry Division had not ordered them and sent them back. Then they were sent to the IX TAC again. And again they were turned away. Delivering a tank to the IX TAC commander made no sense. Somebody must have made a mistake.

There was no mistake. Bradley had ordered the tanks. It was all part of a science project to figure out how to install and power a fragile ground-to-air radio in the cramped compartment of a tank that would rumble across the battlefield, plow through hedgerows, bounce in and out of craters, slosh through mud, and make it work reliably.

Through trial and error, the GIs figured it out. Rover Joes were posted in the lead tanks of each column and operated the VHF radio. They coordinated directly with the pilots. Ground commanders monitored the air radio channel to receive in-flight updates or request target attacks.

Three fighter groups were tasked to provide column cover for Cobra. Of the planned missions, 74 percent were dedicated to column cover and close air-support operations.[30] The entire system was in place in time for the breakout. Quesada was ready. "My fondness for Buck Rogers devices," he wrote home, "is beginning to pay-off."[31] At least that was what he thought. Maurice Rose, his old staff college classmate, hoped he was right.

## THE ROAD TO TESSY-SUR-VIRE

Rose knew that every leader in CCA was as tired as he was. Even when the troops did stop during their wild ride through enemy territory, there was no rest for the leaders. They would traipse back to the command post for new orders, then back to their headquarters to draft new plans, then issue their own orders, and then it was dawn and time to move again. And the more progress they made, the more changes in plans there were. Rose had just issued another new set of orders. At dawn, CCA would be on the road again.[32]

The commander of CCA had reorganized his force into three columns. One task force was to head south to secure the crucial high ground near Percy. Controlling the high ground meant controlling the town and the road junction, and with their control the CCA advance would be able to continue. Meanwhile, CCA's second column was ordered to Beaucoudray to cover the flank of the advance from attacks from behind.

The third column was headed southeast toward Tessy-sur-Vire; taking the town would complete securing CCA's flank because the town marked the crossing site of the Vire River. If CCA controlled the town, then any German counterattack force heading west would be stopped dead in its tracks, stuck with no way to get across the river.

That was the plan.

What CCA did not know was that the German 116th *Panzer* Division was headed toward Tessy-sur-Vire in force.

The CCA column that tried to enter the town included a company of medium tanks, a platoon of light tanks, a company of infantry, an assault gun platoon, a platoon of engineers, medical and maintenance detachments, and an armored reconnaissance platoon. It was only a few hundred men, but it seemed like more than enough combat power for the mission. Since the breakout, CCA had experienced no organized opposition. The counterattacks they had encountered had been hastily organized. The enemy's assaults were not combined-arms operations. They were not supported by artillery or air attacks. A few hundred men should have been more than enough to brush off the resistance they might encounter.

What the task force discovered when it reached Tessy-sur-Vire, however, was not disorganized, but armor from the German 2nd *Panzer* Division. Intelligence had warned the Americans of the division's movement west on July 27, 1944, and it predicted the division would try to cross the Vire River at Tessy-sur-Vire. It was hoped that CCA would get there first. It did not.

When Rose received the report of German tanks in the town, he was worried. He could not ignore a threat headed west right into his flank and continue the CCA advance to the south. If he did so, the whole command might be vulnerable. That would be bad news on a number of counts. A counterattack would cut CCA's supply lines and give the Germans good armor routes for driving back First Army's penetration. All the while, his units were reporting harassment from small detachments of retreating German forces up and down the line. Some units had even been strafed by enemy fighters.

Wars without fronts were just hell.

The situation called for yet another change of plans. CCA was to cede part of its flank to another division so that Rose could turn his attention to driving back the 2nd *Panzer* Division's bridgehead in Tessy-sur-Vire.

While Rose knew the *panzers* were in the town, he knew very little else about the situation. In particular, he did not know what the Germans were going to do next.

What the Germans were planning to do was attack. And they were attacking with some confidence. Another thing that Rose did not know was that the 116th *Panzer* Division was headed straight north aimed at the town with the mission of linking up and reinforcing the 2nd *Panzer*.

Oblivious to the threat of the 116th, Rose sent his troops back into Tessy-sur-Vire in force, backed up by a tank destroyer battalion. They arrived in time to meet the 2nd *Panzer* coming out. What followed was a desperate 13-hour battle in the streets and surrounds of Tessy-sur-Vire.

Lieutenant Colonel Carl Hutton, commander of the 14th Armored Field Artillery battalion, knew exactly how harrowing the battle was. At dawn on July 30, 1944, his battalion was headed toward Percy to reinforce the advance. At 11:30 A.M., Hutton got a call to turn the gunners around. CCA was locked in a precarious battle at Tessy-sur-Vire, and Rose ordered all available support for the task force in the town. Hutton ordered the firing batteries to take up position as soon as possible.

Doctrine usually called for artillery units to be one-third of their range behind the lines, which placed them back far enough to be out of the range of enemy mortars and direct-fire weapons. Tessy-sur-Vire was not a doctrinal battle. The gunners were so close, they were being shot at while they were shooting. They could see the enemy.

Friendly infantry forces began retreating through the artillery positions—not a good sign.

The artillery remained in place until German tanks were within 2,000 yards and then began to leapfrog back trying to just keep out of the range of the enemy armor.

Hutton needed help.

The 14th Field Artillery Battalion Fire Direction Center organized support from three additional artillery battalions that were within range of the battle.

The massed artillery fire blunted the German advance. In turn, the American tanks and antitank guns began to pick off the *panzers*. The tank destroyer battalion alone recorded 11 kills.

What Hutton and Rose did not know was that while their attention was turned on Tessy-sur-Vire, they were saved from the attack of the 116th by Quesada's column cover.

July 30, 1944, was a sunny, clear, perfect Normandy summer day, perfect weather for close air support … not that that made much of a difference to the soldiers fighting in the town. Air support proved to be of little help in the Battle of Tessy-sur-Vire. GI and Germans were mixed together. The planes could not attack.

Planes flying cover for CCA spotted the armored spearhead of the 116th before the Germans saw the first American tank. The cover sorties called for reinforcements. A swarm of fighter-bombers crowded the skies over CCA.

The 116th was doomed before the battle started. The German tanks did not have anything like Sergeant Culin's hedgerow cutter. They did not have an option. They could not negotiate the hedgerows. They were road bound. They were perfect targets for the fighters. They did not stand a chance.

Pilots looked down to see the *panzers* forming a long-winding ribbon of gray on the narrow Norman roads. It was a bomber's paradise. Almost as soon as the tanks were spotted, bombs began to rain down.

The counterattack failed, broken up before it even reached the enemy. By the end of the day on July 30, 1944, what Germans were left of the 2nd and 116th *Panzer* divisions were desperately trying to determine how they could withdraw without being annihilated. The chances of their turning back the breakout were nil.

From July 27–30, 1944, during the exploitation phase of the breakout, IX TAC flew 5,105 sorties. They had not, as airmen had often dreamed, won all the battles on their own, but thanks to GI ingenuity they had made a substantial contribution to ensuring Cobra's strike succeeded.

## WINNING HABITS

Quesada's innovations in air-ground operations were far from an anomaly. In every command and theater, GIs were scratching their heads, debating, discussing, experimenting, innovating, determining how to make air power an asset for the ground war. George Patton was among their number.

With the success of the breakout, Bradley moved up to become an army group commander, relinquishing command of First U.S. Army and activating Third U.S. Army for the drive into Brittany. The command of Third Army went to Patton, who after his relief in Sicily had been anxiously waiting for another combat command.

Patton's air support would come from XIX TAC commanded by Brigadier General Otto P. ("Opie") Weyland. Weyland arrived in England in January 1944. His fighter groups operated under Quesada until the tactical command was activated in France to support the Third Army. Weyland shared Quesada's frustration at the inability of the fighters to provide more effective support for the close battle.

Nobody envied Weyland's assignment as Patton's air general. Old Blood & Guts's distain for air generals was legion. In North Africa, Patton had shown nothing but disdain for the airmen. He wrote snidely of Kuter in his war diary, "some wonder boy."[33] Patton raised such a stink about the state of air support that prompted such a strain among the senior commanders, Eisenhower contemplated resigning.

Early on, however, like Quesada's relationship with Bradley, Weyland and Patton had reached an understanding. Weyland claimed he had "full control of the air. The decisions were mine as to how I would allocate the air effort."[34] In turn, Patton never had anything but praise for his senior air officer.

Patton had many quirks of character, but he respected leaders who could prove they could get the job done. And Weyland did, right from the start, supporting Third Army's rapid advance into Brittany, controlling nine flight groups, some 400 planes.

As with IX TAC, Weyland succeeded by ignoring doctrine and adapting his air forces to meet the needs of the situation. Patton's airman, concluded David Spires, "exemplified the type of practical leader who came to dominate tactical air operations ... . Weyland approached each situation on its own terms."[35] As the Normandy campaign progressed, he and Quesada rivaled each other for initiating creative new ways to serve the ground pounders better.

In fact, as the battle progressed from France to Germany, each of the four American field armies devised its own way to make the air-ground team work better. Everybody innovated.

There was a downside to all this exercise in imagination: procedures varied. In three of the field armies, for example, air-ground communications relied on Army Air Force communications networks, in the other field army, Army communications networks. Only one field army relied on airborne controllers to direct tactical air support. As a result, when the field armies fought side by side, they sometimes found they had difficulty supporting one another because their close air-support systems were not compatible.[36]

Nor was the northern European theater unique. Field expedient air-ground procedures were also developed in Italy.[37] Likewise, in the Pacific innovation and improvisation remained the hallmark of air operations.[38]

Air-ground operations during World War II illustrated the difference between the doughboy army and the GI fighting forces. In both cases, the genius of generals, the ability to organize, and to manage large-scale activities got the Americans to the war. During World War I, doughboy genius did not help take the last mile. The margin of victory often relied on brute force and raw courage alone. World War II was different. The overwhelming material advantages of the American forces got GIs to the fight and got them back into the fight after they were taught bitter lessons in close combat at places such as the Kasserine Pass and the Séves River. But the GIs added something more: they learned in battle and they innovated with technology and they made the force better, more efficient than the top-down directives of doctrine and general genius could ever have hoped to do.

# CHAPTER 7

# An Imagining of Armor

## THE SHAPE OF THINGS TO COME

OMAR BRADLEY HAD ALWAYS imagined the battle of Europe as a fast war of movement. The success of Cobra and the activation of George Patton's Third Army made that vision a real possibility.

In all aspects of human endeavor the future derives its form from the dreams of the present. Imagination matters. War is no exception. In part, World War II looked as GIs imagined it would. They had helped make the shape of things to come.

Armor played a big part of what many GI generals imagined the future of battle would be like. And like most American soldiers, their imagining of tomorrow's wars was, in part, borrowed. It was borrowed from science fiction writers.

Decisions in engineering and manufacturing and decisions in the application of technology to everyday life are not preordained. The application of any technology may often not make optimum use of that technology. It is just the application that is selected. In World War II, for example, the air forces had options for extending the range of their planes. They could build planes that could carry more fuel or they could employ air refueling. The Americans, the British, and the French had been experimenting with air refueling since the 1920s. When manufacturers moved from aircraft made of wood and fabric to metal, planes could carry a lot more weight. Refueling was discarded. Commercial firms designed airframes with greater organic fuel capacity. Designs for military planes followed suit. It was not until after the war that air refueling became integral to military aviation.[1]

Technology is as much about choice as it is about science. Therefore, it is not surprising that many of the choices of the American genius for war were influenced by science fiction. The industrial age was driven by men of drive and vision, not necessarily men of imagination. In contrast, at the turn of the century, imagination was the hallmark of science fiction. It was in the realm of science unbounded by engineering, the world of fiction, where technological choices were first made. And so it is of little wonder that when the time came to make the choices for real, manufacturers and generals often opted for the ones made by the men who conditioned their imaginations.

During the First World War, H.G. Wells, perhaps the preeminent science fiction writer of his day (and a wartime propagandist for the Allied cause), was asked to write the introduction to *Joseph Pennell's Pictures of War Work in England* (1917). The book contained illustrations of the various industrial activities supporting the war effort. "There is a delusion," Wells wrote in the preface, "that war is conducted and controlled by gentleman in red tabs, gold lace, and spurs ... it was only by the end of 1914 that the mass of people began to realize that there was a new sort of war in progress ... . The engineer has got hold of them. The avalanche of change has started."[2] War had become an industrial-strength activity.

To many, Wells would have been an obvious choice to write about the nature of modern war since he seemed to predict so much of it in his writings. In *The War in the Air* (1908), he wrote of large airborne *Drakenships* bombing cities. He also wrote of futuristic war on the ground. *The War of the Worlds* (1898) envisioned an invading armada from Mars that wiped out armies with large, metal, walking-tripod war machines powered by some fantastic combustion engine. It was a popularization of the conceptualization of mechanized warfare before the age of armor.

In the preface of *Pictures of War Work*, Wells warned that there was more of his imagining of war in the offing. "The form and texture of the coming things are not yet to be seen in their completeness upon the modern battlefield. One swallow does not make a summer, nor a handful of aeroplanes, a 'tank' or so, a few acres of shell craters, and a village here and there pounded out of recognition do more than foreshadow the spectacle of modernized war on land."[3] Industrial powers might make the mechanized war of tomorrow far more terrible than the trench wars of the present. The engineer was both the master and the slave of the future, Wells concluded, it all depended on the choices he made.

Before the war ended, debate over how choices would influence the future became joined in earnest. One of the most strident voices belonged to John Frederick Charles Fuller. When tanks were introduced as a wartime innovation, J.F.C. Fuller was a British staff officer in France, responsible for helping to plan some of the first major offensives employing the armored vehicles. He soon became an outspoken advocate for mechanized warfare, drafting a proposal, "Plan 1919," that called for a massive tank offensive backed by air attacks with an aim toward paralyzing the enemy's command. After the war he continued to press, largely unsuccessfully, for tank developments. He retired in 1933, continuing his advocacy for armor as a military journalist and a historian.

Fuller argued that the problem with tank tactics during the Great War was that armor was relegated to supporting the advance of the infantry. That was a mistake. Armor should be used in mass, employing penetration and envelopment tactics (similar to the plan for Cobra). Fuller argued for building mechanical armies with heavy tanks and motorized infantry and artillery to break through followed by light tanks, artillery, and vehicle-borne infantry to race into the enemy's rear; all resupplied by mechanical carriers.[4]

British tank developments during the interwar years were far too timid for Fuller. In 1927 the British formed an experimental tank force, but it led to nothing like the kinds of formations for which Fuller had hoped. "Clausewitz said that 'in war the simple is difficult,'" Fuller wrote in his memoirs in 1936, "he should have added 'in peace it is generally impossible.'"[5] Nothing was simple in the British army, railed Fuller, except simple-headed peacetime generals who failed to grasp the obvious importance of his ideas for the future.

In part, Fuller's proposals may have been unpopular because of his immense ego, difficult personality, and penchant for controversy. In part, Fuller was also shunned for his association with Britain's most outspoken Fascist, Oswald Mosley.[6] In part, however, it was also because many felt, wrote the Canadian Army officer and military historian Roman Johann Jarymowycz, that Fuller's ideas "bordered on science fiction."[7] Automotive technologies were not yet advanced enough to perform the kinds of miraculous feats Fuller envisioned. Most of the tank losses during the Great War, after all, were from mechanical failures. In the real world automotive technologies just did not seem capable of standing up to the rigors of battle.

To many Fuller's ideas seemed fantastic ... to others inevitable.

By the 1930s, the future world of science fiction did not seem like such a foreign country. Alexander Korda's 1936 film *Things to Come* told the tale of a 100-year-long mechanized Second World War that breaks out in the near future (1940). In the face of battles fought by tanks and planes, nations disintegrate into barbarism. The surviving communities are run by warlords until the civilization is resurrected under the guidance of the mysterious "airmen," a utopian people ruled by science. With over a million-dollar budget, it was one of the most expensive and ambitious films of the decade. Based loosely on Wells's book *The Shape of Things to Come* (1933), it proved a box-office failure. The film lacked strong characters and was weighted down with wooden acting and a preachy story. But moviegoers in Britain and America also turned away because after half a decade of the Depression, the rise of Fascism, and the outbreak of a Civil War in Spain (where terrible weapons like modern dive bombers debuted in battle on the doorsteps of Europe), they found the film's foreboding warnings of mechanized war all too real. Audiences were much more enamored with movie's such as the Oscar-winning *The Great Ziegfeld*. The biographical picture with 23 song and dance scenes about the successful Broadway producer helped them forget all their troubles.

## WHITHER THE CAVALRY

While many Americans hoped that mechanized war would remain a reality only in the canons of science fiction, some U.S. officers in the interwar years knew that it would not. Two of them were named Dwight Eisenhower and George Patton. After the Great War both of them reported to Camp Meade, Maryland, for duty in the fledgling U.S. Tank Corps. They spent a lot of time together musing over the future of tanks. "By themselves," records historian and retired military officer Carlo D'Este, "they stripped a tank down to its last nut and bolt and managed to put it back together—and make it run. They tinkered with supporting weapons and endlessly debated tank employment and the tactics of surprise."[8] They were curious about the future of war and technology.

At the time, military men such as Eisenhower and Patton were an exception. It would not remain so. While they disassembled tanks, teenagers were toying with jalopies and they avidly read a growing corpus of juvenile science fiction literature in "pulp" magazines (named for the cheap wood pulp paper they were printed on) like *Amazing Stories* founded in 1926. And they watched future wars on the Saturday movie screen at the Bijou. And it was science fiction with a serious militaristic streak, where bad guys were battled with spaceships, death rays, and futuristic armored vehicles. In World War II, these teenagers would be battalion and regimental commanders and staff officers ... zealots of GI ingenuity. And they expected to fight a mechanized war.

The debate over the kinds of technology these teenagers would have in their war was already well under way when Eisenhower and Patton played at tank mechanic in a drafty garage at Fort Meade, Maryland. Patton had met Fuller in France. In the first years after the war, however, it appears neither he nor Ike seemed to have known much of the ideas of Fuller, or of the other great British advocate for armored forces, B.H. Liddell Hart.[9] That would change. The great debate was just getting started.

There were three options for determining the future of tank developments: (1) make the Tank Corps independent, (2) assign the tanks to the cavalry branch, and (3) place armor under the command of the infantry. The Army's choice would determine how America prepared to employ the technology in the next war.

Option number one, an independent Tank Corps, which would have allowed its officers to chart their own future, much in the way the Air Corps plotted its own course, was never a realistic alternative. After the war, John Pershing disapproved of the idea. And no one was going to argue with the savior of Europe. In 1920, Congress barred the establishment of an independent armor branch by law.[10]

Fuller had made the case for option two, thinking of tanks as the next generation of cavalry, an exploitation force that would primarily operate behind enemy lines. "The horse's legs have been replaced by mechanical forces," Fuller wrote, "so should men's legs."[11] The U.S. cavalry branch, however, never made a serious effort to take control of mechanized warfare. The last chief of cavalry, Major General John K. Herr, proved particularly obstinate. His self-appointed mission was to preserve the place of the horse in modern war. In 1938, he even raised the issue of reinstituting the cavalry saber, which had been abolished in 1934. It was not that Herr opposed developing tanks, it was just that he refused to do so at the expense of eliminating horse cavalry. There simply was not enough money to support both. As late as 1940 he declared, "not one more horse will I give up for a tank."[12]

Armor development came under option three—the responsibility of the infantry. The infantry inherited a substantial inventory of armor from the short-lived Tank Corps, almost 1,000 vehicles. Many of them were parked at the Army Tank School at Fort Meade with dreamers like Eisenhower and Patton … and promptly forgotten.

In 1928, copying the British example, the Americans established their own "gasoline brigade," an experimental mechanized force.[13] As with the British experience, the project did not amount to much. In May 1931, the force was disbanded, and the remaining equipment was sent to Fort Knox, Kentucky, to form a cavalry unit, the 7th Cavalry Brigade Mechanized. Since Congress had directed that tanks belonged to the infantry, the post commander, Colonel Adna Chaffee, a cavalry officer and a zealot for armor (which often earned the rancor of his fellow horsemen), renamed them "combat cars." After that things became even more muddled. The infantry branch was assigned responsibility for developing heavy tanks to support the infantry, while the cavalry was supposed to develop light tanks for reconnaissance and security missions. Since neither branch proved terribly concerned about elevating the tank to a prominent role in warfare, Fuller's vision seemed like it would remain science fiction.

## THE ARSENAL OF DEMOCRACY

While tank developments in the United States lagged, America's capacity to prepare for industrial-strength armored warfare remained unparalleled. American industry was the wonder of the world. And it was a wonder not just in its production methods, but in research and development as well. And one of industry's greatest wonder boys, a self-taught engineer named J. Walter Christie, turned his genius toward the problem of armored warfare.

From 1916 to 1942, Christie produced a variety of designs for military equipment that were tested by the Army. Christie received his first contract for an experimental tank from the Ordnance Department in 1919. His designs were innovative, but in field tests they often proved unreliable. The imaginative engineer's combative personality and frequent disregard for contract specifications did not help matters. "Christie's position—indicative of his arrogance and condescending attitude that would plague his relations with the military for years," writes George Hoffmann, "was that he knew every phase of tank design and construction. He therefore saw no need to follow contract specifications. That did not sit well with Ordnance officers, who insisted that the specifications listed in the contract must be followed."[14] There were, however, bigger problems. By 1924, the Ordnance Department had already invested almost a million dollars in Christie's projects without a clear requirement for his inventions. The lack of consensus among Army leaders on what was needed retarded developments more profoundly than Christie's obstinate personality or the paucity of budget to develop and field modern tank forces.

While the military did little to exploit America's full potential for armored warfare, others were less reticent. The Russians invested in Christie's high-speed tank chaise design. Germans paid even more attention to American technical prowess. There was a reason why Henry Ford's autobiography became an instant best-seller in Germany. Germans had become enamored with the potential of centralized, large-scale, rational industrial production.

The debate over the future of industry in postwar Germany had a political as well as an economic dimension. Some in Germany's fledgling postwar democracy argued that capitalism was the guarantor of the American republic. The ideas of Frederick Winslow Taylor, or *Taylorismus* (scientific management), and *Fordismus* (mass production) equaled *Amerikanismus* and *Amerikanimus* equaled the marriage of democracy and technology that defined what made America great. Others argued that American industry merely produced a highly materialistic society, one that could be bested by an industrialized society committed to a higher calling. When the Nazis came to power, they brought with them a particular ideological view of technology. Technology in modern society had one purpose—to serve the state—and the Nazi state wanted fantastic war machines that could dominate land war-fare.[15] And while America slept, they built them. Americans did not.

In 1939, America's largest mechanized unit, the 7th Cavalry convoyed its 650 vehicles to New York City for the World's Fair, called the "World of Tomorrow." To some the sight of the 112 combat cars might have appeared like a scene right out of *Things to Come*. Only six years after the movie hit the screen, here were the glittering rows of war machines that looked not too different from the film's mechanized armies that devastated the earth. But in truth, the entire force laid out on the fields of Flushing in New York was obsolete by modern standards. At the same time America's Army put its meager armored column on display, Germany invaded Poland, triggering the Second World War.

In the first years of the war, the Europeans led the way in the development of mechanized tactics and technology. When the United States joined the conflict, it would build on those experiences.

After Pearl Harbor, Hollywood, like the rest of America, was roused from complacency. Before the Japanese sneak attack, studios that made promilitary films, such as *Sergeant York,* were accused of war mongering; now Hollywood like the rest of the nation was expected to take up arms. No film illustrated this transformation better than *Casablanca* (1942). The film starred Humphrey Bogart as Rick Blaine, expatriate American and owner of a nightclub that caters to all sorts of characters in an exotic North African city crammed with refuges from Europe. Set before the U.S. entry into the war, Bogart's enigmatic character, who moves from indifference and appease-ment to combating Nazis, served as a metaphor for America's end of isolationism.

The government's Bureau of Motion Pictures, which was established after the outbreak of the war to evaluate the film industry's activities, rated each film's contribution to the war effort. It gave *Casablanca* high marks. From the standpoint of the war information program," the bureau reported, "CASABLANCA is a very good picture about the enemy, those whose lives the enemy has wrecked and those underground agents who fight him unre-mittingly on his own ground. The war content is dramatically effective."[16] The government was pleased, so were moviegoers.

Americans did not even mind that Bogart did not get the girl (Ingrid Bergman). He sacrificed love in the name of something greater—the pursuit of liberty. *Casablanca* was a box-office smash. Americans were ready to go to war.

When the American colossus awoke, it was, according to John Steele Gordon, "one of the most astonishing feats in economic history. In the first six months of 1942, the government gave out more than $100 billion in military contracts, more than the entire gross national product of 1940."[17] The Ford Motor Company alone produced more material than the entire Italian economy, including part of a large fleet of over 86,000 tanks that equipped both U.S. and Allied forces.[18] There was no nation on earth more prepared to undertake industrial-strength warfare.

The automobile industry was at the heart of the mobilization of American industry. When war came the industry had operations in 44 states and 1,375 cities. It employed over 500,000 people. It consumed the vast quantity of raw materials used in the United States. That changed overnight. The government ordered an end to the production of commercial automobiles; the last one rolled off the line on February 10, 1942. The next day the entire industry was turned over to war production. Among its production, the industry turned out 80 percent of the tanks and tank parts.[19]

And American industry gave the Army the tanks it wanted. There were two of them. One was the Stuart "light" tank. The Stuart M3 tank was obsolete when the war started and did not get much better. It weighed only 14 tons and sported a 250-horsepower engine. That made it relatively fast. It could hit speeds up to 36 miles per hour. But the cost of speed was armor and armament. The thickest armor on the M3 was a paltry 1.75 inches and its 37-mm main gun fired a projectile that could not pierce two inches of steel at a thousand yards, making the M3 barely a threat to another M3. The Army redesigned the Stuart with a bigger engine, designated it the M5, and awarded a production contract to the Cadillac division of General Motors.

The Stuart tank was ready for battle in time for the North Africa campaign. It had some utility in the Pacific theater against light Japanese combat vehicles, but in Normandy the Stuarts were next to useless. In bocage fighting, most armored battles took place at short range against heavily armored vehicles; killing power and armor protection was much more important than speed.

The workhorse of the American armor was the Sherman tank. Designed in 1941, some 40,000 of them were made by American factories; the most common version was the M4A3. At 34 tons, it was considered a medium tank. It sported three machine guns and a 75-mm main gun. The hallmarks of the tank were a simple design, great durability, mechanical reliability, good speed, and excellent handling. It could definitely outmaneuver the larger and unwieldy larger German tanks in the confined fighting spaces of the hedgerows.

There was only one problem with the Sherman in a tank fight—the two main German tanks employed in Normandy had thicker armor and more high-powered main guns. A Sherman might be able to hold its own against the older *Panzerkampfwagen* (Pzkw) IV, but it was definitely outclassed by the Pzkw V ("Panther"), which weighed in at 55 tons. A Sherman could defeat a Panther only by a carefully placed shot against its thinner flank or rear armor.

Enemy tanks were not the only problem. American armor was also vulnerable to mines, well-aimed infantry antitank rockets (*panzerfaust*), and the high-velocity German antiaircraft guns that were often used as antitank weapons.

GIs could have had a better tank, but the Americans opted for quantity over quality. They had tried to avoid the problem with industry in World War I, when they had fixated on coming up with innovative, cutting-edge technological designs that would outclass the other world's armies. The problem was by the time they got into production, the Great War was over. Instead, the Americans opted to keep it simple—two tanks, two simple requirements.

There were, of course, other reasons why manufacturers were not more adaptive and innovative. The "fog" of industrial war, debates over the allocation of resources (which were scarce, such as how much steel was available and the amount of room on ships to carry equipment overseas), and bureaucratic infighting limited what could be accomplished.[20]

A decision was also made early on that limited what the Americans thought was needing to be done. From the onset, Lesley J. McNair, the head of Army Ground Forces (AGF), favored antitank systems. McNair looked at war from an industrial-production perspective. Armored commands were inordinately expensive. Everything had to be put on wheels to keep up with the tanks. That meant not only a lot more vehicles and with them requirements for more steel, rubber, and glass, but more maintenance units, and depots, and oil, gas, and grease. McNair thought a heavy investment in tank destroyers would offset the requirement for heavier tanks and more armored divisions. "Certainly it is poor economy to use a $35,000 medium tank," McNair reasoned, "to destroy another tank when the job can be done by a gun costing a fraction as much."[21] And as the air maneuvers of the 1930s reinforced the Air Corps' predilection for strategic bombing, so did the AGF find that the Louisiana Maneuvers validated a preference for heavy dependence on tank destroyers. And, as Henry "Hap" Arnold largely got his way on air matters, McNair heavily influenced decisions regarding ground warfare.

The only problem was that the antitank weapons the Americans fielded were not much of a match for German armor. Each U.S. infantry regiment had a company of towed antitank guns. The GIs called them the "wonder weapon." They were so ineffective it was a wonder the Army ever bought them. They had poor cross-country mobility, little protective plating, and could take on a tank only at point-blank range. In Normandy, they were effective only when perfectly camouflaged and set up in a defensive situation for armor ambushes.

Tank destroyer battalions consisting of M10s armed with 3-inch guns were the primary American antitank weapon for the Normandy campaign. The battalions were a field army asset that could be attached to corps and divisions as needed. The tank destroyer battalions also proved a poor match for German tanks. On occasion, particularly in defensive situations, the tank destroyers acquitted themselves well. They played, for example, a significant role in fighting off the 2nd *Panzer* at Tessy-sur-Vire. More often than not, however, they were used as tank substitutes to support the infantry.[22]

## TOUJOURS L'AUDACE

When it came to armored warfare, the GIs had more problems than just being outgunned and outarmored by the *panzers*. Neither the doctrine nor the organization for armor that the Americans started the war with proved to be adequate.

Before the war, the only thing the Army's capstone manual, titled *Tentative Field Service Regulations, Operations* (1939), had to say about operations of infantry with tanks was that they would probably be "faster." After decades of debate and experimentation, the Army concluded that the role of the armor in the next war would be the same as it was in the last—support the infantry. The manual, according to historian William O. Odom, "simply reflected accepted views and demonstrated capabilities of American tanks … ."[23] Almost nothing had changed. Over the course of the war tank doctrine would have to be revised at least twice.

After the astonishing accomplishment of the *Wehrmacht panzers* during Germany's lightning victory over France, nobody argued anymore that American doctrine was adequate. It would have to change. It was revised in 1942.

The doctrine that the GIs took to war emulated the Germans in that it envisioned armor operating in regiments with supporting arms (like infantry and artillery) attached to support armored maneuver. But this doctrine did not hold up well for close combat in North Africa for either the Germans or the Americans—the Americans least of all. The Kasserine Pass was a failure in many respects, not the least of which was the poor employment of U.S.

armor. Bradley recorded in *A Soldier's Story* what he was told by veterans of the battle from the 1st Armored Division. "Initially, our tankers had galloped like cavalrymen into the offensive," he wrote, "trusting rashly in the speed of their vehicles and in the thickness of their armor. Unfortunately neither helped them when the Germans antitank gunners came within range."[24] The Americans lost 183 tanks and 104 half-tracks (a combination of a wheeled and a tracked vehicle). The 2nd and 3rd Battalions of the 1st Armored Regiment lost so many tanks that for a while they had to be combined into the 23rd Battalion.[25]

Oddly enough, in 1943 Humphrey Bogart, now a box-office superstar thanks to his role in *Casablanca,* starred in one of the few major war films that featured a tanker. In *Sahara,* Bogart, the tough-as-nails crew chief of a tank, is lost in the desert after helping turn back the Germans at the Battle of El Alamein. Along with a small group of stragglers he holds out at a watering hole against hundreds of attacking Germans. It was an exciting and engaging film—and about as divorced from the reality of the American armored warfare experience in North Africa as it could possibly be. Bogart spends most of the film fighting on foot as an infantryman. That is just as well because there were no American armored victories to make movies about. There were no U.S. tank troops at El Alamein.

What American tankers mostly did in North Africa was learn. Military historian Christopher Gabel writes, "new forms of fighting evolved that emphasized intimate cooperation among the arms. Increasingly, tanks and infantry integrated their actions at the small unit level. Patience and thoroughness in small unit armor tactics became more important than dash and speed. Infantry learned to guide the tanks over the terrain, leading them around obstacles, pointing out enemy strong points, and actually protecting the tanks from hostile antitank weapons. In return, tanks knocked out automatic weapons strong points located by the infantry and provided close-range fire support … ."[26] Armored division operations might be armor heavy, but they would have to be combined-arms operations.

Likewise, the organization of America's tank commands required updating. There would be six major reorganizations of the armored forces during the course of World War II.

In 1939, before the German *blitzkrieg* there was no armored force. What the Army had done was complete its plans to reorganize its infantry forces into triangular divisions. They were to be supported by tank battalions provided by the field army.

In 1940, Chaffee was put in command of the newly established Armored Force. In included two prototype triangular divisions, the 1st and 2nd Armored Divisions. In addition to two armored regiments with their complement of light and heavy tanks, there would be a regiment of armored infantry on half-tracks with an open bay in the back for carrying infantry. They were not fighting vehicles. Half-tracks were intended to carry the troops to battle where they would dismount and fight on foot. There were also three armored artillery battalions, with the 105-mm howitzers mounted on tank chaises.

In 1942 there were 14 armored divisions. But as the divisions were being equipped, the plan for how they would be organized and employed had already begun to change. Chaffee proposed establishing a special Armored Corps consisting of three divisions, two armored and one infantry. The corps headquarters had already been designated when, in 1942, McNair scrapped the plan only months after it had been implemented. The highest level of independent armor command in the Army would be the division.

In 1943, McNair again revisited the organization of the armored division. It was, he felt, simply too big, with its complement of almost 16,000 men, 232 medium tanks, and 158 light tanks. He complained the division structure "was so fat there is no place to begin."[27] Combat experience, McNair argued, showed that tanks could never operate without infantry. The infantry divisions needed more tanks; and the armored divisions, which were supposed to be for exploitation operations (and therefore should see less heavy fighting), could make do with less armor. McNair proposed creating more separate tank battalions to support the infantry divisions at the expense of smaller armored divisions. The 1943 reorganization removed 4,000 troops and 56 medium and 83 light tanks from the armored division organization.

In 1944, the 2nd and 3rd Armored Divisions were already in England preparing for the invasion when the reorganization was announced. They went to Normandy as "heavy" armored divisions. The other U.S. armored forces for Normandy were organized as "light" armored divisions with 10,937 troopers, 186 medium tanks, and 77 light tanks.

Even as doctrine and organization evolved, there were still two fundamental issues that had to be resolved before armor could conduct effective combined-arms operations and live up to one of Patton's favorite quotes from the Prussian warrior-king Frederick the Great—*L'audace l'audace, toujours l'audace*. There were no answers to these issues in Army doctrine. They were not resolved in the swamplands of Louisiana. They could not be solved by industrial-age genius with clipboards and stopwatches. Both of the big issues for armor largely got solved on the battlefield, and the resolution was the product of GI ingenuity.

Issue one was determining the best way to "task organize" armored columns for combat. The Germans had developed techniques for organizing combined-arms forces for individual missions or tasks. They called them *kampfgruppen*. The Americans called them task forces. In fact, as the war progressed every army fought at the tactical level employing some kind of combined-arms team that was tailored by commanders on the ground to suit the situation. Even the U.S. Infantry divisions, which were supposed to get supporting units from the field army (such as tank support and extra artillery) for particular missions, found that they almost always needed these assets and they had to organize with the forces in the infantry regiments. Regiments were often referred to as "regimental combat teams," reflecting that their composition included other units from the division and echelons above the division. The difference between the American infantry and armored divisions was that infantry regiments task organized as a matter of course; the armored divisions in Normandy were specifically designed to be task organized.

In March 1942, the Army abolished the fixed armored brigades that comprised the armored division. Instead, each armored division was organized with two independent command headquarters Combat Command A (CCA) and Combat Command B (CCB). The division's two armored and one armored infantry regiments, as well as the rest of the support units, would be organized under them. Each combat command consisted of a mix of tank and armored infantry battalions, at least one artillery battalion, and a collection of other supporting units including an antiaircraft battery, an engineer company, a tank destroyer company, a medical company, and a maintenance company. The remainder of the division, designated the division reserve and commanded by the armored infantry regimental commander, was referred to by the name of the commanding officer or simply called the division reserve or CCR. Eventually, the regimental headquarters were abolished and the third combat command was formally added to the division structure.

Within the combat commands, battalions further task organized into task forces, crossattaching infantry and armored companies and platoons to form combined-arms company teams. Commanders designated the task force by letters (such as "Task Force A") or numbers (such as "Task Force X") or just the name of the commander (for example, "Task Force Roysdon"). The composition of the task force was determined by the mission. In the case of CCB (3rd Armored Division), which supported the 1st Infantry Division's push to Marigny, because they had to fight through the enemy's main defense belt, the units had a lot of infantry support. On the other hand, when Maurice Rose's CCA, 2nd Armored Division, made its dash to the Vire River through a disorganized enemy, the lead task forces were predominantly armored units.

The ability to task organize allowed for a lot of options in employing the armored division's combat power. There was, however, no suitable official guidance on how to exploit this flexibility. Some commanders tasked organized frequently. During Cobra, Rose reorganized almost on a daily basis. His decision to add the tank destroyer force for the Battle of Tessy-sur-Vire proved key. The guns reportedly took out almost a dozen armored vehicles. On the other hand, some commanders preferred to keep units together on a semipermanent basis relying on the cohesion, trust, and confidence of a continuing working relationship between units as the best means to adapt to events on the battlefield. It was a system optimized for leaders who were good judges of men and machines, who understood the capabilities and limitations of each, and how to creatively get the most out of what was available. It was a system custom-built to exploit GI ingenuity.

The second serious issue for the armor was how to coordinate tanks with infantry in close combat. It was a task not well understood before men went into battle. Lack of suitable doctrine was a hindrance. Lack of adequate communications was a killer.[28]

The problem of infantry-armor communications was not a simple one to solve. There was limited space inside a tank. The tank compartment had to provide room for a crew of four, plus ammunition and supplies, as well as radios. Radios could communicate only on one frequency at a time, and there was always more than one person that a tanker would have to talk to. Tank commanders would, of course, want to communicate with the tanks on their left and right. But they also had to talk to higher headquarters, and the artillery, the infantry, reserves, and air support. That meant a Hobson's choice. For radios to communicate with one another, they had to be tuned to the same frequency, called a radio net. There was no physical limit to how many radios could operate on the same net, but there was a practical limit. Only one subscriber could talk at a time. If more than one radio operator tried to transmit at the same time on the same net, their signals would overlap and, likely as not, no one listening on the net would be able to hear anyone else. This was often called "stepping on" another operator communicating on the same net. To make matters worse, if two or more operators transmitted at the same time, they had no way of knowing that their messages had not been heard until they waited for a reply. It could all get very confusing, very quickly. And in the heat of battle, when emotions and adrenaline ran high, and screams could be heard over the radio, it could prove hard to discipline all the operators to wait their turns. Having too many people on one net could be a disaster.

Another problem was that not all infantry and armor radios were compatible. The Army had simply not built radios for individual tanks to communicate with squads of infantry. In the infantry division, for example, only the infantry company commander had a radio that could talk to the tanks. In tank platoons, only the tanks of the platoon leader and the platoon sergeant could talk to the infantry. Even the armored infantry, which was designed to work with armor, had issues. There was no room for both infantry and radios in the half-tracks. That was a problem. The radios needed to be protected from enemy fire and be easily accessible so that close coordination between the half-tracks and the tanks could be maintained.

These problems were not only perplexing, they were not even new. Bradley warned the troops in a pre-D-Day speech that he had seen these kinds of difficulties in North Africa. Infantry-armor communication was a particular bugbear. "Some method of communication ought to fixed up," he advised.[29]

In Normandy, integrating armor and infantry again proved no easy task. The commander of the 9th Infantry Division in Normandy was so frustrated over breakdowns in tank-infantry coordination that he threatened to court-martial any tanker who withdrew, abandoning its infantry support.[30] The first time tanks from the 3rd Armored Division were committed to battle in Normandy, the commander of one of the infantry divisions being supported called "Lightning Joe" Collins, the VII Corps Commander, and cried, "Please get them out of our hair!"[31]

Even after the Americans broke through the enemy lines, there were challenges to employing the infantry-armor team. In fast-moving situations, the armor remained skittish of running head-on into an ambush of *panzerfausts* or the dreaded German antitank guns. On the other hand, unless pressed, infantry could prove reluctant to dismount and clear the path for the tanks. One after-action report complained, "Mech infantry often refused to dismount when ordered by the local OC [officer in charge] if their officer was not in the half-track—they preferred to stay instead [of] searching hedgerows … instead they crouched in their track and sprayed the hedges with MG [machine gun]."[32] The infantrymen were worried about snipers and machine guns, opting for the safety of the half-track and the protection.

Likewise, the armor without aggressive infantry support could become more conservative. "The tanks wouldn't move until the inf[antry] knocked out the [antitank] guns," one officer in the 9th Armored Infantry Battalion reported, "Inf[antry] were constantly ahead of the tanks; tks[tanks] didn't do much firing … said they were getting. Inf[antry] was widely deployed and after they'd cleared up resistance on flanks tanks just rolled up road."[33] It was a challenge for commanders to make sure both the armor and the infantry practiced *l'audace*.

If grunts and tankers wanted to talk to each other in battle and work together as a effective team, they and their leaders pretty much had to figure it out on their own. Some units, such as the 2nd Infantry Division in the Battle of Hill 192, devised intricate hedgerow-busting tactics. Others such as the 1st Infantry Division developed close relationships with their supporting armor unit. In the case of the Big Red One's 18th Infantry Regiment attack on Marigny, it was well supported by a company from the 745th Tank Battalion that habitually supported Colonel George Smith's infantry.

Units also improvised communications. In some instances both tankers and infantry units carried infantry man-portable radios so they could talk to each other. In other cases, tankers installed infantry radios inside their tanks. Others attached a field telephone to the rear of the tank and linked it to the tank's intercom system. In that manner, infantrymen could communicate directly with the tank commander.[34] Whatever tactic or innovation they come up with, it was all done on the job by GIs.


## THE PROFESSOR

No division tackled the issues of making armor an effective part of a combined-arms team better than John S. "Professor" Wood's 4th Armored Division, the spearhead of Patton's Third Army. In the days following Cobra, the division not only led the way into Brittany, it made significant contributions to turning the flank of the *Wehrmacht* forces in Normandy.

Like Eisenhower, John Shirley Wood went to West Point to play football. (He had already had a respectable football career at the University of Arkansas.)

Wood was also smart. He graduated 12th in his class. Wood made a habit of helping his classmates in academics as well as in football. That earned him the nickname "P," cadet jargon for "professor." It stuck with him the rest of his life.

During the Great War, Wood served as a staff officer in France, not a combat line officer. There were no medals or battlefield promotions. His career during the interwar years was thoroughly unremarkable. He passed through a number of modest positions, most with the field artillery. Absent another war, it is unlikely his service would have been much remembered in any way.

In 1940, Patton recruited Wood to join the newly formed 2nd Armored Division. When John Herr, the Chief of Cavalry, heard about the assignment, he asked Wood incredulously, "Are you going down to join that bunch of starry eyed s.o.b's?"[35] He was.

Wood flourished in the armor. Wood was a thinker. When he served together with Patton at Fort Leavenworth, Kansas, and Schofield Barracks in Hawaii, Wood spent many hours in Patton's extensive military library reading, drinking, and debating the tactics for the next war. All that imagining of the future had mattered little in the dreary day-to-day world of the interwar army and a series of lackluster, uninspiring assignments (including

Larger than Life—John Wood, Commander of the 4th Armored Division. (Courtesy, Omar N. Bradley Collection, Military History Institute)

receiving a below-average rating as a "post dump officer.") Armor, however, was different. It fired his imagination.

In June 1941, "P" Wood was appointed chief of staff for one of the newly established armor corps headquarters. The assignment did not last long. The next year General McNair decided that all corps headquarters would be the same, responsible for commanding either infantry or armored divisions. The professor was disappointed, but pleased to leave staff duty for a command position. In May 1942, he took over the newly established 4th Armored Division.

From the outset the professor earned a reputation as a trainer and an experimenter. He had "ideas and was willing to give them without reserve."[36] The professor was particularly interested in testing the limits of the division's ability to task organize. According to one division officer, battalions were "traded off one for another, added to or taken away from combat commands in the middle of training exercises till we learned to make these switches with no diminution of effectiveness."[37] Wood's insistence on dabbling with innovation and trying out unorthodox ideas almost earned his relief before he ever saw a day combat.

The 1941 General Headquarters Maneuvers in Louisiana served as the proving ground for many of the American Army's concepts for land warfare. In many respects, particularly for pointing out the shortfalls in large-scale operations and field logistics, they served well. They were less useful in measuring the value of armor in combat or determining how to best employ tanks in the close battle. But that mattered little to McNair and Ben Lear; by 1942 all the big decisions had been made, the contracts let, the doctrine written. The Army knew how it was going to war. The Tennessee Maneuvers of 1942, which Wood's 4th Armored participated in, had one main purpose: to certify that divisions were ready for duty overseas. That was *not* how Wood saw it.

Wood planned his operations for the maneuvers, much as Patton had done when he commanded the 2nd Armored Division, to experiment with how to get the most out of the shock and speed of an armored force. Lear, who oversaw the training, was more concerned that the exercise went on for the prescribed number of days and that the prescribed tasks required to be performed were conducted and adequately evaluated. According to one participant in the exercise, before leaving for a brief trip to Washington, D.C., Lear lectured all concerned about the "propensity of the 4th Armored Division to move and operate under the cover of darkness, and the inability of [the] umpire to restrain the division in order to drag the maneuver problems out to their planned duration. He stated in no uncertain terms that the problem scheduled to be held during his absence was to go for a minimum of three days, or the responsible individuals would suffer dire consequences."[38] The maneuvers were tests—not free play exercises.

The battle ordered by Lear lasted little more than a day. Wood's command had taken every objective. There was not much the umpires could do. When Lear returned, he was angry—very angry. At the critique of the exercise, he castigated the division's performance pretty sternly. Using the notes provided him by the umpires, he recounted every mistake made. The division chief of staff recalled, "P was boiling mad at this. He asked Lear if he could talk and took the stage … . Lear ordered him off the stage. He shook his finger [under] P's nose. I rushed on the stage, pushed between them and led P to his car and we left for camp … ."[39] Other accounts of the incident vary in the details, but they all agree it was vintage Wood. There was a reason why Wood was also known as "Tiger Jack." When he thought he was right, he would argue with anyone, even generals such as Lear and Patton, who would brook criticism from few men.

In facing up to Lear, Wood had wanted to make a point. Lear, he felt, was too critical of the mistakes made by junior leaders. The professor was zealous in his defense of the division and the practice of allowing junior leaders to innovate, make mistakes, and learn from their experiences, both their failures and their successes.

Long before the division entered battle, Wood had honed one of the most important attributes of great American generalship in World War II. Wood let the greatest generation be the greatest generation. He was a fanatical trainer, but his training methods were not the stuff of the industrial age. They were not the military's version of Taylor's scientific management practices. Rather, Wood's training and leadership techniques were tailored to the character of the GI generation, encouraging leaders to become independent thinkers, operators, and innovators. Lear was an "old army" soldier who still treated war as a matter of sound business practices. Wood thought differently.

It was not the last harsh words Tiger Jack would have with a senior commander. Eventually, it would cost him his job.

The showdown with Lear, however, did not keep the Professor from taking his division to England and Normandy.

When the division finally arrived in France, a good month after D-Day, Wood had to make the case for not immediately throwing his troops into battle. While Bradley was desperate for infantry to help out in the hedgerow fighting, Wood argued against sending his forces in too soon. He had trained his armored infantry to work with the division's tank units; if they were used up in bocage fighting, they would not be ready to exploit the breakout when the time came. When the time came, he told Bradley they would be ready.

Wood won the argument.

## ROAD TRIP

From the first battles in Normandy it was clear that Wood's training paid off. The Professor would issue brief "mission-type" orders (usually verbally), giving commanders their assignments and his intent for the operation. He would let them figure out the best way to get the job done, without a lot of detailed supervision. It was a command style that served him well throughout the campaign—and one well suited to exploiting GI ingenuity.

Professor Wood was 56 years old when he led his division into France. He had no trouble trusting commanders who worked for him who were half his age. One of the best of the breed was Wood's most famous battalion commander—Creighton Abrams.

When the 4th Armored Division debuted in combat during operation Cobra on July 28, 1944, Abrams commanded the 37th Tank Battalion. Over the course of the campaign, few armored commands would go farther and faster than those led by "Abe" Abrams. His first day in battle, however, was hardly a promising start. The division had been attached to the corps on the west flank of the breakthrough; the "hammer" whish was supposed to crush the enemy in front of it after the Germans had been cut off and encircled by Collins's VII Corps. What happened proved far less dramatic. Most of the German forces on the flank of the Cotentin Peninsula withdrew at the first sign of the American envelopment. Some, such as Lieutenant Colonel Friedrich August Freiherr von Heydte, were squandered in a futile counterattack against the 2nd Armored Division. Others fled straight south to assist in the defense of Brittany.

Despite the fact that the Germans had run away, it still took some time to get the 37th Tank Battalion and the rest of the 4th Armored Division into battle. The path in front of them was crammed with American infantry and minefields that had been left behind by the Germans. Clearing the mines and maneuvering through the traffic jams would consume the better part of the day. It was not a promising start for Bradley's fast war of movement.

One of the first rounds fired by the division in anger was shot at what turned out to be troops from the U.S. VII Corps. The 37th Tank Battalion's first engagement with the enemy also happened by accident. On July 30, 1944, while refueling, there were reports of Germans in the woods. Two companies went to investigate and came back with 158 prisoners.[40] It was an easy victory, but in a way a bit disappointing. Instead of lightning war, all the armor had encountered so far were GI traffic jams and demoralized Germans.

The accidental engagements in the first days of the campaign meant only one thing—the enemy's main defensive belt had completely collapsed; Abrams and his battalion would be conducting pursuit and exploitation, the mission that the armored divisions had dreamed about. It was a mission that Abrams had spent two years preparing for.

Creighton Abrams also went to West Point to play football. By the time he graduated from the academy in 1936, he never made better than third-string. He would prove to be a much better soldier. In July 1942, Abrams took command of his battalion in the newly established 4th Armored Division. In the interwar army it was common for battalion commanders to be well over 40, with over 20 years of active service. Abe was 27 years old.

From his first days in command, Abrams began to innovate. According to his biographer, the distinguished military historian and veteran armor officer Lewis Sorley,

> in the battalion headquarters there were only two medium tanks authorized, one for the battalion commander and one for the executive officer. Abrams withdrew a tank and crew from each of his three medium tank companies and those tanks to his S-3 (operations officer), S-2 (intelligence officer), and liaison officer. This permitted him to use those officers in an overwatching role when he committed a tank company to combat. As the level of experience of company commanders progressively declined over the months in combat (due to death or evacuation of incumbents, and their replacement by more junior or greener people), the steadying influence of the accompanying staff officers became more and more important. Underlying Abrams's ability to use that technique were the early organizational changes he made to provide them with tanks.[41]

It was GI ingenuity from the start.

With the success of Cobra assured, CCA, 4th Armored Division was ordered to secure the bridges and dams on the Sélune River, opening up the routes to the Brest Peninsula. It was a classic exploitation mission. CCA task organized into four task forces, each containing some of Abrams's tanks. Abrams commanded one of the task forces, which secured four bridges during the advance. The Americans now basically had an open door into the rest of France. Abrams would routinely accomplish similar missions throughout the European war. Few tankers earned a greater reputation for innovation, tactical prowess, and aggressive combat leadership.

On August 1, 1944, the Third Army under Patton was formally established with the troops of Abrams's battalion and the rest of Wood's 4th Armored Division under the command of "Old Blood & Guts." The division's mission had been to secure Rennes, the capital of Brittany. On establishing Third Army, Patton ordered the tankers to push all the way to Quiberon, taking the port there as well, and, in effect, cutting off the whole peninsula. By the end of the day, the division was not only the first American division to enter Brittany, it had pushed 40 miles toward Rennes.

One of Wood's first actions was to establish liaison with Patton's air force, XIX TAC, commanded by Opie Weyland. The division had had no air support in the first days of the campaign and it was anxious to try out the concept of employing armored column cover and the tank-mounted air support parties. The planes of "Yellow Leader" (codeword for XIX TAC) had a close working relationship with "Eggcup" (codeword for the 4th Armored Division). Over the days ahead Weyland's fighters would cover the entire flank of the advance with airpower. On August 1, 1944, Weyland sent five massed sorties into the area during the day and kept planes in the air all night despite the risks.[42]

The first significant contribution that Weyland's fighters made was that they did not attack Wood's tankers. "The 4th Armored Division was near Rennes," Patton wrote in his notes of the campaign:

> Here a very amusing thing happened. About an hour before sundown we received a report that an armored column was fifteen kilometers southwest of Rennes, moving rapidly. I asked General Weyland, commanding the XIX Tactical Air Command, to send some fighter bombers to stop it. The bombers were unable to find the column, because it actually was the 4th Armored Division moving in from the northeast. However, the planes did do some very effective work knocking out enemy resistance ahead of the 4th Armored Division and this was the precursor of many other such jobs. It was love at first sight … .[43]

Without question, airpower had helped speed the armor's advance.

Getting air support was not all that Wood was interested in. He also wanted to reevaluate the division's mission. The German forces in Brittany were trapped, but rooting them out of Rennes and the port facilities would require some time, a mission Wood felt that could be better managed by follow-on units. Rather than continuing to press westward toward the Atlantic Ocean and a deadend, he wanted to press eastward toward Chartres and make the division the end of a sweeping envelopment of the German force in Northern France.

What followed was a continuing series of misjudgments, miscommunications, and misunderstandings from the army level to the task forces.[44] At the same time, the division began to run low on fuel and remained frustrated at the seemingly slow rate of resupply. There was a reason for that. As the Allies turned to exploit the success of Cobra, operations in Brittany had shifted from the main effort to a secondary concern. The major flow of the Allied supply lines shifted with them. In the end, these factors prevented the 4th Armored Division's exploitation from being as bold as it could have been and delayed in seizing the ports long enough to give the Germans time to organize their defenses and scuttle most of the port facilities, requiring weeks and months of repair before they could be made operational.

Wood grumbled, "Can achieve impossible but not yet up to miracles."[45]

Perhaps Tiger Jack was too hard on himself and his commanders. Even with all the miscues, it was not a bad first few days at war. The division had

German Vehicles Blocking the Advance of the 4th Armored Division Destroyed by Close Air Support. (Courtesy, Army Signal Corps)

covered a lot of ground, cut off a lot of Germans, and helped turn the flank of the enemy army—not bad for a rookie division.

## FARTHER AND FASTER

If industrial-strength warfare was the musical equivalent of fine classical music—a carefully prepared, well-orchestrated, organized, and disciplined flourish of notes—a grand symphony; then GI ingenuity was jazz (the music of the GI generation), improvisational and creative. When they were brought together, as they were in Cobra and the operations in its aftermath, at times they could sound a bit discordant. That was, in part, to be expected; genius does not eliminate the chance and difficulties of war—it is merely the means to prevail against these inevitable obstacles.

On the other hand, in the days and weeks after Cobra, there was clear evidence that the mix of GI ingenuity and the genius that made America great in the Great War could prove a powerful combination. Together they provided "operational flexibility," the capacity to overcome the Army's limitations and flaws in equipment and doctrine, as well as in planning and battlefield decisions of generals; the ability to fight through the fog of war.

It was a pretty damn good army. Patton certainly thought so. He wrote, "as of August 14 the Third Army had advanced further and faster than any Army in history."[46] In fact, Patton's advance seemed so mercurial that Bradley's aide wrote in his war diary, "we aides live in Mortal fear that Patton may unjustly grab credit for the breakthrough which was made and sealed before he became active. Remembered a captain in the PX in London yesterday who said, 'I'll bet Georgie Patton is doing the work there now.'"[47] There was no question, the American Army had proved it was capable of great things.

And few aspects of combat during the European campaign saw more innovation and adaptation than armored warfare. The Americans, of course, were not the only army experimenting with mechanized operations and perfecting them to meet the rigors of battle. Nevertheless, the GIs had done well. It was not what science fiction or J.F.C. Fuller had exactly imagined, but it was good, competent fighting that won battles and did not squander lives.

In fact, the American achievement was extraordinary. The GIs had far less operational experience than the Germans, the British, or the Russians and arguably not the best armored equipment, yet over the course of the campaign leaders such as Patton, Wood, and Abrams and their men proved the equal of any army in Europe.

And they were on their way to Berlin. Or so they thought.

In August 1944, Adolf Hitler did not agree. Having survived an assassination attempt only weeks before and with the Russians pressing on the Eastern Front, the *Fuhrer* was loathed to permit a defeat in the West. He ordered a counterattack in France, one more chance to turn back the sequence of events started with Operation Cobra. On his order the *Wehrmacht* armor began to role, headed toward a town named Mortain.

## CHAPTER 8

# The King of Battle

## WHO WON THE WAR?

ON THE MORNING OF August 6, 1944, Robert Weiss piled his gear into a jeep for the short ride from B Battery, 230th Field Artillery to an infantry position on the top of a hill outside the small town of Mortain. He was rotating to the front for duty as a forward observer. He had been in country for a little more than a week; he was a replacement. The Army seemed to need a lot of replacements for artillery observers. It was his turn. It was Sunday—almost like a real Sunday, not a day at war—warm, hot, and lazy. The roads were crowded. Everybody was moving up. The Allies were advancing; the enemy was retreating.

It took less than a half an hour to cover the couple of miles between the battery and the 120th Infantry Regiment, 30th Infantry Division that occupied the town. It was not much of a town, less than plain, 2,000 folk, bounded on one side by a high rocky ridge and on the other by the Cance River. There was not much room to maneuver. The road necked straight through the town.

It was pretty obvious that the best location for an artillery observer was on top of the ridge. The artillery liaison officer pointed on his map to the highest point. That was where he wanted Weiss. Weiss and his team remounted the jeep and started heading up Hill 314.[1]

It was a forward observer's dream. The view from the heights was incredible. They could see for miles.

It took two things to be an ace forward observer. (1) An artillery observer had to know his own location. That was no problem here. They were on the most prominent piece of ground on the map. Accurately locating themselves was not a challenge. (2) The observer had to know where the target was. That was no problem either. Not only could Weiss and his team see everything, they had all day to identify terrain features, plot chokepoints on the ground where they could hit the enemy all bottled up, and send the coordinates to the artillery so that the battalion could mark them on the firing chart.

It all seemed like a lot of wasted work. Odds were they might never fire a round. The sector was quiet. It was, however, a routine that was required every time they moved into a new position. At least once they finished, they could relax a bit and enjoy the day.

During the afternoon a few missions were fired against some German infantry, probably the remnants of an enemy unit trying to escape the advancing First U.S. Army.

The sky was graying. The long summer Normandy afternoon was coming to an end. Soon Weiss knew they would be finished. There was not much the observers could do at night, particularly in a quiet sector. They could not see any targets, and there was not any enemy anyway, so they probably would not be very busy. There were pre-prepared fire missions to plot—called final protective fires (FPFs). These could be used in the dark if need be. The FPFs were targets plotted right in front of the infantry position in case there was a sneak attack at night. They probably would not be needed.

It looked to be an uneventful evening. Weiss's team found a couple of empty foxholes. They thought they might get some sleep.

There was no sleep.

There were noises in the town, first the crack of rifles, the chatter of machine guns, explosions, and then the creaky rambling of armor, lots of armor, heading toward the town, not away from it—Germans—lots of them—attacking. By 5 A.M., as the division artillery reported, "the pot started boiling over." Weiss ordered his sergeant to call the artillery on the field telephone. They needed fire support, artillery—lots of it.

Artillerymen are fond of quoting from a speech George Patton made to U.S. troops during the occupation of Germany. "You all know who won the war. The artillery did."

In one sense, he was right. Artillery was the greatest killer on the battlefield. More wounds were received from "indirect" fire than any other casualty-producing weapon. Artillery, however, like the other great technological engines of modern war, airpower and armor, required GI ingenuity to make it live up to its potential.

Of the three great weapons of war, despite Patton's exaltation, the contributions of the artillery are the least prevalent in modern memory. John S. "Professor" Wood started his career as an artilleryman. So did William Westmoreland who fought as an artilleryman in Normandy and would go on to command U.S. combat forces in Vietnam. The most well-known artilleryman of the war was Lesley J. McNair, but of course, he made his reputation as the Army's chief trainer. Nobody became famous by being a gunner. There was a reason for that.

Unless an individual was actually on the receiving end of an artillery barrage, it was difficult to understand the power of artillery—not just the killing power of the flying white hot metal thrown off when the round exploded, but the terrifying, deafening shock of a nearby detonation: the ear ringing, bone-jarring, automatic flush of adrenaline that could take a soldier's wits away. In World War I, a soldier with this condition was called "shell shocked." The horror of artillery war, however, was not reproducible in peacetime. In the Louisiana Maneuvers, umpires could fly red flags and tell a battalion commander that his troops had just been wiped out by an enemy barrage, but that meant little to him or his men, except perhaps that they could sit for a while and rest and break out some K rations. It was just numbers. No wonder many infantry commanders did not appreciate their artillery until they saw the face of battle themselves.

There was only one war film that came close to capturing artillery's proper place in modern war. It was *The Battle of San Pietro* (1945). And, it was made by a young Army Signal Corps lieutenant—John Huston. Huston had become a big-time movie director with the success of his 1941 picture *The Maltese Falcon*, where his film noir styling turned Humphrey Bogart into the classic hard-boiled movie detective. In April, Huston received a commission and the assignment to make war documentaries. He made three over the course of the war. All were brutally frank portrayals that came as close as film could come at the time to showing what real war was like.

*The Battle of San Pietro* tells the story of an attack on a town during the Italian campaign in the Liri Valley in 1943. The film is principally told through the point of view of an infantryman on the ground. Much of the motion picture is raw battle footage taken by Army combat cameramen, though some of the scenes are staged and some of the negatives were reversed to make it more obvious that the infantrymen were attacking in the right direction. Even so, it was all about real soldiers in a real war zone.

Making even the staged scenes seem raw and unrehearsed characterized an artistic style known as *cinéma vérité,* "real-life filmmaking," that used people instead of professional actors, no sets, and handheld cameras that would wobble and bob following the action. At one point in *The Battle of San Pietro* the eye of the camera following the infantry flies upward toward the sky and then drops to the ground. Steven Spielberg used similar camera techniques to film the opening Omaha Beach sequences in *Saving Private Ryan.*

When the Army censors first saw the film, they banned it. It was too graphic. Huston was accused of making an antiwar motion picture. He reportedly replied, "Well, sir, whenever I make a picture that's for war— why, I hope you take me out and shoot me." General George Marshall reversed the ban. "This picture should be seen by every American soldier in training," he remarked, "It will not discourage but rather will prepare them for the initial shock of combat." An edited 30-minute version was released in early 1945.

Even in the edited version, the film portrays a pretty gritty image of war. There are a number of scenes in the movie featuring the rain of artillery. One is particularly telling. A small group of infantry works its way across an open, broken field. The camera trudges behind. A short distance away one round explodes. The infantrymen and the camera drop to the ground, prostrate. Nothings happens. No one moves. The camera rolls on—longer. Gingerly, the infantrymen begin to rise. And then they begin to head up the hill again. The power of one small explosion to stop them dead in their tracks and hold them at bay—the terrifying, hopeless feeling of being powerless and exposed, the fear of what artillery really meant to the infantry—were all expressed beyond measure in one brief passage in the film. Hollywood never showed artillery like that.

Artillery operations lacked the capacity for great myth making. The artillery was, after all, blamed for the horrors of the Great War. It was artillery that drove men under grown, burrowing in the earth, living with rats and mud. And despite all of its wrath, the artillery could not break the stalemate of the trenches. Mass killing was not heroic stuff.

All Americans entered the war conceptualizing their heroes as individuals. They were looking for another Samuel Woodfill, an Eddie Rickenbacker, a Sergeant Alvin York. And there were individual heroes who were celebrated during and immediately after the war, such as Jimmy Doolittle, who led the first bombing raid on Japan (played by Spencer Tracy in the 1943 wartime film *Destination Tokyo*) and Audie Murphy, an infantryman and the most decorated soldier in the war (Murphy released a best-selling autobiography in 1949 and played himself in the film version of his book *To Hell and Back* in 1955). Heroism in World War II was also a team sport. Americans loved teamwork, which is why they had a growing obsession with American football. Hollywood fanned that mania; virtually every war film featured a small team, usually with class, ethnic, and geographical diversity. In *Sahara*, Bogart's makeshift command included, among others, three Americans, four Brits, a white South African, and a black Sudanese infantryman. As in the movies, in World War II Americans saw their teams of fresh young boys, as

Stephen Ambrose so famously wrote, as "a band of brothers." They were tank teams, infantry squads, and bomber crews.

The artillery was a kind of team, but not in the sense of the all-American squads moviegoers saw at the theater. It took a lot of men to make artillery work right in World War II. The greatest difference between artillery in World War I and the American redlegs (U.S. troops were called redlegs because at one point artillerymen had a red stripe on their uniform trousers) was accuracy. In World War I, artillery was a weapon of mass destruction, an indiscriminate instrument used to flatten a large area. U.S. artillery fires during World War II were the most precise that could be achieved with the available technology, and it was because of the artillery team—a really big, complex team.

There were five elements to accurate, predicted fire. In other words, there were five variables that had to be measured and calculated. If they were all accounted for in the firing order, which included the direction and elevation of the tube, the number of powder charges to placed in the tube, the type of projectile (such as high explosive or smoke), the type of fuse, and the fuse setting; then the artillery could ensure that a round exploded less than 50 yards from the target.

The five elements of predicted fire were (1) target location and altitude; (2) observer location and altitude; (3) the location of the firing unit and its altitude; (4) the muzzle velocity of the howitzer, the weight of the projectile, and the lot of the powder, as they might have different characteristics depending on when and where they were manufactured and how old they were; and (5) environmental conditions that would affect the burn rate of the powder and flight of the projectile, such as wind, air density, and temperature. All these data were then fed into a mathematical calculation that determined the projectile's flight to the target and expressed the results in firing commands: elevation, azimuth (direction), charge, and fuse setting.

Target and observer locations came from the observers, usually field artillerymen sent forward (similar to the air-support party). Their job was to accurately locate the target themselves and send in the "call for fire," the size and nature of the target (such as the type of enemy troops and their condition, such as whether they were in the open or dug in), location and altitude, the direction from the observer to the target, and the observer's location and altitude). The location of the firing units came from survey parties. Meteorological units provided weather information. Firing batteries took care of the guns. The battalion headquarters was responsible for communications and directing the firing commands. All these men had to work in concert to account for the five elements of accurate, predictive fire. It took hundreds of people to get one round of artillery down range. And of those hundreds, only the forward observer might go through the whole battle and ever see the enemy.

## LAWTON, AMERICA

If any aspect of close combat resembled a process akin to the assembly line it was shooting artillery with its precise language of firing commands, mathematical calculations, and standardized procedures. Artillery in battle, however, was anything but an industrial-age process. And while it might have made a poor candidate for heroic worship, it was an important part of winning the war. But, it could do so only by being an effective part of the combined-arms team. And that required GI ingenuity.

Artillery innovation began long before the war on a sleepy former cavalry post in the Indian Territory astride the frontier town of Lawton, Oklahoma. In 1910, the War Department dispatched Captain Dan T. Moore to Fort Sill to establish the School of Fire for Field Artillery. Moore's modest school eventually grew into the Field Artillery School, which became not only the principal education center for artillery officers and noncommissioned officers, but the main center for developing new equipment and tactics.

The Army did not have the numbers of guns it needed to fight World War II when the Japanese bombed Pearl Harbor. The Americans had, however, already developed the kinds of weapons, organizations, and procedures they needed to fight modern war. In fact, in many ways when the Americans first entered battle in North Africa, they already had better fire support than the Europeans who had been fighting for years. That was due largely to efforts at Fort Sill.

Fort Sill started to experiment with a mechanized platform in the 1920s. In 1923, Fort Sill tried out J. Walter Christie's light-tank chassis to see if it could be used as a self-propelled howitzer. It was a disaster. The mechanical components of the chassis could not withstand the constant pounding of the recoil from the gun. Instead, the Army focused on promoting motor-drawn artillery. There would be a prime-mover vehicle and the gun would be towed behind on a carriage like a trailer. The Chief of Field Artillery pointed out that the Ford Motor Company, General Motors, International Harvester, the Caterpillar Tractor Company, and a half dozen others made heavy four- and six-wheel trucks and tractors that could be adapted to provide up-to-date mechanized artillery when the need came and the money was available.[2]

Not all artillery officers were in favor of completely abandoning horse-drawn artillery. A debate raged over the issue in the service's *Field Artillery Journal*. Some argued that motor-drawn artillery was not reliable. Others argued that it could not match the mobility that horses provided to negotiate rough ground. One letter to the editor argued horse-drawn artillery was superior for night operations because horses had better night vision than humans. "The trend toward motorizing artillery is alarming," wrote Colonel Edward Wentworth in 1937, "horses will give quicker support after dark than motorized vehicles."[3] There were other arguments as well. Horses were more reliable than people. Trucks needed gas. Horses could eat grass. Horses were needed for the post polo team.

Horse-drawn artillery, however, was not cheap. The American West had disappeared. The supply of commercial horses in the United States was in precipitous decline. Horse maintenance was manpower intensive. Horses required extensive training in an age when fewer and fewer people worked in equine-related activities on a daily basis. That drove up training costs even more.

There were arguments that, in the long run, mechanization would be cheaper. In the *Field Artillery Journal*, Captain Creswell Blakeney made the case that it was easier to train truck drivers than horse handlers.[4] And, as Captain Joseph Greene noted, there were "26,000,000 registered vehicles in the United States, every one of which *somebody* drives."[5] Remarkably, in 1933 (perhaps not so remarkable given the scarcity of defense dollars) in the midst of the Great Depression, the Army received funds to begin the transition to motorized artillery—in part, to save money.

Upgrading the firepower of the artillery proved more problematic. The Army was reluctant to abandon its existing substantial arsenal of towed 75-mm guns, the standard caliber light field piece for World War I, even though the Field Artillery's tests showed the gun lacked the punch for modern warfare. That attitude changed in 1940. Observers of the German campaign convinced the Army that the 75 mm's time had passed.

Four years before GIs hit the beaches at Omaha, the Army decided to eliminate the 75-mm howitzer and make the 105 mm the standard light field artillery piece. The 155 mm would serve as medium field artillery. By the time the first divisions deployed to battle, they were up-gunned to this new mix of calibers. In 1943, the 105 mms, thanks to the production of American industry, were available in large numbers.[6] The Army also fielded a complement of heavy howitzers and the mechanized self-propelled light artillery used in the Armored Divisions.

In addition to fielding a modern artillery force, the Field Artillery added a new capability to its arsenal—airborne artillery observers. This was a new capability unmatched by any other army in Europe, but one that was not easy for the artillery to obtain.

Pilots had tried to spot artillery fires during World War I, but it was a cumbersome affair because there was no means of direct communication between the pilot and the artillery unit on the ground, other than dropping notes out of the plane. Radio changed all that. At least, it would have if the Army Air Corps had had any interest in having its planes act as artillery spotters. It did not.

A combination of advances in portable radios, airframe and engine designs, and new construction techniques made possible building light, durable aircraft that could operate from the near front using unimproved air strips (such as roads and open fields). A small group of junior officers at Fort Sill pioneered the idea of airborne artillery observers. Then in field trials they proved it would work.

The problem was wresting the authority of the Chief of the Air Corps, Hap Arnold. The airmen argued that dedicating airplane production and valuable mechanics and pilots to a peripheral mission was a waste of resources. In 1941, the artillery school, largely through luck and guile, obtained formal permission to test the air-observation-post concept. It proved a remarkable success. Tests conducted by McNair with the triangular division were also encouraging. The Army Air Forces tried to kill the program anyway. The battle was fought in the halls of the War Department in the Pentagon. In part, with Dwight Eisenhower's support, the initiative survived.

Eisenhower's commitment to a new way to spot artillery rounds was rewarded. In battle, the air artillery observers proved invaluable from almost the first days they were committed to combat in North Africa.

There was, of course, no doctrine on how the planes should be employed. That was all right. GIs learned how to use them to best effect on the job.

In Normandy, the GIs discovered lots of uses for their planes, and not just to call for fire missions for the infantry. The air observation posts conducted reconnaissance, relayed communications, coordinated air support, and were even used by commanders to help command and control units, with various panels, streamers, and flags used to signal to troops on the ground. Perhaps the most significant innovations were in using the planes behind lines to direct "counterfire" missions. In other words, the airborne observers would find the telltale signs of firing enemy artillery, flash and smoke, and then target the positions with U.S. artillery. In Normandy, every German artillery commander glanced uncomfortably skyward after his battery fired a round. If he saw any signs of the small American planes, his troops had to stop firing and move fast.

None of the missions that were performed by the air observation posts were written down in any War Department manual, anywhere. It was GI ingenuity all over again.[7]

Another significant innovation for World War II was the adoption of new organizations. During the Great War, artillery battalions were assigned to brigades. It was a relatively fixed organization. When a division needed more artillery, the corps commander assigned him another brigade. The allocation of fire support was a relatively crude and inflexible affair. With the creation of the triangular division, the artillery received a new headquarters called the Division Artillery, or the "DIVARTY." The DIVARTY was much like the combat commands in the armored divisions. It was primarily a command and control headquarters that could oversee any number of artillery units of light, medium, or heavy artillery. In addition, the reorganization established separate field artillery groups and brigades that would be assigned to the field army.[8] These too, were not fixed organizations. Battalions in the field army could be assigned to support a corps or a division, or the whole brigade could be tasked to support one or more commands.

Artillery doctrine was designed to promote flexible organization and employment. It was, in fact, a system that proved much more facile than that employed by the other ground forces. In the maneuver arms, units had to be "assigned" to a command. When Rose reorganized Combat Command A for the attack on Tessy-sur-Vire, for example, the task force assumed

Artillery Spotter Planes Parked on an Improvised Airfield in Normandy. (Courtesy, Army Signal Corps)

responsibility for the companies assigned to the command that included positioning, supply, and support. Artillery, however, was more like air support. Fires could be shifted around the battlefield without reassigning units from one command to another. This was accomplished by designating one of four standard tactical missions: (1) direct support, (2) reinforcing, (3) general support, or (4) general support/reinforcing.

Direct support meant that the artillery unit would provide fire support to only one maneuver unit. Reinforcing assigned an artillery battalion or brigade to "reinforce" another artillery unit; in other words, it would fire as ordered by the direct support unit. General support meant that an artillery unit would provide supporting fires to any artillery command that asked for additional fires. General support/reinforcing required the artillery to support all the other artillery units, but to provide first priority to a specific artillery command.

It all sounded a bit complicated to the average infantryman, but the artillery advisors understood it was a fairly clean and simple system. All the maneuver commander had to decide was which mission he wanted, a decision usually made with the advice of his artillery advisor, and then the redlegs took care of everything else.

The standard tactical missions provided for a great deal of flexibility without burdening maneuver commanders with worrying about the logistics or support needs of the artillery. There were standard operating procedures for each mission detailing who would be responsible for positioning units and observers, sending calls for fire, providing survey and resupply, and other tactical matters. As a result, with a single order, the overall maneuver commander could shift the weight of fire support simply by reordering the tactical missions for his supporting artillery.

In practice, the standard tactical missions proved to be well suited to a fast war of movement. When Lieutenant Colonel Carl Hutton had to coordinate fire support to fight off the Germans at Tessy-sur-Vire, all the command arrangements were made over the radio. Hutton's artillery battalion already had one battalion reinforcing him; another was added to provide more reinforcing fires, and additional general support fires were provided by the artillery units on VII Corps's flank.[9]

Of all the weapons of industrial-strength land warfare (armor, artillery, and tactical airpower), the doctrine and the organization of the U.S. field artillery proved the most mature when the first Americans went into battle. It was perhaps for these reasons that the artillery was among the best-trained parts of the force. That was true even in units that were troubled in their battle débuts. William DePuy recalled that, "when we went to war that part of the division which was really well-trained on the combat side was the artillery."[10]

And indeed, it was. Lieutenant Colonel Kenneth D. Reimers, who commanded the division's 343rd Field Artillery Battalion recalled, "from induction centers all over the country came draftees. They were untrained and skeptical men who had no military experience but were smart and willing to learn … six months after the basic training began the 343rd journeyed to Camp Bowie, Texas for the Army Ground Forces test to determine the degree of its training. The result was the highest score ever obtained by a field artillery battalion."[11] Reimers's pride was not exceptional. Most artillery commanders headed to Europe confident in the technical prowess of their troops.

In turn, because artillerymen were generally proficient at their craft, and because doctrine was so well developed, the redlegs could be more innovative and creative at applying artillery in battle. The complex fire-support plan used by the 2nd Infantry Division to march up Hill 192 offered a case in point.

The field artillery not only had a mature doctrine that could adapt well to any style of warfare from static battles to fast-moving mechanized warfare, it also had a command and control system that was both designed to be flexible and could quickly mass the fires of a number of artillery units at the same time. The heart of this system was called the Fire Direction Center (FDC).

In 1931, Major Carlos Brewer, the director of the gunnery department at the Field Artillery School, tackled the difficult challenge of figuring out how to make fires both fast and accurate. At the time, there were two ways to mass fires, in other words, have a number of units shoot at the same target. Both had been around since World War I, and neither worked particularly well. The first was to locate a target on a map, send the location to each firing battery, have it compute firing data, and then send a command for all the units to fire at once. This method was simply too slow and often not very accurate because of errors in determining the location of the firing unit or the target.

The second procedure (when a precise map location was not available) was to have one battery from one gun fire at the target and the observer would give corrections (move left or right, add or subtract range). The observer would continue to call for that one gun to fire and give corrections until he had "adjusted" the round onto the target. Only one battery could adjust at a time because, if more than one battery fired, the observer would have difficulty figuring out which round had been fired by which unit. One at a time was the only way. This method was very accurate, but very, very slow.

Brewer and his staff invented a firing chart, a graphical representation that could be used to plot both the target and the battery positions (accurately determined ahead of time using various survey techniques). The chart put everything on a "common grid." Using this method the observer had only to adjust the fires for one unit. Then, using the chart, all the other units could plot their adjustments in relation to the position of the base unit.

Major Orlando Ward, who succeeded Brewer, added some refinements to the system. He introduced the use of radio, which could be set up quicker than wire lines, and he established a center at the battalion to compute the firing data. The use of tabular firing tables was also introduced to help speed calculations. Now all the firing batteries had to do was receive the firing commands, send them to the guns, and fire. The battalion also took over the duties of "fire direction," telling the batteries where to locate and managing the expenditure of ammunition. Since there were four guns in each battery and three batteries in a battalion, one observer could now mass 12 guns on a single target in 10 or so minutes. As time and experience progressed, the artillery would get much, much faster.

While the new fire direction method had enormous potential, it was controversial, impinging on the traditional prerogatives of the battery commander. Not surprisingly, officers of the old army who were reluctant to give up their horses were loathed to depart with the independence of the firing battery command. McNair, who served as the commandant of the Field Artillery School during the period of the development of the FDC was a strong proponent. There were others who were not. The battle raged in the classrooms at Fort Sill, in exercises in the field, in backrooms at the War Department, and on the front pages of the artillery journal.

Eventually, the independent firing battery went the way of the caisson. In 1941, the Field Artillery School declared that the battalion Fire Direction Center would be adopted throughout the army. The FDC was ready to go to war—at least on paper.

What was *not* known at the time was how versatile and effective the FDC system would prove in massing fires of multiple battalions in combat.

It did not take long to find out.

Artillery proved to be one of the few bright spots in the battle at the Kasserine Pass. Eisenhower dispatched reinforcements from the 9th Infantry Division to stem the mounting disaster at the front. The DIVARTY marched over 700 miles in 100 hours and occupied covering positions at Thala. When the Germans arrived, 84 artillery pieces were waiting. They fired in mass, turning back the German advance.

The artillery saved the day, but not Orlando Ward. Ward, who had helped create the FDC, commanded the 1st Armored Division at Kasserine. He was relieved.

The success of artillery at Kasserine was no fluke. Massed fires also made important contributions to American victories in North Africa at Gafsa and El Guettar.

And it was all the result of GI ingenuity. In the months leading up to the invasion and in the field, the gunners had experimented and refined the FDC techniques invented at Fort Sill, developing tactics and procedures to mass more guns, faster, using both ground and airborne artillery observers. Carl Hutton, who directed the artillery support for the Battle of Tessy-sur-Vire, recorded in his memoirs that while Fort Sill may have changed the doctrine, it was commanders in the field who had to figure out how to overhaul their fire direction system and implement the new battalion-directed procedures so that they worked in battle. For example, Fort Sill assumed that firing commands would go to the batteries via radio. Hutton found that it was better to use both wire and radio, a better chance of assured communications. Little of what they did, he recalled, could be found written in manuals. By the time they faced the Germans in North Africa they had figured it all out on their own.[12] In the end, the results were impressive. One commander concluded, "on any important target I usually mass all the artillery of the division." Omar Bradley boasted with pride that his corps could mass every gun it had, 324 pieces, on a single target—and it was all because of the FDC.[13] In one speech before the D-Day invasion, the old infantryman told the troops of one infantry regiment that one of their principal tasks was concentrating artillery fire. "In the last war," Bradley declared, "we spoke of putting a battery for an hour or less on a target, but now we speak of six or eight battalions concentrating for five minutes." When they hit the ground in Normandy, the First Army commander encouraged, they should use a new technique developed in Italy where all the battalion FDCs calculated the projectiles' flight times from their batteries to the target and fired so that all the rounds landed simultaneously. "Tremendous concentration in a short time," Bradley demanded, "It is called a 'TOT.' 'Time on Target."[14] The artillery had made tremendous progress during the course of the war. The infantry must be prepared to rely on the artillery. For Mortain, that would prove very sound advice indeed.

## UNTERNEHMEN LÜTTICH

Mortain had the makings of another Kasserine. While Cobra had broken through the German defenses in depth, the Americans had not moved fast enough to envelop the mass of the enemy army. They had, however, pushed the German lines way back. And there was little likelihood the line could be held. In particular, the Germans had lost Avranches, and they needed the town to anchor their southern flank and maintain a continuous defensive line. Without Avranches there would be no front line and no defensible terrain upon which a static defensive network could be anchored. In truth, the

German Tank Destroyed by American Artillery in North Africa. (Courtesy, Omar N. Bradley Collection, Military History Institute)

senior German commanders in the field doubted that Adolf Hitler's demand for a bold counterattack could hold France for Germany, but at least a bold strike now might facilitate an organized withdrawal later.

On a map, it looked tantalizingly achievable. The zone of the First U.S. Army was at its thinnest west of Avranches. The distance between Mortain and Avranches looked like a skinny waist on a big-hipped woman. A drive to Avranches would cut the First U.S. Army in two and offer a solid flank to Patton's Third Army.

They would shoot for Avranches. The attack was code-named *Unternehmen Lüttich* (Operation Liege).

The road to Avranches was through Mortain.

Controlling Mortain meant controlling Hill 314.

On August 3, 1944, when troops of the Big Red One had first taken the area as part of the advance following the exploitation of Cobra, one of their actions was to secure the high ground. On August 4, when "Lightning Joe" Collins queried Clarence R. Huebner to check on the progress of the attack, he said, "Ralph be sure to take Hill 314." Huebner replied, "Joe, I already have it."[15] When the 1st Infantry Division pulled out, it turned the vital ground over to the 30th. The Americans were going to leave such key terrain unprotected.

When the Germans came, they wanted the hill back.

Before bedding down for the night, Weiss made sure that communications with the battalion FDC were set and ready to go. The 1st Infantry Division had left its wire lines when it moved out. The battalion used them to communicate with its observers and the infantry. Weiss also had his team lug its 35-pound Model 610 and long antenna out of the jeep and up to its forward position on the ridge. Now there were two ways to talk to the guns.[16]

The team also brought the battery pack, another bulky load that had to be manhandled up the ridge. Without batteries, the radio would not work. Weiss made sure there were spares in the jeep. If the batteries ran low, the team would have to go back to the battalion and get some more. If an observer could not talk to the FDC, both he and the artillery battalion were helpless. (At the Battle of the Séves River, the 90th Division had plenty of artillery and an observer with the troops at the front, but without communications, all that fire support had proven useless.) It was never a good idea for an observer to be short extra batteries.

Shortly before 6 P.M. mortar rounds started hitting the ridge. Weiss knew they were mortars. Their "pop" was unmistakable. The enemy was firing at or near his position. There were two problems with that. (1) If the Germans were trying to retreat, they would have no reason to fire on the American positions and attract attention. (2) Mortars were short-range weapons, usually used for infantry support. That meant they were nearby and so German infantry could not be far off. Was the enemy attacking?

Later in the last fading light of the day, Weiss's team spotted German infantry swarming not 2,500 yards below them in a cluster of buildings. He called for artillery fire on the location. Weiss moved his team down closer to the infantry command post. They waited. It was an uneasy night.

By dawn on August 7, 1944, enemy activity had picked up. The valley was covered in fog. The team called in fire missions based on sounds heard in the milky haze blanketing the ground. The team could not tell what effect the rounds were having.

By 9:30 A.M. the mist had burned off. There were Germans everywhere—infantry on the hillside, vehicles in the town. The team began calling for fire missions nonstop. And the enemy was firing at them—mortars and machine guns. At times tanks and infantry reached within a 1,000 yards of the team's position. It was becoming a hell of a firefight. Weiss sent a man back to the jeep to get the extra batteries. They might be needed.

By August 8, 1944, it was clear that a major counterattack was under way. In fact, the troops on the hill were under assault by forces from two

German divisions. The American infantry was surrounded and Weiss along with them. The U.S. artillery fire was the only thing holding the Germans off the hilltop and holding back a major advance down the highway toward Avranches.

The Germans knew that the heights on the hill stood between them and the next step in the offensive. Killing the infantry and forward observers on the high ground was job one. And they threw everything they had at them —mortars, machine guns, grenades, tank fire, and high-velocity antiaircraft defense guns firing at point-blank range. Even some *Luftwaffe* planes made a run at the U.S. position.

What *Unternehmen Lüttich* lacked was robust fire support. In contrast to the Americans, the Germans went to battle with artillery that was outclassed in virtually every way by the GIs they were fighting.

The Germans had won the battle for France in 1940 with fast-moving armor and minimal artillery support. When they turned to attack the Soviet Union it was thought effective close support over the vast expanse of the Russian front would be more valuable than massed fires. Huge support artillery formations were broken up and divided up among the divisions. Scant investments were made in motorized artillery. Throughout the war, most of the German artillery would be horse-drawn. Industrial production priorities went to tanks over artillery; there simply was not enough capacity to make both a priority. Ammunition production also became a problem, as did the logistical challenge of getting the ammunition to the front with the constant Allied bombings of the rail lines. In turn, more artillery production and ammunition had to be turned over to building up Germany's air defenses. By 1944, the Germans might have wanted to emulate the Allies' abilities to mass fires, but they lacked the resources to do so.[17]

As a result, while the Germans poured a lot of lead into the hill, Weiss and his team were safe, snug in their foxholes. The enemy had the same problem at Mortain that the Americans had at Omaha Beach. Most of the German fire support came from air defense guns, which had a flat trajectory much like naval guns. Weiss's position was just beyond the lip of the ridge, almost impossible for a gun to hit because of the large range-probable error: short rounds plowed into the ridge; long rounds sailed harmlessly over the heads of the GIs.

The force on Hill 314 remained relatively safe. As long as the artillery fired the FPFs that ringed their position with a curtain of exploding steel, the force was fine. As long as the artillery held out, the force was fine. Everything was fine—except, batteries were running low.

## THE SIEGE

While the defenders of Hill 314 were surrounded and battling for their lives, First Army was awaking to the scope of the German threat. Seven divisions would eventually be thrown in to turn the enemy back. By August 8, 1944, the Americans were already pushing back along the southern shoulder of the German advance.

First Army pretty much let Collins, the corps commander, handle the fight. The First Army Commander, however, did make all the difference in the world. The corps was low on artillery ammunition. Courtney Hodges had been in command of the First Army for less than a week (Bradley had been elevated to command the Army Group that oversaw both Hodges's First Army and Patton's Third Army). His assessment of the battle for Mortain was that "the guns weren't firing enough. They weren't shooting enough. The weather was beautiful, but Quesada [Elwood R. "Pete" Quesada, Commander of the IX Tactical Air Command] couldn't do it all, and Hobbs [Leland Hobbs, Commander of the 30th Infantry Division] was catching hell." Hodges asked, "What if I double ammo for 48 hours?" The staff replied, "You'd be down to nothing." The First Army commander declared, "I'm not going to leave the ammo for Hitler, so increase fire by 50 percent!"[18] Hodges ordered that VII Corps should get every round it wanted, even if it depleted the First Army's ammunition stocks. The corps also got priority from the Army's heavy artillery and tactical air support.[19] It was one of the best decisions Hodges made in the whole war.

Meanwhile, the Canadians were undertaking a major offensive (Totalize) that had begun the night before. While the Canadian advance was not as successful as the Allies had hoped, the Third Army was collapsing the Germans' line of communications and looked like it might well link up with the Canadians and cut the spearhead of the German advance right off.

The Germans were awaking to the likely failure of the operation. Battling the Canadian offensive took away from the forces that were available for *Unternehmen Lüttich*. Meanwhile, the Allied fighter-bombers were attacking deep behind the German lines, making the challenge of bringing up reinforcements and supply more difficult. And the damn GIs still held Hill 314. From the hilltop the Americans could bring artillery down on anything in sight, and that slowed the German attack to a crawl.

When the *panzers* tried to slide north of the town the American infantry retreated before them, but the maneuver opened the German's flank to the fires of the 4th Infantry DIVARTY. At least it would have if there were an observer that could see the advancing columns of gray. The division's ground forward observers had been overrun or withdrew in the face of the surprise enemy advance.

One observer, however, did show up on the scene—the assistant division artillery air officer, Lieutenant David E. Condon.

Condon had flown his L-5 observation aircraft to Normandy on June 7, 1944, and he had been flying and fighting ever since. Airborne over the front at Mortain, Condon radioed fire missions to one of the division's supporting artillery battalions; its fires were later reinforced by two other battalions. The division's commanding general concluded that the Germans "would have set us on our heels," but the DIVARTY's accurate fires kept them at bay.[20]

Having failed to turn the flank, the Germans, on August 9, 1944, made a desperate attempt to break through once more, doing something that they had rarely ever done. That night they brought forward every available artillery tube and began to blast away at the 30th Infantry Division front.

Again, the air-observation posts came to the rescue. They called down 30 fire missions in an hour. "Active enemy batteries appeared so rapidly that the Air OPs [observation posts]," recalled the unit history, "were forced to adjust on an enemy battery and pass on to the next one without really working over the first one thoroughly."[21] The enemy artillery might not have all been destroyed, but the harassing fire of the American guns at least forced them to move, preventing the Germans from even trying to mass their artillery.

On the hill, Weiss's team continued to call observed fire on the enemy, while the fighter-bombers of IX TAC worked over the targets behind the front lines. It was an inspired division of labor. Even with innovations such as column cover and armored air-support officers, close air support was too dangerous to use when friendly and enemy troops were on top of each other. During the battle for Mortain, for example, the 120th Infantry Regiment's command post was hit by British fighters. Using the airpower for the deep targets and accurate, observed artillery fires for the close-in targets maximized the strengths of both systems.

But it all depended on the ability of the observers to keep finding targets for the gunners. And that was getting tough. By now, they had been on the high ground for days. They were tired. No, they were utterly, utterly exhausted. They were hoarse. They smelled beyond belief. They cheated death by the hour. They were low on water, ammunition, food, and medical supplies.

And ... they were very, very low on batteries for the radio. Somebody needed to think of something.

## THE INSPIRATION OF DESPERATION

GI ingenuity was genius. That did not mean it always worked. Solving the dilemma of a battalion surrounded by enemy tanks and infantry certainly called for creative thinking. And in the heat of battle, GIs came up with all kinds of very creative ideas.

Sadly, none of them worked worth a damn.

First, they tried using the observation planes to drop supplies to the stranded men on the ground. These planes flew low and slow and were made out of wood. They avoided getting shot down by stealthy flying and innovative tactics. Flying over fields thick with enemy did not work so well. German ground fire drove the planes off before they could get the supplies over the hill.

Next, the Army Air Force tried parachuting in supplies. Most of the drops resupplied the Germans. They tried again. Worse results.

Then, they tried something else.

The division artillery executive officer and the operations officer for Weiss's battalion hit on an idea. One type of artillery round that the gunners employed was not designed to explode. The artillery had a chemical smoke round designed to open in the air and release the smoke over the battlefield. It was called the M-84, base ejection HC smoke. The round contained smoke canisters and a base ejection charge. After firing, the base ejection charge would be set off by the fuse in the nose of the round. The explosion would blow off the base plate and disperse the canisters at the proper altitude.

Perhaps, they thought, the contents of the M-84 could be emptied, filled with supplies, and then fired to the men on the hill. It was August 10, 1944. They were desperate. They could not stand the thought of GIs stranded on the ridge with nothing, while only miles away trucks were packed with lifesaving supplies. They could not stand the thought that the division might lose the most critical piece of ground on the Normandy front for the lack of a couple of batteries and some bandages. As ludicrous as the idea of firing supplies up the hill sounded, they would give it a try.

The first task was to crack open the base plate of the projectile. That was a problem. The artillerymen were never meant to open the projectiles. They had been issued no suitable wrench for the task. So they tried a hammer and screwdriver. To their amazement, that worked without damaging the threads in the base of the projectile that they would need to put the base plate back on later. They were equally fortunate that all the banging on the projectile did not detonate the base ejection charge.

Next they removed the canisters and base charge. Since they could not fire a round without a fuse on the tip of the projectile, they needed some means to ensure that a fuse detonation did not burn the contents of the container. A steel disk was fabricated and stuffed into the nose cone of the projectile behind the fuse. The problem was solved.

The first priority was medical supplies. So, after consulting with the battalion surgeon to determine what was needed most and what might survive firing out of a howitzer, five shells were packed with bandages, cotton, adhesive tape, morphine Syrettes, and sulfa drugs. In another, they placed a unit of plasma heavily wrapped in cotton and bandages.

The next problem was trying to figure out how the rounds would perform after they were fired. Since the weight of the rounds had been changed, their aerodynamic properties would be different than a normal M-84 projectile. And, since the weight of the projectile was a critical part of the five elements of predicted fire, they would have to figure out how to compensate for the new variable. After all, even though they were not trying to kill the enemy, the rounds still had to be accurate. The rounds had to (1) land where the battalion could readily find them and (2) not accidentally kill friendly troops.

Four projectiles were filled with sand to approximate the weight of the medical-laden artillery shells. They would test-fire the sand projectiles, make adjustments, and then use the data to calculate firing data for their experimental rounds.

At 9 p.m. on August 10, 1944, they notified Weiss to watch for an incoming sand round. Weiss alerted the infantrymen, who anxiously served as spotters for the experiment.

The first round was fired with the report, "dud on the way!"

It was not an auspicious start. As expected, the projectile's performance was "very erratic."

It took an hour to adjust fire until they thought they had a fair chance of getting the experimental rounds on to a predictable spot near the top of the hill.

The next command heard was, "medical round on the way!"

At midnight the observers on the hill reported they believed they had spotted where all the rounds had fallen. That was the good news.

A little while later, the artillery observers radioed back that they could not retrieve the projectiles because of enemy sniper fire. That was the bad news.

At 1 a.m., they woke the battalion surgeon, packed six more rounds, and planned to try again at first light. They also got five 155-mm shells, which were considerably bigger, and packed those, too.

As soon as the morning mist lifted, they fired a check "sand" round to make sure their firing data were still accurate. It hit close enough. Then they fired their medical rounds. They all landed within a hundred yards of each other, an amazing feat.

Then they tried to pack batteries into the projectiles. That did not work. They were too big. The battalion communications officer suggested that instead they take three smaller BA 37 batteries and solder the leads together. He reasoned this should work just as well as one big battery. These were ready for firing by midday on August 12, 1944, but the artillery was too busy firing other missions to attempt aerial battery resupply.

The division artillery's unofficial history reported that most of "the supplies were in usable condition." But the report had a very generous definition of "usable." The GIs found some of the medical rounds and managed to pry them open. According to Weiss what was inside was little more than a mass of glop. The terrific velocity imparted to shell when it was fired mashed up anything in the projectile.

Still, while it did not work, it was classic GI ingenuity.

Weiss and his team figured out a better solution on their own. They warmed some of the used batteries in the sun. Heating the batteries allowed them to squeeze a little more life out of each one. By rotating the batteries and cutting down transmission time, they kept on the air.

By August 12, 1944, the Germans had given up and were in retreat. The Americans on Hill 314 were relieved. The only issue that remained to be resolved was how many more Germans would be killed or captured before the enemy evacuated France and the invasion of Germany began.

Hitler stuck the *Wehrmacht's* neck out and Bradley tried to cut it off. The GI general recognized the opportunity to trap the German Army in a double envelopment—two armies trying to swing around the flanks of the enemy from opposite directions. Bradley hoped that First Army, after regaining the initiative at Mortain, would hold the Germans' attention while Third Army swung around behind from one side and the Canadian and British forces from another. The two would meet at Argentan-Falaise.

The maneuver failed to close the gap at Falaise before a number of German units escaped. Historians still vigorously debate why.[22] Nevertheless, Carlo D'Este's assessment that "Hitler's blunder at Mortain and Bradley's decision to envelop and entrap German forces at Argentan-Falaise marked the end of the Normandy campaign, and resulted in one of the most crushing and decisive victories ever attained by the Allies during World War II" is undeniably accurate.[23]

On August 21, 1944, General Omar Bradley held a news conference.

Reporter: "Do you believe that we have won the battle of FRANCE?

Bradley: "Depends on what you mean by the battle of FRANCE. There is nothing in FRANCE that can stop us now."[24]

He was right.

Still there was more to be done. There was a war to be won.

## THE FIREPOWER WAR

It was a long way from August 12, 1944 to May 8, 1945—VE Day, victory in Europe. Along the way the American Army got better. Even divisions, such as the 90th Infantry defeated so soundly at the Séves River, became better fighters. "Partly," wrote DePuy,

> this was because the seasoning curve was steeper while casualties diminished. And it was because battalion and higher commanders found that there were ways to win battles at reduced costs ... . The tactical discoveries of World War II were motivated by the shear necessity of preserving our soldiers and their junior leaders long enough so that they could learn and become effective. This dimension of a leader's responsibility places a discipline upon his selection of tactical concepts.[25]

In Normandy, and other battles during the European campaign, artillery was the right choice. Until leaders and soldiers became more seasoned and skilled, firepower was often the only appropriate answer.

Long after the battlefields of Europe had fallen silent, after Berlin had fallen, Hitler dead, after the hot war had been replaced by a cold one, DePuy explained how GIs had played their part in fighting and winning World War II. He described "his job as an infantry commander in Europe as moving the artillery's forward observers across France and Europe."[26]

DePuy's description was perhaps a bit too much like Patton's aphorism of who won the war. Neither had really meant to argue that battles should or could be won by firepower alone. They both had seen enough of war to recognize the truth of Carl von Clausewitz's contention that there could be no rule book for armed conflict. And they would have agreed with Marshall's advice in *Infantry in Battle*—be leery of "lessons from past wars; mostly, these have proved to be short-sighted, or only situationally valid. Lessons from presumed victories are especially apt to mislead."[27]

Neither Patton nor DePuy believed that artillery was the answer to everything. Indeed, in Normandy less skilled troops quickly came to overly rely on artillery. DePuy's division was a case in point. In the first few weeks of the campaign infantrymen thought artillery was the answer to everything. "The F.O.s [forward observers are doing most of the fighting," Reimers, a direct support artillery battalion commander, recalled,

> the infantry hear nothing but the rustling of leafs [sic] or the snap of a twig and holler for artillery fire. At other times when the Germans fire on them with mortars they sceam [scream], "Get the artillery on those bastards!" The[y] don't give a damned where we shoot as long as we shoot. I'll try putting a stop to this our ammunition supplu[y] is too limited to waste on nothing.[28]

Without strong leadership, solid tactics, and trained and disciplined troops, artillery could become a crutch.

But when it was used right, it made an enormous difference. It was the most mature part of America's Ground Army. And GI genius made it even better. And when the Americans used it to best advantage, at the right time and the right place—it won battles and saved lives. That was the lesson of Mortain.

Perhaps the field artillery proved the most facile of the three great weapons of mechanized land warfare because the technologies that it employed were the most proven. As a result, they combined the best of industrial-strength warfare with GI ingenuity for innovation and adaptation. When the two were fused was when America's Army operated at its best. That was a lesson as well.

## THE SHAPE OF THINGS TO COME

After he retired from the presidency, Eisenhower penned *At Ease: Stories I Tell to Friends*. The book was not a biography, but a collection of reminiscences from his military career and the early postwar years. The title of the last chapter of his book is borrowed from H.G. Wells, "The Shape of Things to Come."

In 1951, Ike recounts in the book, President Harry Truman sent him to tour Europe and assess the prospects for setting up a military alliance, the North Atlantic Treaty Organization (NATO), and then to report his findings in a speech to Congress.

At the time of Ike's trip, the war in Europe had been over for half a decade. Patton was dead as the result of injuries in a car accident during the occupation. Bradley was Chairmen of the Pentagon's Joint Chiefs of Staff. Collins was Army Chief of Staff (Marshall's old job). Marshall had just resigned after serving briefly as Secretary of Defense. Before that, he had been Secretary of State and authored the Marshall Plan for the reconstruction of Europe. Huebner had just retired as a three-star general, commanding all the U.S. troops in postwar Europe. Creighton Abrams was also serving in Europe. Maurice Rose, who led the armor to victory at Tessy-sur-Vire, was killed during the war. Frank T. Mildren, who led the troops up Hill 192, survived the war. He wrote a history of the battle for his paper at Staff College. Robert Weiss, the forward observer on Hill 314, survived as well, went home, and practiced business and tax law. Humphrey Bogart was starring in the *African Queen;* John Huston directed.

America had moved on.

While the mission in Europe was to think about the future, Eisenhower could not help but to reflect on the past and what it portended for the days after tomorrow. When he returned, he went back to West Point to reflect and write the speech he would deliver at the Capitol.

> For the next four days, I kept to the Thayer Hotel at West Point. A center of gaiety every other time I had been there, the place was now almost deserted. This pleased me, for in its quiet, no longer under the gun of early starts and late hours, I could review all that I had seen and heard during the trip. Hours on end I worked over the talk. Few speeches have ever given me so much trouble ... . the three principal points I wanted to make were: that the preservation of a free America required our participation in the defense of Western Europe; that success *was* attainable ... and our own major role should be as a storehouse of munitions and equipment ... .[29]

Ike's reflections were an odd combination of hopefulness and nostalgia. Eisenhower, who knew much of war, who fought wars, and lost friends, was a man of peace. He argued for NATO, built nuclear weapons, talked tough with the Soviets, but in the end he hoped that the age in which America had to send its citizens as soldiers to fight and die in foxholes would one day come to a close. Ike hoped that America's industrial power might be enough to deter war. In the future, he hoped there would be no need for GI ingenuity, for teaching American kids the tradecraft of killing, for learning on the job, for playing catch-up in the modern ways of war.

It was a noble, but unrealistic hope. Despite the victory in Europe for a second time, America would have to draw on doughboy genius and GI ingenuity again. And as technology moved forward, the American soldier would have to add something more to remain the master of the battlefield.

# CHAPTER 9

# Warriors

## BUNGLE IN THE JUNGLE, 1965

ARMY CHIEF OF STAFF Harold K. Johnson was unhappy with how things were going in Vietnam—it was no great secret. At one point he considered resigning. He did not believe the war was being fought the right way. He commissioned a study—A Program for the Pacification and Long-Term Development of Vietnam (PROVN). The study concluded, indeed, the war was being fought the wrong way—too much emphasis on the big war against the North Vietnamese Army, not enough on making South Vietnam a stable country.[1] One of Johnson's biggest concerns was the too liberal use of air and artillery. "It's very popular to say send a bullet instead of a boy," Johnson complained but, "I think we overemphasize firepower."[2] The destruction and ill will caused by the indiscriminate use of artillery and bombing, he contended, slowed development, alienated the populace, and accomplished little. It cost more in feeding instability than it gained in adding security.

One of Johnson's chief culprits was William DePuy, who commanded the Big Red One. "His credo was simple," contends Army War College professor Henry Gole, a retired Army officer, "infantry develops the situation minimizing risk to the American soldier and then destroys the enemy with the overwhelming use of firepower. That logic runs like a red thread from his experiences in Normandy in 1944 ... ."[3] And DePuy practiced what he preached.

Johnson was right—the wasteful use of firepower was valueless. Gole was right—DePuy encouraged the grunts in Vietnam to liberally use the powerful instruments of modern battle. But, they were also both wrong. DePuy was not in love with a single way of war. In Normandy, he would have preferred infiltration tactics, where GIs attacked at night, in small groups, without massive doses of firepower, using stealth and guile rather than brute force. Standing off against the Soviets in Europe during the Cold War, he advocated heavy suppressive fires with direct-fire weapons, long-range tank and antitank weapons, and heavily armored and armed infantry fighting vehicles.

DePuy eschewed single solutions to warfare.

It is true that in Vietnam, DePuy's prescription looked something like what his infantry learned how to do in France—the cautious maneuver of infantry with the hammer of firepower. In part, DePuy pushed for similar solutions because they were similar kinds of armies, with similar kinds of problems. They were armies of citizen-soldiers who learned a lot of what they knew about fighting at the front. They were not armies that could start out applying advanced techniques such as infiltration warfare and pacification. They had not been trained for it.

DePuy's answer to the criticism of his tactics in Vietnam would probably have been something like this. If America wanted to start out fighting a different kind of war, it should have trained a different army, but it did not. As a result, the Army would have to start by relying on what always worked best —a heavy dose of industrial-strength warfare and then a growing reliance on GI ingenuity.

## TECHNO-WAR

Few historical legacies are more confusing, contradictory, and just plain wrongheaded than the myths about how the American ground soldier fought in Vietnam. One of the first, strongly held, and patently false myths was that America lost because it tried to refight World War II, attempting to fight a conventional war against an unconventional enemy. One of the most extreme expressions of this thesis is Loren Baritz's *Backfire: A History of How American Culture Led Us into Vietnam and Made Us Fight the Way We Did* (1998). The American Army, Baritz argued, believed that it was invincible, a belief based in large part on a blind faith in technology to win on every battlefield.

Baritz's conclusions certainly mirrored beliefs expressed in popular culture. And the trends in popular culture were nowhere more clearly expressed than in Hollywood. Indeed, the evolution of filmmaking in regards to the Vietnam War illustrates how Americans went from fondly remembering World War II GIs to denigrating the sacrifice of grunts at the front in Vietnam.

In the period between the end of World War II (1945) and the decline of popular support for the Vietnam War after the Tet Offensive of 1968, Hollywood made World War II, as Studs Terkel famously described, "The Good

War," *and* then it turned every war that followed into a World War II. When Gregory Peck battled for control of *Pork Chop Hill* (1959) during the Korean War, the movie would have looked little different if he were leading a company up a ridge in the battle for the Lili Valley. One of the first Hollywood movies about Vietnam, *The Quiet American* (1958) turned Graham Greene's 1955 novel on its head. In Greene's novel the American, Pyle, is a morally ambiguous character. In the film, he is played by real-life World War II hero Audie Murphy as an idealistic crusader fighting a just cause against the evils of Communism. It was a reprise of Bogart's awakening to the struggle against Nazism in *Casablanca*.

No movie tried to make Vietnam more like the mythical World War II seen in the Hollywood motion pictures of the 1940s than *The Green Berets* (1968). The film's star, John Wayne, was personally interested in turning Robin Moore's 1965 novel into a motion picture. Wayne supported the war effort. He even wrote President Johnson and asked for the administration's endorsement.[4] There was never any question but that a Vietnam film staring John Wayne, as the epitome of the World War II action hero, would have the look and feel of an old-fashioned American wartime film. One review called the final product "a cliché-ridden throwback to the battlefield potboilers of World War II."[5] That it was. Remarkably it also proved to be a box-office hit. Perhaps Americans were already nostalgic for the good war they believed that they had lost, or perhaps disillusionment had not yet sunk so deeply into middle America where Wayne's films still represented the personification of everything all-American. It was, however, without question the last major successful Hollywood film glorifying the American way of battle that would come out for some time.

The major American war films about Vietnam after 1968, *Apocalypse Now* (1979), *The Deer Hunter* (1978), and *Platoon* (1986), had nothing in common with a classic John Wayne combat movie such as *The Sands of Iwo Jima* (1949). They were a different kind of caricature of war. Instead of techno-war done good, it was techno-war gone bad.

What was lost, however, was not the American way of war, but the myth of the American way of war as personified on celluloid and in bad history books. The Army that Baritz complained blundered in Vietnam, the techno-war machine of World War II, never existed, except perhaps on film.

## LOOKING BACK

In part, Hollywood and cultural historians like Baritz got Vietnam so wrong because they never got World War II right. What characterized the American approach to combat operations during World War II was a combination of competent management of large-scale activities (a skill inherited from World War I) and innovation and adaptation to meet the conditions on the ground, a talent it took from America's citizen-soldiers. Rather than slavishly relying on technology, GIs were skeptical of what they were given and what they were told to do. If it did not work, they fixed it. If they did not like it, they changed it. They had the healthy inquisitiveness of an engineer and the confidence to rely on trial and error. And as the war went on, the longer they tinkered with the machines of war and the ways of battle, the better citizen-soldiers got at mastering both.

The tragedy of America's postwar years was not that the Army refused to do anything other than refight World War II, but that it seemed to all too easily let slip the genius that had made all the difference in places such as Normandy. What made the American Army great began to dissipate the day the war ended.

As happened to the Army after World War I, as soon as the peace treaty was signed demobilization began. In fact, when some troops in Europe felt the demobilization was not going fast enough, they actually rioted in protest.

The Army, as after World War I, got smaller. There were fewer men. There was less equipment. The equipment was older. There was less money to train. There were more missions than people.

The Army had faced the same problem after the First World War. But the Army after World War I had managed to retain at least the core of what had made its military great, doughboy genius—the ability to organize large industrial-scale activities. The spark of this genius remained alive in the Army institutions and individuals. The war colleges, the staff schools, and mentors continued to preach the intellectual skills required to make an industrial-age nation fight industrial-strength warfare. And they had a ready-made cadre of civilian middle managers, trained in the industrial workshops of America, mentally prepared to execute big ideas, and waiting to be called up. When World War II came, the doughboy mindset was ready to go.

In 1940, GI ingenuity, however, was something new. It was something that had come to America in the interwar years. It was something that emerged from a society that had grown up in the modern technological age. And when national security demanded that the technological age be adapted to the battlefield, the kids that were raised side by side with automobiles and telephones and radios were the ones best prepared to take on the task.

The Army did not teach GI genius. Lesley J. McNair's Army Ground Forces (AGF) did many things well, but teaching GI genius—replicating the conditions of battle and figuring how to make gizmos work in combat was not one of them. When McNair tried to add "realism" to training, to him that meant simulated explosions, sleepless nights, and running around in the woods in a helmet. The tasks required during the exercises, however, were prescribed and unimaginative. What AGF training failed to do was present the intellectual face of real war—the problems and conundrums that required the exercise of GI ingenuity. In fact, when a leader like Tiger Jack Wood tried to be creative during the Tennessee field maneuvers, he was castigated for "fighting the problem." It is worth asking—how much better would American forces have been if the generals had made a greater effort at exploiting GI ingenuity when they began training America's mass army in 1940 rather than when they began fighting with it in 1943?

After 1945, what the Army lost that was most important were men schooled in the practice of GI warfare. They went home to college, family, and General Motors. At the same time, after World War II the Army created a peacetime training system that did not try to replicate the gift to innovate in battle. In spirit, the Army's postwar training system was pretty much a copy of the World War II Army Training Program. "The Army fought in Vietnam," concluded U.S. Army Training and Doctrine Command (TRADOC) veteran General Paul Gorman, "with its close combat training little improved over that of McNair's AGF during World War II, or the Army's training base during Korea."[6]

As a result, when America's citizen-soldiers were called to battle in Korea and Vietnam, they had to do what the greatest generation did, learn how to fight wars on the job and bring GI ingenuity to bear in battle once again.

The Army did not try to refight World War II in Korea and Vietnam. But, the good things that it did in both wars occurred for much the same reason that GIs succeeded in the Second World War. In both Korea and Vietnam, soldiers and leaders adapted and innovated, just like the soldiers of the greatest generation. In Korea, during the static last phase of the conflict, GIs taught themselves how to fight trench warfare, because that was the nature of the war and the kind of fighting that was demanded. In Vietnam, tactical and material innovation was a hallmark of Army operations.[7]

In the cases of World War II, Korea, and Vietnam, America had to make citizens into soldiers in a hurry. The difference between World War II and Korea and Vietnam was that in the Second World War leaders learned and fought; in Korea and Vietnam, they learned and left. In France, most combat leaders stayed with their troops until they were fired, promoted, or became casualties. In Korea and Vietnam, when leaders learned and teamwork and innovation were achieved, the benefits soon evaporated with rotation policies that sent individual soldiers home after a tour of combat duty. The declining experience of combat leaders was what led innovative commanders such as DePuy to always keep things very simple in battle and rely on firepower.

Senior leadership was also a problem. Good generalship required understanding both the character of industrial-strength warfare and tactical and technical innovation and adaptation. Just knowing how to run the assembly line was not enough.

During the era from Korea to Vietnam, the Army promoted two kinds of generals; without a shooting war in between, it was hard to tell one kind from the other. Westmoreland and Abrams were a case in point. William Westmoreland was a product of doughboy genius—smart, hardworking, and ambitious. He could run things. There was no question about that. But, he lacked all the talents needed to be a modern genius for war. He was a veteran of both World War II and Korea. He directed the big battles in Vietnam rather well, including delivering a crushing defeat on the North Vietnamese Army in response to the Tet Offensive of 1968. But he lacked a realistic, proactive way to win the war, and he lacked an appreciation for GI genius.

On paper, Abe Abrams looked much like the same kind of soldier. Abe, however, had what it took to be the consummate twentieth century soldier. He was a master of big problems and a GI innovator of the first order. It took an Abrams to take Harold Johnson's PROVN plan and actually put it into practice. Abrams effectively stabilized Vietnam and fielded a Vietnamese Army that could defend the country. If the United States Congress had not cut off aid and support in 1975 when North Vietnam invaded, Abrams's achievement might be more well recognized today.[8]

In peacetime, the Army had a difficult time telling an Abrams from a Westmoreland. They were all just tough-talking, good-looking guys in uniform, with close-cropped haircuts. The Army training, promotion, and professional developments systems were not sophisticated enough to tell the difference. This was another part of the problem of sustaining GI ingenuity in the post-World War II years.

## BACK FROM THE BRINK

In 1973 the Army was in a death spiral. It was dying not because it was doing as Baritz claimed, trying to repeat the Army's success in World War II; it was dying because the Army would not let go of its greatest failure after World War II—failing to institutionalize the practice of GI ingenuity. That needed to change.

After Vietnam, Abrams followed Westmoreland as chief of staff. He had an idea that would never have occurred to Westmoreland. Westmoreland was proud of the Army systems that had elevated him to command. Abrams was proud of the people, but thought the people succeeded, in spite of, not because of the system. Abrams was out to change the system.

Abrams Commanding U.S. Troops in Vietnam. (Courtesy, Army Signal Corps)

A big part of the mission of changing the Army fell to Abram's Assistant Vice Chief of Staff. After his appointment as TRADOC commander, DePuy oversaw the overhaul of the Army's training programs. He undertook the most significant restructuring of training since World War II. The most important piece DePuy added was the one thing McNair had not accomplished, adding realistic combat decision making. Depuy, assisted by Paul Gorman, started the Army's training revolution.[9] Their goal was not just to make training sound and look like battle, but to give leaders the moral and intellectual tests they would face in combat.

The Army's training revolution was intended to win the next war in Europe. Instead, it was vindicated in the sands of Iraq and in the mountains of Kosovo and Afghanistan. That Americans triumphed at all on battlefields so different from the central plain of Europe was testament enough to the Army's ability to train its leaders to adapt to the realties of modern war. What also distinguished post-Cold War combat was the capacity to win quickly. In many of America's wars, if Americans lost the first battle, they at least demonstrated (as they did at Soissons during World War I and in North Africa during World War II) how much more there was to learn on the job.[10] America's wars of the late twentieth and early twenty-first century were different. GIs started winning from the start.

## THE HOLLOW ARMY

The training revolution of the 1970s proved doubly important because the Army after Vietnam saw some of its most dramatic cuts in forces structure and resources since World War II. And much of it happened on Abrams's watch when he was the Chief of Staff. After Vietnam, Congress moved quickly to downsize the military and cut funding. The Army became a "hollow force" with inadequate troops, training, and equipment. By the end of the decade, Army Chief of Staff Edward "Shy" Meyer told President Jimmy Carter that only four of the service's 16 active divisions stood ready for battle.

The Reserves were even worse off. Recruiting plummeted after the war. Nearly one out of every two volunteers for the new postdraft "all-volunteer force" was a high-school dropout or scored in the lowest category on the Army's intelligence test.

It was an "OK Army." There was no money to modernize weapons and equipment. That task had been deferred to pay for the war. But that was OK—units did not have enough people to train on the equipment, anyway. Even if they had had the people to fill the ranks, there was not enough money to pay for training and maintenance. It was all OK—as long as America did not actually have to fight anybody.

The Army was in trouble in large part because the economy was in trouble. When President Lyndon Johnson initiated a round of federal spending in the mid-1960s, the impact on American business was disastrous. Johnson insisted on funding both the war effort in Vietnam and a plethora of domestic social programs. That required increases in taxation. With the economy already at near records of unemployment, the result was a vicious round of "stagflation," skyrocketing prices and scant economic growth. Unemployment was 3.5 percent at the height of the Tet Offensive in 1968 (statistically a fully employed economy). It was 5.9 percent in 1971. By 1973 the stock market average was performing as sluggishly as it had in the 1930s. Inflation was unprecedented in peacetime history. Nobody was much interested in funding defense.

The 1980s saw a restructuring of the U.S. economy and an upturn in the business cycle that began a long period of economic growth. After a mild recession in 1990–1991, the United States entered an unmatched period of economic growth coupled with the introduction of a flood of new information technologies including the proliferation of the Internet and personal computers.

As the economy recovered, so did the military. In the 1980s, an adrenaline shot of funding from the Reagan administration saved the services. Some parts of the force, such as the National Guard, still never got the resources it needed, but by the end of the Cold War, after a decade of investment, it again was an Army of which to be proud. However, without the intellectual rebuilding of the Army that started under DePuy in the 1970s, there might have been no base to build on. As the Army did during the interwar years, after Vietnam the service preserved its "intellectual" capital. And when it came time to rebuild, the Army was ready.

## WARRIORS

Since the end of the Cold War, the Army has also tried to keep pace with the nature of the society in which it lives. America at the turn of the new century is a fundamentally different nation than it was at the end of World War II, as different in character as GIs were from doughboys. America today is driven by an information-age economy built on the capacity of the computer chip. As with ages past, the new character of this industrial era will inevitably be reflected in how the nation fights. That means America's soldiers in the twenty-first century will need to add a new kind of genius to tap the industrial and human potentials of the postindustrial American society.

The Army already has some idea of what this genius might be. As with ages past, today's generals stole their vision of the future from the science fiction of the future. That vision of tomorrow comes not from *Star Wars* (1977) but *Star Trek* (1966–1969). *Star Wars,* after all, was just World War II in space, complete with battle sequences modeled on combat footage from dogfighting P-47s. On the other hand, the NBC television series featured the captain and crew of the starship *Enterprise* on a mission to explore and police outer space. What is notable about how Captain James T. Kirk (William Shatner) commands his ship is that he appears to be able to contact and be aware of what every individual is doing, and he can direct their actions with a single verbal command because they are all linked together by "computer." All the systems on the ship are integrated.

When generals were asked after the Cold War what kind of Army they wanted, how they envisioned computers changing the nature of war, what they described sounded suspiciously like *Star Trek* with themselves standing on the bridge of the starship. The TRADOC commander at the time, General William Hartzog (1994–1998), owned up even to having a pair of "Spock ears" (Kirk's executive officer was an alien named Spock, played by actor Leonard Nimoy, sporting pointed rubber ears).

That generals at TRADOC might have been inspired by reruns of a 1960s sci-fi TV series should not seem like too much of a stretch. They were following in a long-standing tradition of American soldiers who found inspiration from imaginative writing. Colonel William Triplet fought as an enlisted soldier with the Thirty-Fifth Division in the Meuse-Argonne. As a commissioned officer, he fought in combat with an armored division during World War II. During the interwar years, "since 1935," he recalled, "I had supplemented my inadequate pay by writing fantasies about futuristic weapons or tactics ... in the 40s or 50s against the Munga invaders. The Infantry Journal paid me at the top rate of five cents a word." After the journal published a story he wrote based on a futuristic six-wheeled jeep, he was summoned to his commander's office. "Triplet ... any ideas that you have while you're working for me, if they're any good they're TOP SECRET."[11] While it is true, there were always some officers who were more concerned about saving the horse and cavalry saber than anything else, there were always men like Triplet who hungered for what new technology might bring. Hartzog would have related well to Triplet's appetite for imagining what future militaries might look like.

And imagining the future was not just something limited to the Army. After the Cold War, visionary officers in all the services began talking about the creation of a "system of systems" or network-centric warfare, where all the components of the force were linked together so they could share information.[12] Instead of conducting combined-arms warfare, where the challenge was to figure out how to have separate systems such as artillery, armor, and airpower cooperate with each other, the twenty-first century challenge was building a single system that integrated all of these capabilities.

In calling for the establishment of information-age forces, the generals and admirals in the Pentagon were not just parroting science fiction; they were trying to emulate business and management practices that were becoming common in the marketplace. Companies such as FedEx can identify where any package is, at anytime, anywhere in the world. Wal-Mart can monitor what every register in its stores is selling and send that information to buyers, stock managers, advertisers, and suppliers. That is systems integration. The American military wants to be able to do the same thing in war: know what the system knows—and get the right information, to right person, at the right time, to do the right thing. Systems integration is the twenty-first century skill of modern warriors—and the next generation of American military genius.

## THE MODERN LOUISIANA MANEUVERS

Gordon R. Sullivan was the Army's first post-Cold War Chief of Staff (1991–1995). Carl Vuono was actually Chief of Staff when the Berlin Wall came down in 1989, but his turn in George Marshall's old chair was consumed with fundamental decisions of downsizing the Army as America had done after its other wars. Sullivan was arguably the first chief to have the time to think very seriously about what America's Army would look like in the twenty-first century.

Sullivan chose to call the centerpiece of his effort "The Modern Louisiana Maneuvers." It was both the most perfect and the oddest of choices.

"LAM," as staff officers took to calling Sullivan's initiative, was the perfect choice because Sullivan, as Marshall, faced a similar challenge: developing a new Army for a new era. "I was compelled," Sullivan said, "by the power of Marshall's ideas and by his intent to conduct experiments that would be the basis for designing new units and battlefield processes … . Borrowing Marshall's title was a signal that business as usual was not good enough … ."[13] Sullivan intended LAM to start turning the Army into an integrated system, an information-age force.

LAM was also an odd choice. Given all we know about the shortfalls in McNair's efforts to use the general headquarters maneuvers to develop new concepts and verify that commands were ready for battle, the exercises were not something to emulate in total. After all, McNair argued the maneuvers validated antitank doctrine, and he certified that the 90th Division was ready for battle.

Sullivan's task was to capture the spirit, the practice of McNair's maneuvers. LAM, as Sullivan envisioned it, was not to be series of exercises with regular troops, but a plethora of integrated experimental activities and studies that would be used to inform major decisions about how to reengineer the Army. The centerpiece, according to LAM historian James Yarrison, was "digitizing the battlefield, using automated interactive exchanges of positional and other information to provide a common, relevant picture of the battlefield. The development and emplacement of these digital linkages would enable the forces so equipped to operate more responsively, to anticipate their own and their opponents' next moves, to gain better protection through greater dispersion and to avoid fratricide through better combat identification."[14] LAM offered one of the first coherent and comprehensive expressions of an integrated systems approach for postmodern war. It was a vision of harnessing computers to drive every aspect of battle. It was a vision of the warrior.

LAM set up for business at DePuy's old command, TRADOC. The officer in charge was an upcoming Army brigadier general, a Vietnam veteran with reputations both as an out-of-the-box thinker and a plainspoken soldier. His name was Tommy Franks.

"Our task from General Sullivan," Franks recalled, "was to take a hard look at the most important things the Army did, the structure of our units, our training methods, and procedures we used to develop and procure new weapons and equipment."[15] One of the first tasks Franks focused on was adapting systems integration to military practices. And one of the first places he turned was the private sector. "The Schneider Trucking Company," Franks found, "had been the first firm to install GPS [a global positioning system, satellite-based navigation system first developed by the military to guide long-range cruise missiles] receivers with coded software, allowing dispatchers and managers to see instantly where any of their more than 400,000 trucks was at any time, anywhere in the nation. Each vehicle had a transponder that broadcast not only its position, but also its unit number and cargo. The military application of the technology was obvious, so one of our task force teams contacted the company. Now armored, mechanized infantry, and logistics commanders could track their forces ... ."[16] It was the first step in digitizing the service.

Sullivan and Franks started a trend. Each service chief that followed made another step toward building an information-age, integrated army. Following Sullivan's lead the next Army Chief of Staff, Dennis Reimer (1995–1999), initiated his own framework for analysis—the Army After Next Project. According to Army War College analyst Steven Metz, the project was an ongoing series of war games, workshops, studies, and conferences whose purposes were to postulate "the feasible strategic environments of the 2020–2025 period and speculate on the sort of technology, force structure, and operational concepts the U.S. Army might need."[17] Reimer, who had served as aide-de-camp to Abrams during his tenure as Chief of Staff (before he succumbed to cancer), used the project to make the argument that the future area would be heavily invested in information technologies, a multilayered system of integrated sensors, weapons systems, and organizations. The next chiefs of staff, Eric K. Shinseki (1999–2003) and Peter J. Schoomaker (2003–) began developmental and reorganization programs to develop these capabilities under an initiative called "Future Combat Systems."

## GLOBAL WAR, GLOBAL ARMY

Initially, the Army took a different direction than the other services. The Navy and the Air Force invested more of their post-Cold War effort in replacing their existing systems. They wanted better planes and faster ships. And they invested more effort in getting to the battle quicker, particularly in austere places where U.S. forces had not gone before. This was often called "expeditionary warfare." While the Army was focusing on "digitization" and wiring things to computers, the other services were focusing on getting there first, with the most.

And initially, it seemed that the Army had guessed wrong in what it would take to be the master of twenty-first century warfare. After 1989 the demand for military forces all proved to be in unexpected places and have unexpected needs. And the Army with its massive requirements for logistical support and transportation seemed too slow to keep up. In particular, the Army came under significant criticism for its perceived inability to quickly deploy forces to support U.S. operations in Kosovo (1999).[18] In fact, when General Eric Shinseki first introduced what became the Future Combat Systems program in 2001, a large part of the rationale he gave was that it was designed to make units lighter so they could deploy faster.

Perceptions change. The success of conventional military operations in Afghanistan (2001) and Iraq (2003) proved to be a turning point in postmodern warfare. Under the command of Tommy Franks, who now was a four-star general responsible for overseeing both operations, American soldiers fought in ways they never had before. The precision-guided long-range weapons, unmanned aerial vehicles, satellite reconnaissance, command posts stuffed with computers, and the blistering pace of operations all suggested that future wars might be as different from the struggles of the Cold War as World War II was from World War I.

While faster deployment was desirable, command of information was essential. Today, all of the Defense Department's modernization programs have some aspect of integrating systems and infusing information-age capabilities as a centerpiece of their initiatives. Even the Army's Future Combat System program, as it has developed, has placed less emphasis on rapid deployment and more on building an information-system backbone to support land warfare.

Some military visionaries took the notion of a system-of-systems force to the extreme, sounding like the information-age version of J.F.C. Fuller. Admiral Bill Owens, a former Vice Chairman of the Joint Chiefs of Staff, gave his book on future warfare the evocative title *Lifting the Fog of War* (2000), suggesting how far some were willing to go. Owens predicted that the friction of battle so famously described by Carl von Clausewitz might be largely overcome by militaries going into battle sporting near perfect knowledge. Genius was no longer required. That was an overstretch.

Indeed, the victories in Afghanistan and Iraq did not resemble Owens's vision of frictionless battle or Baritz's convoluted notions of techno-war. Of the many integrated technologies that the Americans employed, some worked better than expected; some proved less mature than many had hoped; some failed miserably.[19] The spirit of Clausewitz was alive and well. When integrated systems failed in Iraq and Afghanistan (as when the generals' plans failed in Normandy) soldiers picked up the slack. In some cases, they responded with personal courage and valor, a staple needed in any war. In other instances, GI ingenuity, a skill that since Vietnam has been trained and fostered in Army leaders, made the difference.

When the 126th Armored Battalion deployed to Iraq in 2005, it faced a fearsome problem. While Coalition Forces had made short work of the Iraqi Army during the 2003 invasion, insurgents still roamed parts of the country terrorizing troops and civilians with IEDs—improvised explosive devices. The Army's basic troop-carrying and patrolling vehicle, the Humvee, was no match for these powerful devices often buried as land mines or carried by cars or trucks. The Army tried adding armor to the light-skinned vehicles, but the insurgents started making bigger bombs.

The Brigade Commander, Colonel Michael Steele, said something had to be done. Among the troops of the 126th was a group of citizen-soldiers from Michigan: mechanics, electricians, and carpenters. The best way to defeat an IED, they argued, was to either keep it from exploding or not be there when it went off. They constructed a six-foot boom that could be mounted on the Humvee. On the boom they mounted dangling chains, a thermal imaging camera, and infrared countermeasure devices. These could be used to detonate the IED or identify suspicious locations before the Humvee rolled over the top of a land mine. Some units added jamming devices that could block the signals of cell phones and garage door openers, which the insurgents had rigged as remote detonating devices.[20] Sergeant Curtis G. Culin would have been proud. It was GI ingenuity all over again.

In other cases, there were interesting examples of GI geniuses meeting warrior integrators. During the 1st Cavalry Division's tour of duty policing downtown Baghdad, the division commander recalled,

> To help those junior leaders [lieutenants and sergeants] we came up with Cav-Net A knowledge transfer system where individuals can post emerging enemy and friendly TTPs [tactics, techniques, and procedures] on SIPRNET [secure internet protocol network]. A platoon sergeant could see the newest TTP on the CavNet just before he conducted PCIs [pre-combat inspections, where troops were checked to see if they had all their equipment for the next mission] or briefed his platoon on its upcoming patrol, or he could post what he saw or learned during his patrol on the CavNet. This is *revolutionary*. Let me give you

an example. In one part of the city, we saw Muqtada al Sadr [radical Iraqi cleric who directed attacks against American occupation forces] posters being rigged with IEDs. The natural response of an American Soldier is to rip down the poster. A soldier in one part of the city noticed wires coming out of the poster and discovered it was booby trapped. He posted the info on CavNet that night. Days later, because a Soldier had checked the CavNet, a platoon in another part of the city checked out posters and found them booby-trapped too.[21]

The 1st Cavalry Division took its secure Internet, a means for promoting systems integration, and created a new use for it. And the division did it on its own, in the middle of ongoing operations. It was the spirit of the modern warrior fused with the practicality of GI "can do it."

## THE FOG OF PEACE

Indeed, the character of American soldiers and their army in the twenty-first century seems in many ways reminiscent of the greatest generation—in both strengths ... and failings.

Franks seemed like the perfect twenty-first century general: personally courageous, an industrial-strength manager, a GI innovator, and a warrior integrator. Where Franks ran into trouble was in fighting the war after the war—little surprise there. In the fight for peace, Franks found fog and friction at every turn. In the end, the occupation of Iraq proved far more difficult than winning the war.

Where American soldiers have had trouble since the end of the Cold War should not have been too difficult to predict. They have struggled with peacekeeping missions such as Somalia, the occupation in Iraq, and tracking down terrorists in places such as Afghanistan. Even here, however, there are unmistakable signs of GI ingenuity at work, soldiers figuring out on the ground how to do what nobody taught them—police a town, negotiate a deal, care for civilians. And they might have started out doing these things right from the start if at the end of the Cold War the Army had sooner restructured its training, professional development, and education programs to better anticipate future missions.[22]

Indeed, if Americans had studied the history of World War II more closely, the shortfalls in the postconflict operations in Afghanistan and Iraq would have been eminently predictable. During World War II, general genius got the soldiers to the battlefield, but on the battlefield their grandiose plans (such as the invasion of Omaha and the breakout at St.-Lô) were flawed. They were saved by GI courage and GI genius. The occupations after World War II were much the same story.

After years of planning and preparation for the postwar occupations, in practice the large-scale plans were not sufficient to deal with the fog of peace. Nothing turned out as expected. The problems faced were more complex, difficult, and protracted than the Americans anticipated. In the end, the occupations succeeded, in large part, because the GIs did what they did during the war. They learned by trial and error. They improvised. They innovated. They kept at it till they got it right. Commanders, like Clarence Huebner, took the army they had and turned it into the one they needed. One of their initiatives was to reorganize conventional military forces into constabulary units that were better suited to occupation duties.[23]

In the end, the process by which Abrams undertook and implemented "Vietnamization" and the manner in which Army leaders established plans to deal with the insurgent threats in Iraq and Afghanistan proved to be not too different in character and took about the same amount of time. It was GI ingenuity blundering to victory once more.

In the future, if the American Army wants to do better, if it wants to win the peace as efficiently as it wins wars, and if it wants to perform all the national security missions it may be called on to perform as skillfully as it fights battles, then it will have to adapt America's genius for war to all the challenges it will face in the twenty-first century.

In some ways the challenge to this generation and the next generation is the same as it was to the greatest generation and the doughboy generation —adapting the capabilities of technology to the reality of conflict. The good news is, as strategist Steven Metz wrote, "No military is better at this than the American, in large part, because no culture is better at this than the American."[24] As long as that remains so, the freedoms and liberties of free nations secured on battlefields like Normandy will remain secure.

# Fantastic Voyage

## A REMEMBRANCE OF THINGS PAST

There is nothing in Normandy now but monuments. Still, while the war is more than a half century gone, while the greatest generation is raising its last salutes, and while the reality of war has been overwhelmed by ribbons of Hollywood celluloid, there is something to be gained by walking the fields of Normandy.

On the fields of Normandy are monuments to all the things that made the American Army great in battle. In the cemetery above Omaha rest many of our boys. To walk past the white stones is to walk down a seemingly endless row of markers, each one chiseled with—Private, Infantry; Private; Infantry; Sergeant, Private, Private, Private, Sergeant. These gardens of stone remind us of the fundamental requirement for success in any Army—the sacrifice and valor and selfless service of boots on the ground. Character and courage are fundamental to genius.

Bravery and numbers, however, are not enough. It took the genius of generals to raise, equip, train, and get an Army to the fight. There is one stone in the Omaha cemetery that bears that remembrance. The name on it: Lesley McNair. America's Army would never have gotten to the front without him. The genius for industrial-strength warfare was learned in the Great War and honed in the fight against Hitler by men such as McNair.

There is no stone monument to GI ingenuity in Normandy. But, there is the perfect remembrance. The Norman countryside is little changed since Creighton Abrams's tanks and Clarence Huebner's infantry fought their way through the bocage. The hedgerows themselves are the best reminder of how smart leaders figured out how to lead brave men past unanticipated obstacles.

The modern warriors are there, too. Every year the history department at the military academy at West Point (the department founded by the visionary historian and educator Colonel Tom Griess, a World War II veteran who served in the Pacific) takes a group of cadets to Normandy to visit the battlefields. There they learn of the American genius for war: the genius perfected by their grandfathers and borne in the hearts of their great-grandchildren. In their brains, the cadets carry the seeds for the genius of this generation—adding to a skill set that includes courage, management, and innovation is the skill of integrating complex systems—the wisdom of making new technologies applicable to the age-old challenges of war.

## FEAR FOR THE FUTURE

The American genius for war at the dawn of the twenty-first century is a combination of courage, industrial-strength generalship, GI ingenuity, and systems integration. While the current generation of soldiers learned Normandy's lessons (and brought the advantages of their own era to the test of war), they still face the challenges that confronted Omar Bradley, George Patton, Dwight Eisenhower, and Abrams during their careers—enduring the fate of an army when not at war.

As America reduces operations in Afghanistan and Iraq, as likely as not there will be pressures to reduce defense spending, as there were after World War I, World War II, and Vietnam. That could be troubling. The post-Cold War drawdown took its toll on the military. Defense spending as a percentage of Gross Domestic Product (GDP) (the total value of goods and services in the U.S. economy) sank to its lowest levels since the outbreak of World War II. The Clinton administration took a prolonged procurement holiday and cut the force to the razor-thin minimum needed to get by.

Although defense spending increased at the end of the Clinton years and then rose sharply under Bush, much of these resources have gone to support operations in Afghanistan and Iraq. And these operations strained the force —helicopters wearing out at five times their expected rate, and trucks going into overhaul five times faster than expected. America's military served the nation well, but it is a tired warhorse.

After Iraq and Afghanistan, it could be 1920 or 1945 or 1973 all over again. There is always pressure to balance the budget on the back of defense cuts.

Cutting funding levels before resetting the military for its next mission is a bad idea. The military has been stretched, and it shows. The National Guard alone has had to transfer more than 74,000 soldiers from one command to another just to fill the ranks deploying overseas. Since 9/11, the Army has transferred more than 35,000 pieces of equipment from nondeploying units to forces in Iraq, leaving the stay-behind commands lacking more than a third of their critical equipment.

Without adequate budgets, today's soldiers, like their fathers, grandfathers, and great-grandfathers before them, will have trouble maintaining the military the nation needs. That is a problem.

Nowhere is the danger of losing the Army America needs greater than in the parts of the Army required to train and educate the intellectual capital of the force—the place where general genius, GI ingenuity, and warrior integrators are nurtured. Military schools have changed only modestly since the end of the Cold War. Preparing to fight a known enemy required certain skills and knowledge, and professional education focused on those narrow areas. As a result, officer schools and development programs have continued to train and promote leaders with skills and attributes to meet the needs of the twentieth century, not future challenges. Note a case in point—despite the fact that the U.S. military has conducted an average of one peacekeeping, peacemaking, or postconflict operation every two years since the end of the Cold War, military education and training programs offered scant preparation for the postwar challenges in Iraq. And the money to do even the traditional things the Army has always done is atrophying. That is a real danger.

## SHOW ME THE MONEY

The lack of funds for the future is not a problem created by one political party or the other. It reflects the changing nature of modern governments. Government in the developed world has expanded substantially during the past century. The United States stands at the apex of this trend. One of the best measures of the burden that the federal government, as a whole, imposes on the national economy through its spending policies is the percentage of GDP taken up by outlays. During America's first 140 years, the federal government rarely consumed more than 1 or 2 percent of GDP. In accordance with the U.S. Constitution, Washington focused on defense and certain public goods, while leaving most other functions to the States or the people themselves. That changed in the twentieth century. Between 1962 and 2000, defense spending plummeted from 9.3 percent of GDP to 3.0 percent. Nearly all of the funding shifted from defense spending went into mandatory spending (mostly entitlement programs), which jumped from 6.1 percent of GDP to 12.1 percent during that same period.

The importance of this evolution cannot be understated. For most of the nation's history, the federal government's chief budgetary function was funding defense. This two-thirds decline in defense spending since 1962 has substantially altered the makeup and the structure of the U.S. national defense.

Today, spending on defense and homeland security in the United States stands at about 4.0 percent of GDP, the highest level of investment since the end of the Cold War. However, this represents, on average, less than half what the nation spent before the fall of the Berlin Wall and a fraction of the 40 percent of GDP spent on the military during World War II. And, unlike the Cold War period, post-Cold War defense spending is faced with unprecedented competition for federal dollars with mandatory government spending on entitlement programs.

Mandatory outlays for programs such as Social Security, Medicare, and Medicaid are consuming, and will continue to consume, ever-larger percentages of federal spending and total GDP. As a result, they will apply increasing pressure to crowd out the resources available to the government's traditional primary mission—providing security to the nation. And that will likely change how future wars are fought.

Nor is the United States unique in facing this dilemma. European nations, which already spend on average less than 2 percent of their GDP on defense, and spend much more of their national budgets on social services and entitlements, face similar predicaments. As potential economic and military power-houses such as China and India move from the ranks of the developing to the developed, they will also confront the same kinds of challenges. In fact, India and China may encounter even more pressure to rein in defense spending since they will have much larger populations demanding higher levels of social services.

None of this means that modern militaries will not spend money to fight wars. They always do. But it does mean they may do like the democracies did during the years of the Depression before World War II: skimp on defense, encourage aggression, and pay for the lack of preparedness at a future Kasserine Pass.

## A FEW GOOD MEN … AND WOMEN

Demographic changes could well exacerbate the strain of America's ability to fight modern war. During World War II, the United States mobilized over 8 million for its Army without sacrificing the productive capacity to serve as the arsenal for democracy. That is something America might never be able to do again.

As nations develop, their population growth slows and the average age of the population increases, as does the cost of manpower. The result is an increasingly shrinking population available to run with the dogs of war.

In the future, the changes caused by the dynamics of demographics will accelerate, altering the character of modern military forces and their attributes as an instrument of battle. Although the rate of population increases in developed countries will slow, the total size of the population will continue to grow—and less of the national polity will be suitable for military service.

The cost of military manpower will also increase as armed forces find themselves competing with the private sector for talented young people. The total size of militaries in relation to the nation as a whole will likely continue to decrease in the years to come. At the same time, as populations age, militaries will likely diversify those they seek to bring into the ranks to compensate for the shrinking pool of traditional military-age males.

Over the next few decades, the U.S. military and other national forces in the developed world might include more women, individuals with disabilities, noncitizens, and older persons.

At the same time, the use of conscription as a form of military service could well decline. With a trend toward fielding forces armed with more technology and more sophisticated skills, short-service conscription will be seen increasingly as inadequate, not allowing sufficient time to train forces and requiring excessive costs to frequently retrain new recruits. Likewise, with militaries becoming smaller in developed nations, conscription will be seen increasingly as socially divisive because it will be difficult to equitably draw on the available eligible pool of recruits. In all likelihood, military drafts will be viewed as inefficient and ineffective means for mobilizing manpower in developed, liberal democracies.

Finally, the impact of economic and demographic trends on the developed world could exacerbate the gap between how nations and nonstate actors wage war in the twenty-first century. The span between the military capabilities of undeveloped, failing (and failed) states, developing nations, and the developed world will only grow in the decades ahead.

As a result, the twenty-first century could well see a witch's brew of countries and nonstate actors, such as transnational terrorist groups, fighting with very different means, employed in a polyglot of ways, toward a dizzying array of divergent ends. Some analysts call these "asymmetric" wars. Such conflicts will be a real test for the American genius in war.

## THE ARSENALS OF DEMOCRACIES

Another way in which the world of today and tomorrow is fundamentally different from days of the greatest generation concerns the American industrial base. America is no longer a nation of manufacturers. Today, the United States imports goods and services from around the world. The U.S. industrial base is the planet.

And military services are not just supplied by militaries. The trend for militaries to increasingly outsource logistical and support functions is well established. Added to that, however, is the emerging use of private sector companies to provide traditional combat services, ranging from training soldiers to patrolling streets.

Reliance on private sector assets in war is likely irreversible. Unlike the public sector, the private sector is bred for efficiency. Left to its own devices it will always find the means to provide services faster, cheaper, and more efficiently than governments.

In addition, governments are losing their monopoly over the research and development that creates new technologies with military applications. During World War II and into the Cold War, the government financed much of the cutting-edge technologies that resulted in new combat capabilities. Today, government is virtually dependent on the private sector for cutting-edge research and development. And not all of it is being conducted inside the United States.

War in the twenty-first century will be neither a private nor a public matter, but a civil activity that spans both worlds, with each realm having a substantial amount of autonomy and influence. Harnessing the global private sector will be another significant challenge for America's warriors.

## IT IS A SMALL WORLD AFTER ALL

While today's Army tries to nurture its genius through the challenges of the years ahead, it is not too soon to ask what will be the next version of American genius. Fifty years from now the dominating technologies America brings to the table may be very different. And it will require a new form of military genius.

The future is a foreign country. Knowing it does not come easy. That is why soldiers so often have turned to science fiction for their inspiration. They may do that again.

Science fiction may have already offered one glimpse of the next wave of military genius. Today's generals probably saw it when they were in junior high school. In *Fantastic Voyage* (1966) a group of scientists board the research vessel *Proteus*. (It is commonly believed the movie was adapted from a novel by writer Isaac Asimov; actually the script was written first by Harry Kleiner, and Asimov was paid to write a novelization that came out before the movie.) The *Proteus* is shrunk to microscopic size and injected into a human being where the scientists perform lifesaving surgery. The film won an Oscar for special effects—and complaints from reviewers that the cast included sexpot movie queen Rachel Welch, but she was never seen in the film in any state other than fully clothed.

*Fantastic Voyage* was classic 1960s science fiction. The film dropped the metaphors for Cold War confrontation, which dominated the 1950s films (though the plot featured a Soviet-American rivalry over the miniaturization technology). The technology was the star. *Star Trek,* for example, was widely popular with young people and developed a cult following as they became adults because it merged cool new technologies with story lines that addressed relevant social issues such as racism, war, and nuclear proliferation. Contemporary plots made the technology seem even more plausible.

There was a reason why technology got star billing in the science fiction of the 1960s. So many of the technologies featured in the movies of the 1950s had, by the 1960s, become science fact (men had flown in space, built atom bombs, and put satellites in orbit). Americans believed that what they saw on the screen today might be reality tomorrow. In the 1960s Americans took their science fiction seriously. *Fantastic Voyage* proved so compelling and popular because it featured technologies that had not been showcased in films before and displayed them with state-of-the-art special effects.

In the course of modern warfare, science in battle has not perfectly mirrored science in fiction. The tanks that rolled across France did not look exactly like the Martian war machines. Nor may humans ever maneuver submarines through bloodstreams. But, that does not mean *Fantastic Voyage* was not on to something. Indeed, the next technologies that transform how armies fight wars may be the technologies of the very small. The next great technological advances will likely be those that deal with the molecular level.

One is biotechnology. Biotechnology is one of the fastest growing commercial sectors in the world. The number of biotechnology companies in the United States alone has tripled since 1992. These firms are research intensive, bringing new methods and products into the marketplace every day. Many of the benefits of this effort are largely dual use, creating knowledge, skills, and capabilities that may transform the nature of peace and war. Rapid advances in biotechnology are being accelerated by commensurate advances in information technologies known as bioinformatics. What they may bring to the nature of war remains to be seen. Weapons and sophisticated countermeasures may not be the only potential contribution to new ways of war. Biotechnology may reshape medical practices (on and off the battlefield) and human performance, allowing for unprecedented levels of individual achievement and endurance.

Another is nanotechnology. Nanotechnlogy involves developing or working with materials at the level where at least one dimension falls within the range of 1–100 nanometers, the tiniest fraction of a human hair. Working at such a small scale offers unique capabilities, such as being able to control how nanodevices interact with other systems at the atomic or molecular level. Current research areas include materials, sensors, biomedical nanostructures, electronics, optics, and fabrication, but the future applications may be limited only by the imagination.

Materials that have been modified at the nanoscale can have specific properties incorporated into them. For instance, materials can have coatings that make them water-repellent or stain resistant. Nanoscale electronics can help to shrink computer circuits to microscopic size. Fabrication at the nanoscale level offers the potential of creating devices from the atom up, as opposed to having to shrink materials down to the needed size. For example, using nano-technologies manufacturers have restructured the avionics of the Air Force's new F-22 aircraft, replacing over 1,000 parts with 36 microelectrical-mechanical machines.

What all this means is that if these and other similar technologies come to fruition, gravity will no longer matter. Weight might not matter. Operations that today require iron mountains of supplies and masses of men may be accomplished by machines the size of dust. By the middle of the twenty-first century the American genius for battle may be as masters of molecular warfare.

## TECHNOLOGY AND WAR

Technology has always been a factor in shaping the future of war, but its impact is far from deterministic. Technology does not define future ways of war. The conduct of warfare is shaped by larger cultural, economic, and political factors and strategic choices. That is a lesson from Normandy for all times.

The impact of future technologies will likely be the same. They might unleash or accelerate social and cultural changes that reshape the nature of war, but it is unlikely they will simplify or define how combat is conducted. Technology will always be a "wild card" in war's future. The American genius for war has always been rising above the tidal wave of technological change. In Normandy it was GI ingenuity. Tomorrow?

# Notes

## CHAPTER 1

1. Henry G. Gole, "DePuy and Vietnam, 1964–1968," in *The Most Dangerous Years, The Cold War, 1953-1975,* ed. Malcolm Muir and Mark F. Wilkinson (Lexington, KY: The Virginia Military Institute, 2005), 190.

2. Quotes are from the letter "Personnel Relieved or Transferred During My Period of Command," December 29, 1966, William E. DePuy Letters, Military History Institute; for DePuy's comments on his leadership style, see, for example, William E. DePuy, "Remarks to the Army Museum Conference," April 16, 1974, Historical Office, U.S. Army Training and Command, Fort Monroe, VA.

3. Bruce Palmer Interview, Military History Institute.

4. In 1980, Army Chief of Staff General Edward C. Meyer coined the term "Hollow Army" in congressional testimony to describe the shortage of soldiers available to fill the service's field units. The term is now widely used to characterize shortages of personnel, training, and equipment that significantly impinge on military readiness. See Department of Defense, CJSC Guide to the Chairman's Readiness System, September 1, 2000, p. 3. See also Department of the Army, Historical Summary Fiscal Year 1989, updated May 19, 2003, p. 4, http://www.army.mil/cmh-pg/books/DAHSUM/1989/CH1.htm.

5. Paul Herbert, "Deciding What Has to Be Done: General William E. DePuy and the 1976 Edition of FM 100-5, Operations," Leavenworth Papers No. 16, Fort Leavenworth, Combat Studies Institute, 1988, pp. 21–23.

6. Charles E. Kilpatrick, "Lesley J. McNair Training Philosophy for a New Army," *Army Historian* (Winter 1990): 11–15.

7. "Gen. McNair Talks," *Army and Navy Journal* (October 11, 1941): 143.

8. William E. DePuy, Oral History, Military History Institute, p. 202.

9. Harold J. Meyer, *Hanging Sam: A Military Biography of General Samuel T. Williams: From Pancho Villa to Vietnam* (College Station: University of North Texas Press, 1990), 81.

10. Omar N. Bradley, *A Soldier's Story* (New York: Henry Holt and Company, 1951), 296–97.

11. Martin Blumenson, *Breakout and Pursuit* (Washington, DC: Office of the Chief of Military History, 1961), 201.

12. U.S. Forces, European Theater, *Report of the General Board: Organization, Equipment, and Tactical Employment of the Infantry Division, Study No. 15*, p. 7.

13. S3, 357th Infantry Regiment, Training Memorandum No. 1, July 16, 1944.

14. William O. Odom, *After the Trenches: The Transformation of U.S. Army Doctrine, 1918–1939* (College Station: Texas A&M University Press, 1999), 132–42.

15. Gerald Astor, *Terrible Terry Allen: Combat General of World War II—The Life of an American Soldier* (New York: Ballantine Books, 2003), 221–29. Astor provides a detailed analysis of Allen's relief. He concludes it was unjustified.

16. John Colby, *War from the Ground Up: The 90th Division in World War II* (Austin, TX: Nortex Press, 1991), 17.

17. 90th Division Operations Memorandum, No. 2, June 19, 1944.

18. D.K. Reimers, unpublished manuscript, U.S. Military History Institute, p. 116.

19. Letter, Eisenhower to Marshall, July 5, 1944, quoted in Joseph Patrick Hobbs, *Dear General: Eisenhower's Wartime Letters to Marshall* (Baltimore: The Johns Hopkins University Press, 1971), 195.

20. Ibid.

21. Unless cited otherwise, the combat narrative of the 90th Division's attack is taken from Colby, *War from the Ground Up*, 137–44; Blumenson, *Breakout and Pursuit*, 201–4; U.S. Army, *Peragimus, "We Accomplish": A Brief History of the 358th Infantry* (Weiden, Germany: Ferdinand Nickl, 1945).

22. *The Infantry in Battle* (Washington, DC: The Infantry Journal, 1939), 35.

23. Colby, *War from the Ground Up*, 149.

24. Colby, *War from the Ground Up*, 149. Williams, in fact, according to DePuy, was one of the few skilled senior combat leaders in the division. DePuy, *Oral History*, 31.

25. Harold J. Meyer, *Hanging Sam*, 87–88.

26. D.C. Little, "Artillery in Support of the Capture of Hill 192," *Military Review* (March 1948): 31.

27. Blumenson, *Breakout and Pursuit*, 149–53.

28. Frank T. Mildren, "The Attack of Hill 192 by the 1st Battalion, 38th Infantry (2nd Division) July 11, 1944 (Normandy Campaign, Personnel Experience of a Battalion Commander)," unpublished monograph, Command and General Staff College, Fort Leavenworth, KS, 1946–1947, p. 5.

29. Department of the Army, German Defense Tactics Against Russian Breakthroughs, Pamphlet No. 20-233, October 1951, p. 35; Fritz Ziegelman, "History of the 352d Infantry Division," MS B-432, Combined Arms Research Library, Fort Leavenworth, KS, p. 3; see also Timothy A. Wray, "Standing Fast: German Defense Doctrine on the Russian Front During World War II: Prewar to March 1943," Combat Studies Institute, Fort Leavenworth, KS, 1986; James Jay Carafano, *After D-Day:*

*Operation Cobra and the Normandy Breakout* (Boulder, CO: Lynne Rienner, 2000): 26–27.

30. Ibid., 34–35.

31. Army Ground Forces Observation Board, European Theater Operations Report, No. 201, "Use of Dozer Tanks and Landing of Tanks in Amphibious Operations," p. 1.

32. U.S. Forces, European Theater, *Reports of the General Board*, Study No. 52, "Armored Special Equipment," pp. 14–17.

33. Army Ground Forces Observation Board, European Theater Operations Report. No. 191, "Notes on Interviews with Various Commanders in Normandy," pp. 2–3, Exhibits A, B, and C.

34. Michael D. Doubler, "Busting the Bocage: American Combined Arms Operations in France, 6 June–31 July 1944," Combat Studies Institute, Fort Leavenworth, KS, 1988, pp. 31–33.

35. The BAR was a heavy automatic infantry rifle that weighed about 20 pounds. It was durable and reliable. Each squad was assigned a BAR. They proved so popular most squads usually figured out ways to get a second weapon. The practice became so common that the Army eventually authorized to each squad two weapons.

36. *St-Lo,* American Forces in Action Series, Historical Division, War Department, August 21, 1946, Facsimile Reprint, 1994, CMH Pub 100-13, United States Army Center of Military History, Washington, DC, p. 61.

37. A slightly different account of the division's tactics is given in U.S. Army, 1st U.S. Army Group, "Battle Experiences," No. 8, pp. 1–8; see also Mildren, "Attack of Hill 192," 6. Some units used submachine guns instead of the second BAR.

38. Mildren, "Attack of Hill 192," 7.

39. Charles R, Cawthon, *Other Clay* (Niwot: University of Colorado Press, 1990), 87.

40. Mildren, "The Attack of Hill 192," 7.

41. Unless cited otherwise, the combat narrative of the attack on Hill 192 is taken from Mildren, "The Attack of Hill 192"; Little, "Artillery in Support," 31–37; and *St-Lo,* 58–68.

42. Army Ground Forces, Report No. 34, "741st Tank Battalion," p. 1.

43. *Rounds Complete: U.S. Army 65th Armored Field Artillery Battalion* (Philadelphia: Fidelty Press, 1947).

44. *St-Lo.* In the preface, the Army described the narrative as "Twelfth in the series of studies on particular combat operations, *St-Lo* is the story of a corps in the First Army during the bitter July battle that led up to and made possible the great breakthrough from the Normandy beachheads. This was the period of the most intense hedgerow fighting. XIX Corps' part in it has been chosen to illustrate this type of combat. The record of other First Army units in this operation has been covered only in outline.

This study is based upon a first narrative by 2nd Lt. David Garth, prepared in the field from military records and from notes and interviews recorded during the operation by members of the 2nd Information and Historical Service Detachment. The manuscript of this historical officer has been edited and partially rewritten with the help of additional documentation by Col. Charles H. Taylor of the Historical Division."

45. *St-Lo*, 65.

46. Blumenson, *Breakout and Pursuit*, 152.

47. Little, "Artillery in Support," 36–37.

48. Described in Michael Doubler, *Closing with the Enemy: How GIs Fought the War in Europe, 1944–1945* (Lawrence: University of Kansas Press, 1998), 65.

49. Carafano, *After D-Day*, 263.

50. *The Infantry in Battle*, 35.


## CHAPTER 2

1. Paul Fussell, *The Great War and Modern Memory* (New York: Oxford University Press, 1975), 43.

2. Ibid, 51.

3. Bradley, *A Soldier's Story*, 317–18.

4. Mathew S. Holland, *Eisenhower between the Wars* (Westport, CN: Praeger, 2001), 215–19. For a detailed history of the maneuvers, see Christopher R. Gabel, *The U.S. GHQ Maneuvers of 1941* (Washington, DC: United States Army Center of Military History, 1991).

5. Forrest C. Pogue, *George C. Marshall: Ordeal and Hope 1939–1942* (New York: Viking, 1966), 100–101.

6. Robert A. Griffin, ed., *School of the Citizen Soldier* (New York: D. Appleton-Century, 1942), ix.

7. Ibid., 261.

8. Ibid., 262.

9. Christopher Bassford, *The Reception of Clausewitz in English* (New York: Oxford University Press, 1994), 122.

10. Clausewitz apparently borrowed his definition of genius from the philosopher Immanuel Kant. Genius was "a talent for producing that for which definite rule can be given." Beatrice Heuser, *Reading Clausewitz* (London: Pimlico, 2002), 72.

11. Carl von Clausewitz, *On War*, ed. and trans. Michael Howard and Peter Paret (Princeton, NJ: Princeton University Press, 1986), 282.

12. Michael I. Handel, "Clausewitz in the Age of Technology," in *Clausewitz and Modern Strategy*, ed. Michael Handel (London: Frank Cass, 1986), 53–55.

13. Katherine L. Herbig, "Chance and Uncertainty in *On War*," in *Clausewitz and Modern Strategy*, 100-101.

14. Clausewitz, *On War*, 100.

15. This is described in Philip Bobbitt, *The Shield of Achilles: War, Peace, and the Course of History* (New York: Alfred A. Knopf, 2002), 69–74. Bobbitt also describes the historiographical debate over the complex relation between military developments and the process of state formation in Europe.

16. John Steele Gordon, *An Empire of Wealth: The Epic History of American Economic Power* (New York: Harper-Collins, 2004), 262.

17. Ibid., 286–96.

18. Ruth Schwartz Cowen, *A Social History of American Technology* (New York: Oxford University Press, 1997), 212.

19. Gordon, *An Empire of Wealth,* 232.

20. Allan R. Millett, *The General: Robert L. Bullard and Officership in the United States Army, 1881–1925* (Westport, CN: Greenwood, 1975), 3.

21. Ibid., 157, 200–201; 208–209.

22. Douglas V. Johnson II and Rolfe L. Hillman, Jr., *Soissons, 1918* (College Station: Texas A&M University Press, 1999), 26.

23. George C. Thorpe, *Pure Logistics the Science of War Preparation* (Washington, DC: National Defense University Press, 1986), 1.

24. Ibid., 4.

25. Edward M. Coffman, *War to End All Wars: The American Military Experience in World War I* (Madison: University of Wisconsin Press, 1968), 23, 37.

26. See B. P. Hughes, *Open Fire: Artillery Tactics from Marlborough to Wellington* (Chichester: Antony Bird Publications, 1983).

27. Boyd L. Dastrup, *King of Battle: A Branch History of the Field Artillery* (Fort Monroe, VA: Office of the Command Historian, U.S. Army Training and Doctrine Command, 1992), 145–150.

28. William J. Snow, *Signposts of Experience: World War Memoirs of Major General William J. Snow, USA-Retired* (Washington, DC: United States Field Artillery Association, 1941), 17.

29. Snow, *Signposts,* 208–24.

30. Rebecca Robbins Raines, *Getting the Message Through: A Branch History of the Signal Corps* (Washington, DC: United States Army Center of Military History, 1996), 171–72.

31. Linda R. Robertson, *The Dream of Civilized Warfare: World War I Flying Aces and the American Imagination* (Minneapolis: University of Minnesota Press, 2003), 11–23.

32. Dale E. Wilson, "The Birth of American Armor," in *Camp Colt to Desert Storm: The History of U.S. Armored Forces,* ed. George F. Hoffman and Donn A. Starry (Lexington: University of Kentucky Press, 199), 8–11; see also Dale E. Wilson, *Treat 'Em Rough! The Birth of American Armor, 1917–20* (Novato, CA: Presidio, 1989).

33. George S. Patton, Jr., "History of the 304th (1st) Tank Brigade Tank Corps," Box 49, Military Writings 1918–1920 File, George S. Patton Jr., Collection, Library of Congress, Washington, DC.

34. Unless noted otherwise, the battle narrative of Soissons is taken from Johnson and Hillman, *Soissons, 1918.*

35. United States Army Center of Military History, *The United States Army in the World War, 1917–1918*, vol. 5, *Military Operations of the American Expeditionary Forces,* reprint edition (Washington, DC: United States Army Center of Military History, 1989), 315.

36. While the story of the experiment is famous, it might actually not be wholly true. Charles Wrege and Amedeo Perroni, "Taylor"s Pig-Tale: A Historical Analysis of Frederick W. Taylor's Pig-Iron Experiments," *Academy of Management Journal* XVII (1974): 6–27.

37. John B. Wilson, *Maneuver and Firepower: The Evolution of Divisions and Separate Brigades* (Washington, DC: United States Army Center of Military History, 1998), 54.

38. Johnson and Hillman, *Soissons, 1918,* 137.

39. Thorpe, *Pure Logistics,* 3.

40. Robert H. Ferrell, *Collapse at the Meuse-Argonne* (Columbia: University of Missouri Press, 2004), 16.

41. *The Infantry in Battle,* 390.

42. Gordon, *An Empire of Wealth,* 289.

43. Charles E. Heller, "Chemical Warfare in World War I: The American Experience, 1917–1918" Combat Studies Institute, Fort Leavenworth, KS, September 1984, p. 87.

44. Carlo D'Este, *Patton: A Genius for War* (New York: HarperPerennial, 1995), 254.

45. German artillery innovation is described in Bruce L. Gudmundsson, *On Artillery* (Westport, CT: Praeger, 1993), 87–103.

46. D'Este, *Patton,* 260.

47. William S. Tripplet, *A Youth in the Meuse-Argonne, A Memoir, 1917–1918* (Columbia: University of Missouri Press, 2000), 168.

48. Quoted in D'Este, *Patton,* 254.

49. Charles J. Biddle, *Fighting Airmen: The Way of the Eagle* (Garden City, NY: Doubleday & Company, 1968), 95.

50. Tripplet, *A Youth in the Meuse-Argonne,* 167.

51. Ferrell, *Collapse in the Meuse-Argonne,* 107.

52. Kenneth E. Hamburger, "Learning Lessons in the American Expeditionary Force," United States Army Center of Military History, CMH-Pub 24-1, p. 22.

## CHAPTER 3

1. Fussell, *The Great War and Modern Memory,* 221.

2. Townsend Ludington, "John Dos Passos, 1896–1970: Modernist Recorder of the American Scene," *The Virginia Quarterly Review,* http://www.vqronline.org/viewmedia.php/prmMID/7640.

3. Rober Sklar, *Movie-Made America: A Cultural History of American Movies* (New York: Vintage, 1975), 77.

4. Quoted in Lawrence H. Suid, *Guts and Glory: Great American War Movies* (Reading, MA: Addison-Wesley, 1978), 26.

5. Suid, *Guts and Glory,* 29–30.

6. Quoted in Cowen, *A Social History of American Technology,* 210.

7. Robertson, *The Dream of Civilized Warfare* 267–304.

8. Suid, *Guts and Glory*, 25.

9. Edwin Howard Simmons, *The United States Marine Corps: A History* (Annapolis, MD: Naval Institute Press, 1998), 112.

10. Lowell Thomas, *Woodfill of the Regulars: A True Story of Adventure from the Arctic to the Argonne* (London: William Heinemann, 1930), 6.

11. *Infantry in Battle*, 398.

12. *Review of the Secretary of War 1932* (Washington, DC: Secretary of War, 1932), 35, 56–59.

13. Dastrup, *King of Battle*, 186.

14. Henry G. Gole, *The Road to Rainbow, Army Planning for Global War* (Annapolis, MD: Naval Institute Press, 2003), 17–26; Harry P. Ball, *Of Responsible Command: A History of the U.S. Army War College* (Carlisle Barracks: U.S. Army War College Alumni Association, 1994), 165–256.

15. Dwight David Eisenhower, "Brief History of Planning and Preparing for Procurement and Industrial Mobilization," course paper for the Army Industrial College, October 2, 1931.

16. Kerry E. Irish, "Apt Pupil: Dwight Eisenhower and the 1930 Industrial Mobilization Plan," *Journal of Military History* 70, no. 1 (January 2006), 59.

17. David A. Hounshell, *From the American System to Mass Production: The Development of Manufacturing Technology in the United States* (Baltimore: Johns Hopkins University Press, 1984), 331–36.

18. Bruce Condell and David T. Zabecki, eds., *On the German Art of War: Truppenführung* (Boulder, CO: Lynne Rienner, 2001), x.

19. This is described in Robert M. Citino, *The Path to Blitzkrieg: Doctrine and Training in the German Army, 1920–1939* (Boulder, CO: Lynne Rienner, 1999).

20. Condell and Zabecki, *On the German Art of War*, 17.

21. Ibid.

22. Robert M. Citino, *Decisive Victory: From Stalemate to Blitzkrieg in Europe, 1899–1940* (Lawrence: Kansas University Press, 2002), 181–85.

23. "Blitzkrieger" *Time* XXXIV, no. 13 (September 25, 1939), http://www.time.com/time/archive/preview/0,10987,761969,00.html.

24. Quoted in Ronald H. Spector, "The Pacific War and the Fourth Dimension of Strategy," in *The Pacific War Revisited*, ed. Günter Bischof and Robert L Dupont (Baton Rouge: Louisiana University Press, 1997), 43.

25. Russell Cartwright Stroup, *Letters from the Pacific: A Combat Chaplain in World War II*, ed. Richard Cartwright Austin (Columbia: University of Missouri Press, 2000), 42.

26. Griffith, *School of the Citizen Soldier*, 215.

27. Thomas P. Hughes, *American Genesis: A Century of Invention and Technological Enthusiasm, 1870–1970* (Chicago: University of Chicago Press, 2004), 9.

28. Hughes, *American Genesis*, 243.

29. David F. Noble, *America by Design: Science, Technology, and the Rise of Corporate Capitalism* (New York: Alfred A. Knopf, 1977), 41.

30. Douglas Kinnard, *From the Paterson Station: The Way We Were* (Philadelphia: Xlibris Corporation, 2000), 49.

31. Hughes, *American Genesis*, 5.

32. John B. Wilson, *Maneuver and Firepower*, 55.

33. William H. Baumer, Jr., *How to Be An Army Officer* (New York: Robert M. McBride and Company, 1940), 217.

34. Charles E. Kilpatrick, "Orthodox Soldiers: U.S. Army Formal Schools and Junior Officers between the War," in *Forging the Sword: Selecting, Educating, and Training Cadets and Junior Officers in the Modern World*, ed. Elliott V. Converse III (Chicago: Imprint Publications, 1998), 99.

35. Stephen Ambrose, *D-Day, June 6, 1944: The Climatic Battle of World War II* (New York: Simon & Schuster, 1994), 352.

36. Carafano, *After D-Day*, 38.

37. Charles E. Kilpatrick, *An Unknown Future and a Doubtful Present: Writing the Victory Plan of 1941* (Washington, DC: United States Army Center of Military History, 1990), 115.

38. The discussion of the redesign of the Army division is extracted from Glen R. Hawkins and James Jay Carafano, *Prelude to Army XXI: U.S. Army Division Design Initiatives and Experiments 1917–1995* (Washington, DC: United States Army of Center of Military History, 1997).

39. *Report of the Secretary of War to the President 1937* (Washington, DC: Government Printing Office, 1937), 34; Memorandum from the Chief of Staff, War Department, subject: Reorganization of the Division and Higher Units, November 5, 1935, File 53-72, Military History Institute; Memorandum from the Chief of Staff, War Department, subject: Initial Report of the Organization Committee on the Modernization of the Organization of the Army with Special Reference to the Infantry Division, July 30, 1936, File 53-72, Military History Institute; Memorandum from the Chief of Staff, War Department, subject: Test of Proposed Division, February 8, 1937, File 53-72, Military History Institute; see also Chronology, Triangularization of the Infantry Division, File HRC 322, United States Army Center of Military History; for a summary of European developments, see Jonathan M. House, *Toward Combined Arms Warfare: A Survey of 20th Century Tactics, Doctrine and Organization* (Fort Leavenworth, KS: United States Army Command and General Staff College, 1984).

40. For a discussion of the division design objectives and tactical principles, see Memorandum for the Assistant Commandant, The Army War College, subject: The Infantry Division Organization from the Viewpoint of Tactical Employment, April 29, 1933, File 397-13, Military History Institute; Major General Fox Conner, lecture delivered at the Army War College, September 18, 1931, File 383-A-8, Military History Institute.

41. Robert R. Palmer, *Reorganization of Ground Troops for Combat* Study No. 8 (Historical Section-Army Ground Forces, 1946), 4; see also Special Report based on Field Service Test of the Provisional 2nd Division conducted by the 2nd Division,

U.S. Army (1939) and Highlights of Report by Commanding General, 2nd Division, of the Field Service Test of the Proposed Infantry Division.

42. Steve F. Dietrich, "In-Theater Armored Force Modernization," *Military Review* 73 (October 1993): 36–37.

43. Palmer, *Reorganization,* 33–40; *History of the Armored Force Command and Center* Study No. 27 (Historical Section-Army Ground Forces, 1946), 29–43. During the war, the Army continued to modify the design, going through six major revisions. Based on combat experience, the need to conserve manpower, and further increase flexibility, designers eliminated the regiments, added a reserve combat command (CCR), increased the ratio of infantry to tanks, and reduced the number of battalions. The division strength dropped from over 14,000 men to less than 11,000.

44. Quoted in Christopher R. Gabel, *The U.S. Army GHQ Maneuvers of 1941* (Washington, DC: United States Army Center of Military History, 1991), 5.

45. Carafano, *After D-Day,* 39.

46. See, for example, Henry D. Russell, *The Purge of the Thirtieth Division* (Macon, GA: Lyon, Marshall, & Brooks, 1948). Russell, a National Guard officer, commanded the division when it was mobilized. He was relieved.

47. Morton J. Stussman, *60th Follow Thru* (Stuttgart: Scheufele, n.d.), 19.

48. Gabel, *The U.S. Army GHQ Maneuvers of 1941,* 49.

49. "Comments on First Phase Second Army vs. Third Army Maneuvers," 22 September 1941, Combined Arms Research Library, Fort Leavenworth, Kansas, pp. 2-6.

50. Gabel, *The U.S. Army GHQ Maneuvers of 1941,* 55.

51. Ibid., 171.

52. One of the most significant misjudgments in Wedemeyer's analysis was in calculating the number and type of divisions that could be established. Wedemeyer calculated that 215 divisions could be fielded. This was based on estimating that each command would need a "division slice" of 30,000 soldiers. The division slice accounted for the combat (e.g., tanks and antitank units), combat support (e.g., artillery and air defense), and support (e.g., supply units) units that each division would need to support it in battle. In practice, the division slice requirements turned out to be about 60,000 per division. Thus, while Wedemeyer got the overall size of the force about right, he grossly overestimated how many divisions could be produced. Kilpatrick, *An Unknown Future,* 101–11; see also Maurice Matloff, "The 90-Division Gamble," in *Command Decisions,* ed. Kent Roberts Greenfield (Washington, DC: United States Army Center of Military History, 1990), 365–82.

53. The effort to make the film is described in John Perry, *Sgt. York: His Life & Legacy* (Nashville: John Perry, 1997), 235–76; see also Michael E. Birdwell, *Celluloid Soldiers: Warner Bros.'s Campaign against Nazism* (New York: New York University Press, 1999).

54. Suid, *Guts & Glory,* 38.

## CHAPTER 4

1. Metal identity tags, commonly called "dog tags," were issued to GIs shortly after reporting for duty. They were required to be worn at all times and were used as a means for identifying wounded or killed soldiers. It contained the following information: name, serial number, religion, next of kin, blood type, and tetanus inoculation information. Two tags hung from separate cords around the neck. In 1943, a chain was issued instead of a cord. One of the tags always remained with the body. The second was used by graves registration personnel for filling out forms with an "addressograph" machine, and it was then used as a temporary grave marker.

2. Mel Gussow, *Don't Say Yes Until I Finish Talking* (New York: Doubleday, 1971), 198–99.

3. Robert F. Coakley, "Reflections on Writing the Green Books," *Army History* (Summer 1993): 37–39; Stetson Conn, "Historical Work in the United States Army: 1862–1954," Military History Institute, 1980, 115–56.

4. For a cogent study of the use of ULTRA, see Ralph Bennett, *Ultra in the West: The Normandy Campaign of 1944–45* (New York: Charles Scribner's Son, 1979).

5. Gordon, *An Empire of Wealth,* 370.

6. Ambrose, *D-Day,* 25.

7. *Saving Private Ryan* (New York: Newmarket Press, 1998).

8. *Combined Operations: The Official Story of the Commandos* (New York: The Macmillian Company, 1943), 145.

9. Francis Trevelyan Miller, *The Complete History of World War II* (Chicago: Progress Research Corporation, 1945), 734.

10. Gordon A. Harrison, *Cross-Channel Attack* (Washington, DC: Office of the Chief of Military History, 1951), 55.

11. Ibid., 191. In a footnote Harrison states that the lessons are contained in chapter five. The several mentions of the Dieppe raid in the chapter are fairly superficial with no analysis. Harrison does offer an example where advice from the Dieppe commanders was ignored.

12. Leo J. Daugherty III, "Away All Boats: The Army-Navy Maneuvers of 1925," *Joint Force Quarterly* (Autumn-Winter 1998–1999): 111.

13. Dion Williams, "Blue Marine Expeditionary Force: Joint Army and Navy Exercises, 1925," *Marine Corps Gazette* 10, no. 2 (September 1925): 87.

14. Quoted in Gole, *The Road to Rainbow,* 50.

15. Quoted in ibid., 48.

16. Steven Ross, "American War Plans," in *Military Planning and the Origins of the Second World War,* ed. B.J.C. McKercher and Roch Legault (Westport, CN: Praeger, 2001), 151.

17. Mark A. Stoler, *Allies and Adversaries: The Joint Chiefs of Staff, the Grand Alliance, and U.S. Strategy in World War II* (Chapel Hill: The University of North Carolina Press, 2000), 2.

18. Samuel Eliot Morison, "Thoughts on Navy Strategy, World War II," *Naval War College Review* (Winter 1998), http://www.nwc.navy.mil/press/Review/1998/winter/art6-w98.htm.

19. Michael Schaller, "General Douglas MacArthur and the Politics of the Pacific War," *The Pacific War Revisited*, 27.

20. Quoted in Carlo D'Este, *Eisenhower: A Soldier's Life* (New York: Henry Holt and Company, 2002), 445.

21. D'Este, *Patton,* 508.

22. Ibid., 508, 511; Stanley P. Hirshson, *General Patton: A Soldier's Life* (New York: HarperCollins, 2002), 368–69.

23. Hobbs, *Dear General,* 118, 119.

24. Ibid., 33; see also 133.

25. Hirshson, *General Patton,* 388.

26. Hobbs, *Dear General,* 147.

27. Adrian R. Lewis, "The Navy Falls Short at Normandy," *Naval History* (December 1998), http://www.usni.org/navalhistory/Articles98/NHlewis.htm.

28. First United States Army, Memorandum No. 3, Artillery Information Service, April 1944, Record Group 407, File 101-16.0-ART, National Archives and Records Administration, College Park, MD.

29. Samuel Eliot Morison, *The Two-Ocean War: A Short History of the United States Navy in World War II* (New York: Galahad Books, 1997), 578.

30. Thomas Parke Hughes, *Elmer Sperry: Inventor and Engineer* (Baltimore: Johns Hopkins University Press, 1971), 232–33.

31. Ibid., 579.

32. Quoted in Albert N. Garland and Howard McGraw Smyth, *Sicily and the Surrender of Italy* (Washington, DC: United States Army Center of Military History, 1965), 170.

33. Quoted in Ladislas Fargo, *Patton: Ordeal and Triumph* (New York: Ivan Obolensky, 1963), 291.

34. Lewis, "The Navy Falls Short at Normandy."

35. Ambrose, *D-Day,* 270.

36. Report, First United States Army, June 21, 1944, p. 1, Morris Swett Library, Fort Sill, OK.

37. Joseph H. Alexander, "Marine Corps Armor Operations in World War II," in *Camp Colt to Desert Storm,* 197–201.

38. Richard P. Hunnicutt, *Sherman: A History of the American Medium Tank* (Novato, CA: Presidio Press, 1978), 422–29.

39. Charles H. Corlett Papers, Box 2, pp. 234-235, Military History Institute.

40. Battle Summary No. 39. Operation "Neptune," The Landings in Normandy, June 6, 1944, pp. 94, 95.

41. Ibid., 90.

42. Lida Mayo, *The Ordnance Department on Beachhead and Battlefront* (Washington, DC: U.S. Army Center of Military, 1968), 22–230.

43. Ambrose, *D-Day,* 323.

44. Clarence R. Huebner, *Memorial Album* (Society of the First Division, 1947).

45. Blythe Foote Finke, *No Mission Too Difficult! Old Buddies of the 1st Division Tell All about World War II* (Wheaton, IL: Cantigny First Division Foundation, 2004), 171.

46. Adrian Lewis, *Omaha Beach: A Flawed Victory* (Chapel Hill: University of North Carolina Press, 2001), 11.

47. Huebner, *Memorial Album.*

48. For the controversy on the failure to detect the 352nd Division, see David Hogan, *A Command Post at War: First Army Headquarters in Europe, 1943–1945* (Washington, DC: United States Army Center of Military History, 2000), 49.

49. Quoted in Ambrose, *D-Day,* 323.

50. Unless noted otherwise, the combat narrative of Captain Dawson is taken from *From Omaha Beach to Dawson's Ridge: The Combat Journal of Captain Joe Dawson,* ed. Cole C. Kingseed (Annapolis, MD: Naval Institute Press, 2005).

51. Quoted in Joseph Balkowski, *Omaha Beach: D-Day, June 6, 1944* (Mechanicsburg, PA: 2004), 168.

52. The Germans had no such plans. They feared retaliation by the Allies. The Allies had readied some gas bombs for the invasion, but their supply of chemical weapons and the means to deliver them were very modest. See Brooks E. Kleber and Dale Birdsell, *The Chemical Warfare Service: Chemicals in Combat* (Washington, DC: United States Army Center of Military History, 1966), 70, 156, 167; First United States Army, Report of Operations, 95.

53. John B. Ellery, unpublished manuscript, 8, First Division Museum, Cantigny, Wheaton, IL.

## CHAPTER 5

1. Owen Connelly, *Blundering to Glory: Napoleon's Military Campaigns* (Lanham, MD: SR Books, 1999).

2. Suid, *Guts & Glory,* 257, also 251.

3. Martin Blumenson, *The Patton Papers, 1940–45* (Boston: Houghton Mifflin, 1974), 486.

4. R.L. Brownlee and William J. Mullen III, *Changing an Army: An Oral History of General William E. DePuy, U.S. Army Retired* (Military History Institute, 1987), 13; see also Hogan, *A Command Post at War,* 63–64.

5. Hogan, *A Command Post at War,* 9.

6. Ibid., 61; see also Carafano, *After D-Day,* 22.

7. Speech Delivered by Lieutenant General Omar Bradley, March 27, 1944, Box 43, Chester B. Hansen Papers, Military History Institute.

8. Charles H. Coates, "Interviews with Various Infantry Commanders in Normandy, France, 6 June–8 July 1944," Report to the War Department Observation Board (August 5, 1944), Combined Arms Research Library, Fort Leavenworth, KS.

9. "Eisenhower Warns of Losses; Urges a Check on Optimism," *New York Times,* July 11, 1944, p. 1.

10. Hobbs, *Dear General,* 195.

11. This is described in Blumenson, *Breakout and Pursuit,* 52–102.

12. Chester Hansen, War Diary, July 15, 1944.

13. Carafano, *After D-Day,* 89–91, also 84–88, 203, 219, 231.

14. Ibid., 77, also 84.

15. Ibid., 84–85.

16. Bradley, *Soldier's Story,* 342.

17. Hansen, War Diary, July 12, 1944.

18. Henry E. Giles, *The G.I. Journal of Sergeant Giles,* ed. Janice Holt Giles (Boston: Houghton Mifflin, 1965), 56.

19. Hansen, War Diary, July 25, 1944.

20. Cable, Eisenhower to Marshall, July 22, 1944, in *The Papers of Dwight David Eisenhower: The War Years,* vol. 3, ed. Alfred D. Chandler, Jr. et al. (Baltimore: Johns Hopkins University Press, 1970), 2023.

21. Hansen, War Diary, July 26, 1944.

22. Brownlee and Mullen, *Changing an Army,* 8.

23. Paul F. Gorman, *The Secret of Future Victories* (Fort Leavenworth, KS: Combat Studies Institute Press, 1992), v.

24. Hansen, War Diary, July 25, 1944.

25. Blumenson, *Breakout and Pursuit,* 245.

26. Ian Gooderson, "Heavy and Medium Bombers: How Successful Were They in Tactical Close Air Support During World War II," *Journal of Strategic Studies* 15 (September 1992): 372.

27. Charles W. McArthur, *Operational Analysis in the U.S. Army Eight Air Force in World War II,* vol. 4, p. 192 (Providence, RI: American Mathematical Society, 1990).

28. Carafano, *After D-Day,* 106.

29. McArthur, *Operational Analysis,* 192; John J. Sullivan, "The Botched Air Support of Operation Cobra," *Parameters* (March 1998): 103.

30. Charles G. Patterson, Oral History, The Courtney Hodges Story, papers, pp. 3, 4, Military History Institute.

31. McArthur, *Operational Analysis,* 192.

32. Carafano, *After D-Day,* 120.

33. Cable, Eisenhower to Bradley, July 24, 1944, in *The Papers of Dwight David Eisenhower,* 2028.

34. 18th Infantry Regimental War History (DRAFT), 1944, p. 105, First Infantry Division Museum.

35. Hansen, War Diary, August 8, 1944.

36. Clarence Huebner War Diary, July 9, 1944, First Infantry Division Museum.

37. Unless cited otherwise, the combat narrative for the 1st Division attack is taken from 18th Infantry Regimental War History (DRAFT), 1944, pp. 105–8; Carafano, *After D-Day,* 193–207.

38. Mason Papers, Supplement B, D-Day Normandy Invasion, Operation Cobra, From Omaha Beach to Aachen, First Infantry Division Museum, p. 75.

39. 18th Infantry Regimental War History (DRAFT), 1944, p. 106.

40. U.S. Strategic Bombing Survey, Europe War, G-2 Target File, 2478, Box 140, Record Group 243 National Archives and Record Administration.

41. Huebner, War Diary, July 26, 1944.

42. Ibid., July 27, 1944.

43. Max Hastings, *Overlord: D-Day and the Battle for Normandy 1944* (New York: Simon & Schuster, 1984), 252.

44. Mason Papers, Supplement B, p. 55.

45. 18th Infantry Regimental War History (DRAFT), 1944, p. 106.

46. Gooderson, "Heavy and Medium Bombers," 390.

## CHAPTER 6

1. Carafano, *After D-Day,* 237–41.

2. Eddie V. Rickenbacker, *Rickenbacker: His Own Story* (Greenwich, CN: Fawcett Publications, 1967), 152.

3. R. Earl McClendon, *Autonomy of the Air Arm* (Washington, DC: Air Force History and Museums Program, 1996), 59–60.

4. Quoted in James D. Perry, "Air Corps Experimentation in the Interwar Years—A Case Study," *Joint Force Quarterly* 22 (Summer 1999): 45.

5. James Parton, *"Air Force Spoken Here," General Ira Eaker and Command of the Air* (Maxwell Air Force Base, AL: Air University Press, 2000), 97.

6. Ibid., 45–46.

7. Ibid., 48.

8. Lee Kennett, "Development to 1939," in *Case Studies in the Development of Close Air Support,* ed. Benjamin Franklin Cooling (Washington, DC: U.S. Government Printing Office, 1990), 47.

9. Odom, *After the Trenches,* 163.

10. For the impact of American manufacturing skill on the development of aviation, see Richard K. Smith, "The Intercontinental Airliner and the Essence of Airplane Performance, 1929–1939," Box 71, Record Group 259, Auburn University Special Collections and Archives.

11. Haywood S. Hansell, "The Development of the U.S. Concept of Bombardment Operations," lecture at the Air War College, Maxwell AFB, AL, February 16, 1951, Hansell Collection, United States Air Force Academy Library.

12. Steven A. Parker, "AWPD-1: Targeting for Victory: The Rationale Behind Strategic Bombing Objectives in America's First Air War Plan' *Aerospace Power Journal* (1998), http://www.airpower.maxwell.af.mil/airchronicles/apj/apj89/sum89.html.

13. William Edward Fischer, Jr., *The Development of Military Night Aviation to 1919* (Maxwell Air Force Base, Maxwell, AL: Air University Press, 1998).

14. Carafano, *After D-Day,* 52.

15. Kennett, "Development to 1939," 36–37.

16. Ninth Air Force, Summary of Operations Report, July 5, 1944, Chief of Staff Journal, July 6, 1944, No. 533.305-4, Air Force Historical Research Center, Maxwell Air Force Base, AL.

17. Shawn P. Rife, "Kasserine Pass and the Proper Application of Airpower," *Joint Force Quarterly* 20 (Autumn/Winter 1998–1999): 73.

18. D'Este, *Patton,* 481.

19. Albert W. Garland, Howard McGaw Smyth, and Martin Blumenson, *Sicily and the Surrender of Italy* (Washington, DC: United States Army Center of Military History, 1965), 105–8.

20. Daniel R. Mortensen, "The Legend of Laurence Kuter Agent for Airpower Doctrine," *Airpower and Ground Armies: Essays on the Evolution of Anglo-American Air Doctrine, 1940–1943,* ed. Daniel R. Mortensen (Maxwell Air Base, AL: Air University Press, 1998), 108.

21. Ibid., 125.

22. Carafano, *After D-Day,* 49.

23. Thomas Alexander Hughes, *Over Lord: General Pete Quesada and the Triumph of Tactical Air Power in World War II* (New York: The Free Press, 1995), vii.

24. Ibid., 57.

25. Quoted in ibid., 63.

26. Bradley, *Soldier's Story,* 337.

27. Hansen, War Diary, June 17 and 18, 1944.

28. Quoted in Hughes, *Over Lord,* 157.

29. For this and other technical innovations in Normandy, see ibid., 185–91.

30. Carafano, *After D-Day,* 214–15.

31. Ibid., 228.

32. Unless noted otherwise, the combat narrative of the Battle of Tessy-sur-Vire is taken from Carl I. Hutton, *An Armored Artillery Commander in the European Theater,* unpublished manuscript, pp. 114-115, Morris Swett Library, U.S. Army Field Artillery School; Headquarters, 14th Armored Field Artillery Battalion, Operations Annex, July 29 and 30, 1944; Glen T. Pillsbury et al, "Employment of the 2d Armored Division in Operation Cobra, 25 July–1 Aug 44," Research Paper prepared by Committee 3, Officers Advanced Course, The Armored School, Fort Knox, May, 1950, United States Armored Center and Patton Museum, Fort Knox, KY.

33. Quoted in D'Este, *Patton,* 481.

34. Quoted in David Spires, "Patton and Weyland: A Model for Air-Ground Cooperation," in *Airpower and Ground Armies,* 150.

35. Ibid., 159.

36. Kenneth A. Steadman, "A Comparative Look at Air-Ground Support Doctrine and Practice in World War II," Combat Studies Institute, Combined Arms Center, U.S. Army Command and General Staff College, Fort Leavenworth, KS, 10.

37. Ibid., 9.

38. Thomas E. Griffith Jr., "Airpower in the Pacific—A Case Study in Innovation," *Joint Force Quarterly* no. 26 (Autumn 2000): 32–37.

## CHAPTER 7

1. Gregory G. Wilmoth, "False-Failed Innovation," *Joint Force Quarterly* no. 23 (Autumn/Winter 1999–2000), 55–56.

2. *Joseph Pennell's Pictures of War Work in England* (London: William Heinemann, 1917), v.

3. Ibid., vi.

4. George F. Hofmann, "Army Doctrine and the Christie Tank: Failing to Exploit the Operational Level of War," *Camp Colt,* 94.

5. J.F.C. Fuller, *Memoirs of an Unconventional Soldier* (London: I. Nicholson and Watson, 1936), 429.

6. Mosley also tried to recruit Wells to his cause. Philip M. Coupland, "H.G. Wells's 'Liberal Fascism'", *Journal of Contemporary History,* 35, no. 4 (October 2000): 577–94.

7. Roman Johann Jarymowycz, *Tank Tactics: From Normandy to Lorraine* (Boulder, CO: Lynne Rienner, 2001), 42.

8. D'Este, *Eisenhower: A Soldier's Life,* 151.

9. Stephen E. Ambrose, *Eisenhower: Soldier, General of the Army, President-Elect, 1890–1952* (New York: Simon & Schuster, 1983), 71–72; D'Este, *Patton,* 206, 208, 213.

10. Jarymowycz, *Tank Tactics,* 24.

11. Quoted in Hofmann, "Army Doctrine and the Christie Tank," 95.

12. General Robert Merrill Lee Papers, Patton Museum, Fort Knox, KY.

13. Kenneth Steadman, "The Evolution of the Tank in the US Army, 1919–1940," Combat Studies Institute, Combined Arms Center, U.S. Army Command and General Staff College, Fort Leavenworth, KS, pp. 2–3.

14. Hoffmann, "Army Doctrine and the Christie Tank," *Camp Colt,* 100–101.

15. Hughes, *American Genesis,* 284–94.

16. Bureau of Motion Pictures Report, http://www.digitalhistory.uh.edu/learning_history/casablanca/bmp_report_casablanca.cfm.

17. Gordon, *An Empire of Wealth,* 353.

18. Ibid., 353–54.

19. Alan Gropman, "Industrial Mobilization," in *The Big "L": American Logistics in World War II,* ed. Alan Gropman (Washington, DC: National Defense University Press, 1997), 34.

20. See Charles W. Bailey, *Faint Praise: American Tanks and Tank Destroyers During World War II* (Hamden, CT: Archon, 1983).

21. Quoted in U.S. Army Tank Destroyer Center, "Tank Destroyer History," Camp Hood, TX, part 1, chap. 1, p. 13.

22. Christopher Gabel, "Seek, Strike, and Destroy: U.S. Army Tank Destroyer Doctrine in World War II," Combat Studies Institute, September 1985, pp. 54–56.

23. Odom, *After the Trenches,* 145.

24. Bradley, *A Soldier's Story,* 40.

25. Rick Atkinson, *An Army at Dawn: The War in North Africa, 1942–1943* (New York: Henry Holt and Company, 2002), 383–84.

26. Christopher Gabel, World War II Armor Operations in Europe,"*Camp Colt,* 153.

27. Kent Roberts Greenfield, Robert R. Palmer, and Bell I. Wiley, *The Organization of Combat Troops* (Washington, DC: U.S. Government Printing Office, 1949), 322.

28. For a summary of tank-infantry coordination problems, see H.L. Hillyard, "Employment of Tanks by the Infantry Division," *Military Review* XXIV (June 1947): 50–60; G-3 Section, Supreme Headquarters, Allied Expeditionary Force, "Employment of Tanks and Infantry in Normandy," Military Review XXIV (December 1944): 13–17.

29. Speech Delivered by Lieutenant General Omar Bradley, March 27, 1944, Box 43, Chester B. Hansen Papers, Military History Institute.

30. Activities of General Eddy, July 21, 1944, War Diary of General Manton Sprague Eddy, March 4, 1944 to September 30, 1944, U.S. Army Infantry Museum, Fort Benning, GA.

31. Quoted in Blumenson, *Breakout and Pursuit,* 117.

32. Quoted in Jarymowycz, *Tank Tactics,* 212.

33. Report, Major Godfrey, Commander, 9th Armored Infantry Battalion, Action at Lananneyen, Military History Institute.

34. U.S. Forces, European Theater, General Board Study No. 50, "Organization, Equipment, and Tactical Employment of Separate Tank Battalions," p. 6.

35. Quoted in Hanson W. Baldwin, *Tiger Jack* (Fort Collins, CO: The Old Army Press, 1979), 105.

36. Ibid., 113.

37. Quoted in ibid., 145.

38. Quoted in ibid., 121–22.

39. Quoted in ibid., 123.

40. Unless noted otherwise, the combat narrative of the 37th Tank Battalion is taken from Blumenson, 357–58; Lewis Sorley, *Thunderbolt: General Creighton Abrams and the Army of His Times* (New York: Simon and Schuster, 1992), 48–51.

41. Sorley, *Thunderbolt,* 40.

42. Reminiscences of General Otto P. Weyland, Aviation Project, pp. 10-13, Oral History Research Office, Columbia University Library, New York.

43. George S. Patton, Jr., *War as I Knew It* (Boston: Houghton Mifflin, 1975), 76–77.

44. In contrast to Blumenson's analysis, for a more critical assessment of the issue and the controversy over Patton's role, see Hirshson, *General Patton,* 502–10. Hirshson also argues that Patton's role prior to the activation of Third Army was minimal. See pp. 497–501. See also Martin Blumenson, *The Battle of the Generals: The Untold Story of the Falaise Pocket—The Campaign that Should Have Won World War II* (New York: William and Morrow, 1993), 155–66.

45. Quoted in Blumenson, *Breakout and Pursuit,* 365.

46. Patton, *War as I Knew It,* 81.

47. Hansen, War Diary, August 6, 1944.

## CHAPTER 8

1. U.S. forces often identified features by the maximum altitude. The French name is Mont Joie. Some accounts, including the official account of the United States Army Center of Military History, refer to the terrain feature as Hill 317. This comes from identifying the hill using modern topographic maps rather than contemporary French maps. Mark J. Reardon, *Victory at Mortain: Stopping Hitler's Counteroffensive* (Lawrence: University of Kansas Press, 2002), 311, n. 6.

2. Dastrup, *King of Battle,* 190.

3. Edward N. Wentworth, "Two Views on Transport," *Field Artillery Journal* (January–February 1937): 18, 19.

4. Creswell G. Blakeney, "Horse vs. Motor—Recruits," *Field Artillery Journal* (January–February 1937): 21.

5. Joseph I. Greene, "Who Is in the Driver's Seat?" *Field Artillery Journal* (January–February 1937): 22.

6. Janice McKenney, "More Bang for the Buck in the Interwar Army: The 105mm Howitzer," *Military Affairs* (April 1978): 80–86.

7. See, for example, Edgar F. Raines, *Eyes of the Artillery: The Origins of Modern U.S. Army Aviation in World War II* (Washington, DC: United States Army Center of Military History, 2000), 213–15.

8. For an overview of the employment of field artillery groups and brigades, see U.S. Forces, European Theater, *Report of the General Board, Study of the Field Artillery Group, Study No. 51,* pp. 8–12, 17; U.S. Forces, European Theater, *Report of the General Board, Study of the Organization and Equipment of Field Artillery Units, Study No. 89,* 24–25, Combined Arms Research Library.

9. Hutton, *An Armored Artillery Commander,* 114–15.

10. Quoted in Gorman, *The Secret of Future Victories,* II-74.

11. Reimers, unpublished manuscript, Military History Institute, pp. i, ii.

12. Hutton, *An Armored Artillery Commander,* 34.

13. Quoted in Dastrup, *King of Battle,* 211.

14. Speech Delivered by Lieutenant General Omar Bradley, March 2, 1944, Box 43, Chester B. Hansen Papers, Military History Institute.

15. J. Lawton Collins, *Lightning Joe: An Autobiography* (Novato, CA: Presidio Press, 1994), 250.

16. Unless noted otherwise, the battle narrative of Mortain is taken from Robert Weiss, *Fire Mission! The Siege of Mortain, Normandy, August, 1944* (Shippensburg, PA: Burd Street Press, 2002); Norman F. Fay and Charles M. Kincaid, "History of the Thirtieth Division Artillery," (Military History Institute, 1945), 27–38.

17. J.B.A. Bailey, *Field Artillery and Firepower* (Annapolis, MD: Naval Institute Press, 2004), 338–40.

18. Patterson, Oral History, 146.

19. Hogan, *A Command Post at War,* 28.

20. H.W. Blakeley, "Artillery in Normandy," *Field Artillery Journal* 39 (March–April 1949): 52, 54.

21. Fay and Kincaid, "History of the Thirtieth Division Artillery," 37.

22. See, for example, Blumenson, *The Battle of the Generals,* 261–73.

23. D'Este, *Eisenhower,* 571.

24. Press Conference, Headquarters, Twelfth Army Group Forward, August 21, 1944, Box 43, Chester B. Hansen Papers, Military History Institute.

25. Gorman, *Secret of Future Victories,* II-81.

26. Herbert, "Deciding What Has to Be Done," 16.

27. Gorman, *Secret of Future Victories,* IV-3.

28. Reimers, unpublished manuscript, p. 90.

29. Dwight D. Eisenhower, *At Ease: Stories I Tell My Friends* (Eastern Acorn Press, 1989), 368.

## CHAPTER 9

1. Lewis Sorley, "To Change a War: General Harold K. Johnson and the PROVN Study," *Parameters* (Spring 1998): 93–109.

2. Quoted in Gole, "DePuy and Vietnam," 188.

3. Ibid., 189.

4. Suid, *Guts & Glory,* 222.

5. Ibid., 232.

6. Gorman, *The Secret of Future Victories,* II-87.

7. See, for example, James Jay Carafano, "Fortresses and Firepower in Vietnam," *Field Artillery* (August 1988): 37–42; John H. Hay. Jr., *Tactical and Material Innovations* (Washington, DC: Department of the Army, 1974).

8. See, for example, Lewis Sorley, *A Better War: The Unexamined Victories and Final Tragedy of America's Last Years in Vietnam* (New York: Harvest, 2000).

9. John L. Romjue, Susan Canedy, and Anne W. Chapman, *Prepare the Army for War* (Fort Monroe, VA: Office of the Command Historian, 1993), 21–40.

10. See, for example, Charles E. Heller and William A. Stoft, eds., *America's First Battles* (Lawrence: Kansas University Press, 1986). One exception was the first major U.S. combat forces in Vietnam. This unit was a specially trained airmobile command. See Harold G. Moore and Joseph L. Galloway, *We Were Soldiers Once … and Young: Ia Drang—The Battle That Changed the War in Vietnam* (New York: Random House, 1992).

11. William S. Triplet Papers, Recollections from Service on the Infantry Board, Folder 2 of 2, 1940–1942, Box 5, Military History Institute.

12. See, for example, Arthur K. Cebrowski and John J. Garstka, "Network-Centric Warfare: Its Origin and Future," *Proceedings* (1998), http://www.usni.org/Proceedings/Articles98/PROcebrowski.htm.

13. Quoted in James L. Yarrison, *The Modern Louisiana Maneuvers* (Washington, DC: United States Army Center of Military History), vi.

14. Ibid., vii.

15. Tommy Franks, *American Soldier* (New York: HarperCollins, 2004), 168.

16. Ibid., 175–76.

17. Steven Metz, *Armed Conflict in the 21st Century: The Information Revolution and Post-Modern Warfare* (Carlisle Barracks, PA: Strategic Studies Institute, 2000), 31.

18. John Gordon IV, Bruce Nardulli, and Walter L. Perry, "The Operational Challenges of Task Force Hawk—Kosovo," *Joint Force Quarterly* (Autumn–Winter 2001).

19. See, for example, Congressional Research Service, "Network-Centric Warfare: Background and Oversight Issues for Congress," June 2, 2004.

20. Ryan Lenz and Jason Straziuso, "Troops Do Their Own Humvee Upgrades," Associated Press, January 14, 2005.

21. Peter W. Chiarelli, "The 1st Cav in Baghdad," *Field Artillery Journal* (September–October 2005): 7.

22. James Jay Carafano, "Post-Conflict and Culture: Changing America's Military for 21st Century Missions," November 20, 2003, http://www.heritage.org/Research/NationalSecurity/HL810.cfm; James Jay Carafano and Alane Kochems, "Rethinking Professional Military Education," July 28, 2005, http://www.heritage.org/Research/NationalSecurity/HL810.cfm.

23. Described in James Jay Carafano, *Waltzing into the Cold War: The Struggle for Occupied Austria* (College Station: Texas A&M University Press, 2002).

24. Metz, *Armed Conflict*, xviii.

# Index

# About the Author

JAMES JAY CARAFANO is a fellow at the Kathryn and Shelby Cullom Davis Institute for International Studies at The Heritage Foundation. He has served as an Assistant Professor of History at the U.S. Military Academy, a military historian at the U.S. Army Field Artillery School, and Director of Military Studies at the Army's Center of Military History. He has been a Fleet Professor at the U.S. Naval War College, a visiting professor at the National Defense University and Georgetown University, and a Senior Fellow at the Center for Strategic and Budgetary Assessments. Before retiring as an Army Lt. Colonel, he served as Executive Editor of Joint Force Quarterly, the Defense Department's premiere professional military journal. Dr. Carafano has written *Waltzing into the Cold War: The Struggle for Occupied Austria* and *After D-Day: Operation Cobra and the Normandy Breakout,* Military Book Club selection.

# Stackpole Military History Series

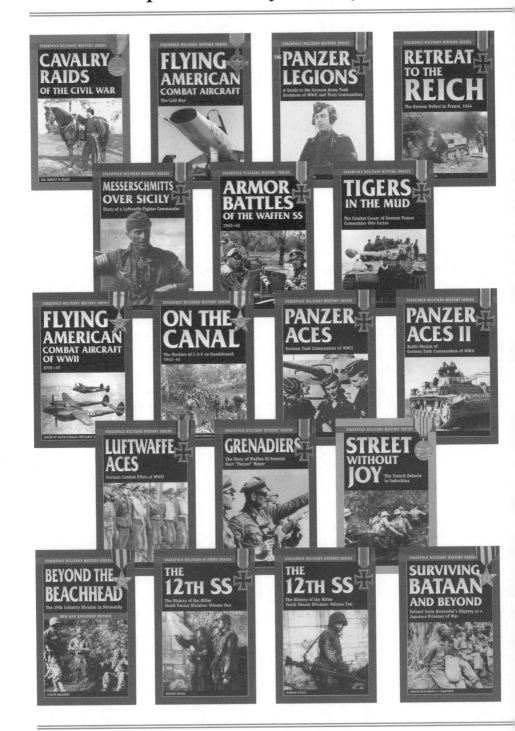

# *Real battles. Real soldiers. Real stories.*

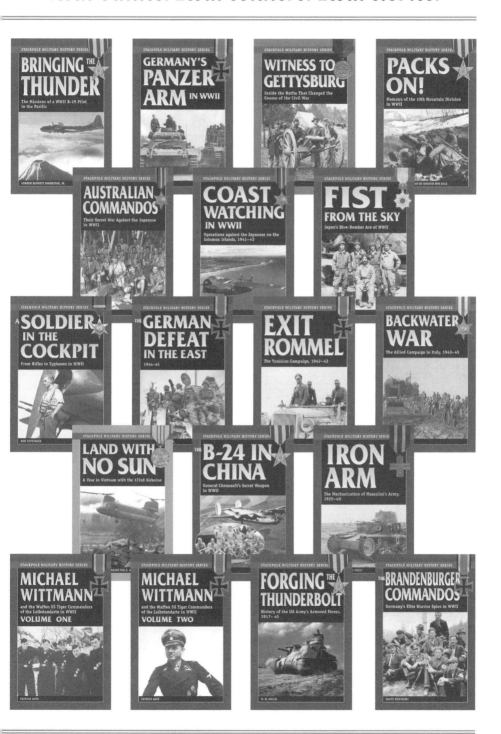

# Stackpole Military History Series

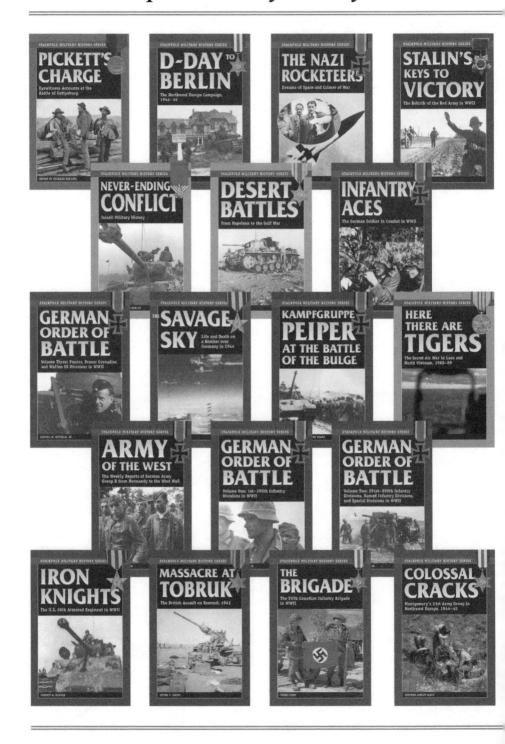

# *Real battles. Real soldiers. Real stories.*

# Stackpole Military History Series

# D-DAY TO BERLIN

## THE NORTHWEST EUROPE CAMPAIGN, 1944–45

*Alan J. Levine*

The liberation of Western Europe in World War II required eleven months of hard fighting, from the beaches of Normandy to Berlin and the Baltic Sea. In this crisp, comprehensive account, Alan J. Levine describes the Allied campaign to defeat Nazi Germany in the West: D-Day, the hedgerow battles in France during the summer of 1944, the combined airborne-ground assault of Operation Market-Garden in September, Hitler's winter offensive at the Battle of the Bulge, and the final drive across the Rhine that culminated in Germany's surrender in May 1945.

*$16.95 • Paperback • 6 x 9 • 240 pages*

**WWW.STACKPOLEBOOKS.COM**
**1-800-732-3669**

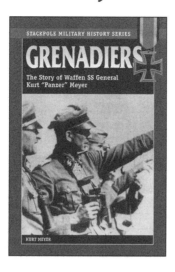

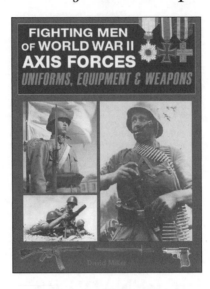